Winning Résumés for Computer Personnel

By
Anne deSola Cardoza, M.A.
President
Personality Assessment Features
San Diego, California

BARRON'S

All inquiries should be addressed to:
Barron's Educational Series, Inc.
250 Wireless Boulevard
Hauppauge, New York 11788

Library of Congress Catalog Card No.: 93-23142

International Standard Book No. 0-8120-1758-7

Library of Congress Cataloging-in-Publication Data
Cardoza, Anne.
        Winning résumés for computer personnel / Anne deSola Cardoza.
            p. cm.
        Includes bibliographical references (p.   ) and index.
        ISBN 0-8120-1758-7
        1. Résumés (Employment) 2. Electronic data processing personnel—
        Employment. I. Title.
        HF5383.C368   1994
        650.14'0240904—dc20   93-23142
                                                                CIP

PRINTED IN THE UNITED STATES OF AMERICA
4567   987654321

CONTENTS

INTRODUCTION

Writing a résumé directed to the computer industry? Stop right there. Let's examine how much in control you feel, and how much you feel on automatic pilot. Does repackaging your competencies seem unreal or humiliating?

If your current résumé isn't getting you interviews, this book will help. In this book you will learn how to write winning résumés as commercial sales tools—résumés that are powerful, competitive, and unforgettable. You will learn how to position yourself first in the eyes of future employers.

Whether you want to work in virtual reality (computer) entertainment theme parks from Singapore to Silicon Valley, donning touch-sensitive gloves and 3-D goggles; create computerized medical or architectural simulations for modeling and training; program scientific, social, or financial information; illustrate ads; or use a computer for word and record processing in an office, you will need to communicate how you can benefit an employer to compete for a job.

Computer companies receive the most diverse résumés in the world, because the jobs information providers perform grow more diverse daily. However, everybody working in the computer industry is doing the same job, essentially: distributing or packaging information. Today organizations are restructuring. The computer industry is changing rapidly, and the information being distributed is diverse. The contents of books and other published material are no longer restricted to text and graphics. The technology for distribution of information changed in the 1990s to CD-ROM (compact disc-read only memory) and CD-Interactive (compact disc interactive) publishing. That means the computer marketplace is expanding into an all-inclusive information industry linking all the senses.

Instructional design corporations are scrambling to fill jobs in digital multimedia. Book publishers are developing CD-ROM titles for collections of historical fiction and interactive suspense novels with alternative outcomes. Employers are migrating from the "business-as-usual" processes of the past to an "information product" mindset. The impact these migration strategies are making on job hunting with paper résumés in an electronic world is awesome.

Another challenge facing job hunters is that fewer jobs in general will be offered during the 1994 to 2005 decade. Colleges are turning out more graduates to compete for fewer positions. According to the U.S. Department of Labor, between 1994 and the year 2005, "the number of college graduates will outpace the number of available jobs by 20 percent each year." The number of older, laid-off workers returning to college is increasing as well as the number of younger college graduates—despite fewer people in their twenties in the population.

Competition for computer-related information industry jobs is increasing. It's important to target several closely related fields for flexibility as well as specialty. Pick a high-growth area within the computer industry, such as the application of computer technology to health care systems, training, artificial intelligence, or multimedia presentation graphics. The application of digital multimedia to training, communications, and entertainment will offer some of the best jobs in the computer industry in the coming decades.

Be inventive. Seek out cooperative programs where companies try out employees who are still in school by hiring them for a semester.

If you are an older worker not in school, create your own telephone marathon. Phone companies and ask for jobs—just as college fundraisers call alumni asking for donations. If the companies can't offer jobs, then ask for information and referrals.

Fundraisers for cultural and college alumni organizations know exactly how to ask for money from business owners. Fundraisers use persuasion techniques to sell "the teamwork attitude" as a benefit and ask for money in return.

In this book, you will learn to use professional fundraising techniques to repackage your résumé for the computer industry (also known as the information industry). Your goal is to persuade employers to offer you an interview and, ultimately, a job.

The information industry, known as an "enabling technology," relies on the teamwork attitude. Computer companies are always seeking better ways to harness the energy, knowledge, and experience of computer users and workers. Every aspect of the computer industry is growing more interactive and user-friendly.

Look at your résumés, cover letters, interviews, and follow-up letters as windows of opportunity to free your inner voice. A résumé verifies that you have been recognized, valued, and discovered. The act of writing your résumé plugs you into your own inner energy. It's a mirror that reflects your self-esteem, because you do what you are.

In this book, you will learn how to write and market your résumé. The latest way to market your résumé is through video-conferencing internationally. Video conference systems now link U.S. offices with those overseas in high-tech job searches. U.S.-based job applicants talk screen-to-screen with employers in Asia or elsewhere for preliminary screening. Video-conferencing (instead of faxing résumés) shrinks a large pool of job hunters to a few who will receive personal interviews without the expense of flying overseas or cross-country.

The idea of video-conferencing job candidates overseas came out of observing computer hobbyists linking modems to electronic bulletin boards in many countries. However, most companies still obtain résumés by advertising, employee-referral incentives, college recruitment, tuition reimbursement, direct mail, and employment or outplacement agencies.

Ironically, the last place an employer looks for a résumé is to the individual who contacts the company without first being asked. Therefore, by contacting organizations before they are swamped by a rush of résumés, chances are you'll stand out from the crowd.

When all résumés begin to look alike, employers may finally hire the job applicant with the most enthusiasm. Between the detailed lines of your résumé, will an employer see your positive attitude, energy, and enthusiasm?

When employers ask for "a good closer," they are talking about enthusiasm for the company and the product or service. A great résumé doesn't close the sale. Your pitch in the interview is the real closer. It summarizes in one sentence every advantage you can offer the company.

Your résumé measures how much you believe in yourself. If you really believe in what you do, you'll never have to painfully work at finding the right career. You'll value what you do so much that you'll enjoy doing the job for the salary. To be valued by others, you must first value yourself. Are you still using the word failure for setback?

When you write to an employer, you are really expressing the strength within yourself. Finding a job is all about repackaging information about yourself. Now let's look at how to repackage your competencies to achieve results.

RESUMES THAT GET YOU A JOB

EMPLOYERS HIRE YOU FOR ADVANTAGES AND BENEFITS

Each year in the United States 10 million employees are terminated from their jobs. Another 10 million workers leave voluntarily. Every five years the entire work force turns over. Twenty million job seekers annually wonder how to repackage their competencies. Résumés are viewed as safety nets. Is your résumé easy to understand?

Only three questions clarify goals in a résumé:

1. Where have you been?
2. How long have you been there?
3. Where are you going?

These are the same three goal-clarifying questions asked of travelers by every border crossing guard in the world. Writing a résumé is similar to crossing a boundary. Moving forward challenges you to seek a better future. Employers hire you for reasons of their own. Many are concerned with the clarity of your goals.

Presenting Yourself

An employer looks for familiar patterns in your résumé, patterns that are found in the company. The corporation or educational institution sees your résumé as a predictor of the organization's future. You are hired for concrete, common sense reasons. You are hired to solve problems. You are hired because you present the least possible risk to the company and the best benefits to its profit and production. An employer invests hundreds of thousands of dollars in your salary, insurance, on-the-job training, perks, and other benefits during the time you're working for the firm.

Sometimes you are hired because you made it your business to learn all you can about the company. You adopted the company and showed your enthusiasm concerning its goals.

Small business entrepreneurs see your résumé as a future spinoff of their plans for expansion. In contrast, an employer might look at a carelessly written résumé and see self-rejection. Or an employer might only observe whether your skills fit the exact needs of the company at a given time.

Emphasize Your Key Abilities

Everyone in the computer industry is hired to organize. Yet the most common complaint of personnel departments is that the résumés coming in aren't organized to emphasize the applicant's most beneficial abilities.

A résumé aimed at the sales department of a computer company should look very different from one targeting a job as a training manager. A résumé for a job as a graphic artist or corporate animator will emphasize different attributes than one that is addressed to the director of research and development.

What Are Your Natural Abilities?

Designing a résumé around your purpose in life means emphasizing what you do well naturally. Before you begin to plan a résumé, ask yourself the following five questions:

1. What kind of mental or physical work would you do as a labor of love without being paid?
2. What job would you choose if you knew you could not get fired as long as you were doing your best?
3. What work activities offer you enough mental and physical challenges for lifelong growth?
4. Does your résumé show how you spend your time and money doing what you love to do?
5. Before you write, ask yourself what you consider successful about the work experiences you've listed on your résumé.

Recognize Opportunities for Success

If the activities you enjoy most can't go on your résumé because they aren't related to your career, it indicates an opportunity you have finally recognized. Change your career. If you don't want to change your career, then change jobs within the same career. Find a position with new or different duties.

For example, if you are a medical transcriptionist doing word processing on a computer all day and don't enjoy it, perhaps you would enjoy being a manufacturer's representative selling medical records software to hospitals as you travel. You might enjoy meeting new people and talking about the efficiency and benefits of software, instead of keyboarding data.

If you would prefer a more recreational career, you might try working as a counselor at or owner/manager of a computer camp. Computer camps allow children or adults to learn about computers while vacationing in a recreational environment.

UNDERSTANDING THE ORGANIZATION'S CHARACTER AND NATURE

Are you familiar with the character of the organization you want to work for? Like people, companies have different personalities that reflect the attitudes and preferences of whomever is in charge.

Comparing your personality type to the character of an organization before you apply there is known as taking the personality-centered approach to job hunting.

By matching your personality type with the character of an organization, you can create optimum productivity in any situation where you have to work with others. When the work is satisfying, you will do your best. In contrast, when you are in frequent conflict with your co-workers or bosses, you'll be more interested in looking elsewhere for a job.

Employers want your personality type and work preferences to fit the character of their organization. Each employer has developed patterns and habits, and may look for these same patterns in your résumé.

Why Organizations Act As They Do

How do you find out a company's character? Ask an employer these two questions: 1) Where is the company going? 2) What is its mission or philosophy? You want to know what the company is all about.

The company may describe itself as either a benchmarking or a visioning organization. For in-depth information on benchmarking, visioning, and the character of organizations, read *The Character of Organizations,* by William Bridges (Consulting Psychologists Press, Palo Alto, 1992). Let's take a brief look at the definitions of benchmarking and visioning companies.

Benchmarking Companies

The corporate world often uses the term benchmarking; it appears in several books on organizational behavior. Benchmarking organizations model themselves after other companies that make something very successfully as a way to determine how things ought to be made. Benchmarkers emulate the best and most popular. An example is the company that tries to model itself after Intel (today) or IBM (a decade before the compatibles appeared in the marketplace).

Visioning Companies

Visioning companies are always looking toward the future for new possibilities, new ways of doing things. These new ways must satisfy a great need. Visioning companies seek out new ideas, new ways to think—however wild, imaginative, creative, and fantastic they seem, as long as they work. The word *visioning* is often used in the computer industry, especially in interactive multimedia and fiber optics research, to mean forward-looking, user-oriented, intuitive kind of thinking that turns ideas into new products.

Interactive multimedia industry magazines, such as *New Media*, or *CD-ROM Professional*, contain ads for companies that offer visioning products that were developed from visioning ideas.

Examples of visioning company products include CD-ROM machines to put your book on laser disk, Philip's Imagination Machine (CD-I technology), interactive industry magazines, and virtual reality equipment. San Francisco is the official headquarters for the interactive multimedia industry, the ultimate in visioning. For further information on interactive communications, write to San Francisco Multimedia Development, 2601 Mariposa St., San Francisco, CA 94110 (415) 553-2300 or to Ed-Tech Review, National Association for the Advancement of Computing in Education, PO Box 2966, Charlottesville, VA 22902 (804) 973-3987.

Examples of visioning ideas that the computer industry is presently developing into actual projects and business ventures include the following:

- virtual reality equipment or desktop animation software for public entertainment and for training surgeons, pilots, architects, designers, and soldiers
- hypermedia and new media publications
- robots for industrial, educational, and military security
- artificial intelligence for financial database management and predicting growth stocks
- software for fashion designers
- videotape and computers in desktop animation
- satellite-linked cable, computers, and wireless phones
- interactive-CD for distance learning or entertainment
- fiber optics to link multimedia information highways and libraries
- electronic tracking
- media laboratories
- branching pathway fiction with alternate adventures
- computer game icon agents
- telecommunications, conferencing, and phone line-computer-satellite links
- electronic universal information libraries
- university courses by computer-to-home link-ups (distance education)

Know the Organization's Needs

A company's character defines how it communicates its needs. The organization shows you the hole that has to be filled. The character of your résumé defines how you communicate what you are about and where you are going. Visioning people need to be matched with visioning organizations. Benchmarking employees feel better when they are working with benchmarking companies.

Before you send your résumé blindly to any company, understand what kinds of help that organization needs. Getting hired has a lot to do with being in the right place at the right time.

Fitting in with the Group vs. Work Competency

You are hired not only for your skill competency, but also because you fit in with the group. Comfortable fit is foremost to the employer. Comfortable fit works both ways. More people are terminated for personality conflicts than for incompetency or tardiness.

Every advertising agency on Madison Avenue knows "you don't get a second chance to make a first impression," as stated in the marketing classic, *Positioning: The Battle For Your Mind.* Positioning works the same way for job hunters in the computer industry. The company's first impression of you is your cover letter followed by your résumé.

The first impression is like a mirror held up to a company's image. When an employer looks at your résumé, that person wants to see similar skills, talents, and goals.

Your résumé also reveals which part of the computer industry feels right for you. It's an image of you, your personality, and your preferences on paper.

Impulsive vs. Compulsive Organizations

Like people, companies come in impulsive and compulsive types. It's important to match a compulsive, routine-seeking job hunter who offers dependability, loyalty, service, and duty with the same type of employer.

The compulsive company emphasizes the security of and need to belong to a large, solvent firm offering steady work. Routine isn't seen as stressful while climbing the corporate ladder. Examples include: hospitals, government, schools, and the military. Other examples of compulsive companies are banks, utilities, law enforcement, computer security, and accounting firms, electronic systems suppliers, the electronic home response industry, home health care software suppliers, and the more traditional computer giants.

Equally important for the impulsive applicant is to be matched with an independent, change-oriented, and innovative employer. The impulsive company emphasizes time flexibility, creativity, achievements, analysis, communication, and a nonlinear fast track to the top. Advancement in an impulsive organization is based on ingenuity, intuition, inventiveness, and impressive profits.

Examples of impulsive computer industry organizations include cutting edge virtual reality companies, software firms dealing with the newest in CD-ROM interactive learning machines and software, educational software and video production firms, computer games manufacturers, artificial intelligence research firms, the most successful computer publications, the computer training management industry, computer human resources specialists, special effects/corporate animation/computer graphics, and simulation software design firms.

To match your résumé (and ultimately you) to either impulsive or compulsive companies, ask what magazines the company's president and your potential supervisor read. Does your future employer enjoy science fiction as inspiration? Even the computer industry has its own compulsive and impulsive publications. Try to find out whether the publications your employer reads are impulsive (like *The Futurist, New Media, CD-ROM Professional, Desktop Communications, Publish, QuickTime Forum, Verbum, Computer Pictures, Wired*) and scientifically oriented mass media magazines like *Omni* and *Discover;* or whether they are mainstream, traditional business-oriented magazines such as *Forbes* and *Fortune.*

The compulsive computer industry publications follow the computer giants more than the independent company spinoffs. Impulsive periodicals follow the smaller, start-up companies, the independents, and new technology or products that compete with the giants.

How else can you tell whether the firm you select is impulsive or compulsive? Does the firm emphasize utility, the present moment, and the practical? Is the company making the computer equivalent of the safety pin? Does it look back in time to tradition in order to move forward new technology? Does it run a tight ship? It could be compulsive.

Does the organization make its tremendous profit by selling imagination? Does it sell interactive multimedia, hypertext, hypermedia, learning as entertainment, or virtual reality? Does the organization look at consumer needs and offer education as fun? Can the creative employees work flexible hours? It could be impulsive.

Knowing whether you are compulsive or impulsive in work habits helps match your résumé with a company that emphasizes your purpose in life, values, and natural abilities.

Does Your Résumé Reflect the Employer's Traditions?
When a change-oriented résumé lands on the desk of an employer looking for tradition in the most rapidly changing of businesses, you have a battle between logistics and analysis.

Consumer need for user-friendly education as entertainment technology collides with the old notion of number-crunching computers based on the universal need to count and store. The employment result pits tradition against new media that changes the way people learn and play. Every new job applicant in the computer industry struggles with change and tradition.

NETWORKING

Most people enjoy networking with others employed in coveted positions. It's draining to job hunt alone.

Professional associations use recorded telephone job referrals to increase membership and attendance at evening networking meetings. The purpose of networking is to help you feel more in control of your job search by making helpful contacts.

Networking With Your Résumé
Job hunting can be a full-time job. Always carry copies of your résumé; distributing your résumé in person while networking may result in job offers.

According to numerous firms providing career services, sending résumés to blind advertisements in the classified section of a Sunday newspaper results in 90 percent fewer hirings than making face to face verbal contact with an employer under relaxed conditions. It's also easier to call and ask for an informational interview to find out about a company than to cold call and ask for a job.

Hand out résumés and business cards at trade shows, conventions, conferences, seminars, computer exhibits, or fairs. Then follow up by interviewing employers for job-related information for your file on companies and employers.

Interviewing an employer in person is the best way to find out whether the character of an organization matches your personality type (and résumé format or focus).

You will probably be given the company tour and remembered. Clip any news articles you read or write about the company's newest product when each is published. Keep these in a file to help you match your technical skills to possible new job openings.

Networking That Works

Getting a foot in the door by passing your résumé to the most important people in the exhibitors' booths at software users' conventions works well. Reviewing software for publications, even the free computer user magazines and newsletters, gives you visibility in the computer industry. Article writing, product reviewing, and informational interviews are ways of networking that appeal to the marketing communications, sales, software, electronic publishing, technical communications, advertising, and public relations departments.

Article writing is a good networking strategy if you have services to sell. How-to articles publicize the abilities of computer repair technicians, technical trainers, animators, and software designers.

Public Speaking to Gain Visibility

The quickest way to get your résumé in front of an employer is to invite several employers to volunteer to speak for an hour at a computer conference. Ask your local computer industry trade journal, computer user newspaper, or a national software users' group whether you can plan a users' seminar or conference for them at their expense to showcase their products and services.

Volunteer to set up a panel of speakers or experts, a seminar, conference, event, software users' group meeting, convention, exhibit, trade show, or workshop at the expense of the national and local software users' groups, the computer trade press, or software or hardware manufacturers and distributors. The majority of software and hardware manufacturers or distributors would be glad to advertise what they have to sell to a captive audience full of potential clients, customers, or colleagues.

They might even suggest that you take a commission as an event planner for organizing and publicizing the event. If they don't, plan it anyway as a volunteer to create visibility for your own résumé.

How good or bad the seminar is will reflect on you as its planner. Invite business community members with interests related to the event theme: computer graphics, desktop publishing, multimedia, educational software, management of information systems, artificial intelligence applied to the stock market, or whatever your chosen field of interest. Charge attendees a small fee to cover the cost of the room and supplies.

Open the conference to students and vendors. Let them talk, give a few demonstrations, and hand out their cards. Then give them your résumé and business card. Every job applicant needs a business card printed professionally with name, address, phone, and primary skill or area of expertise.

Volunteer yourself to speak on panels at conventions. Even if you only speak five to ten minutes about your computer education, experiences, or internships, or introduce the other panelists, it's the most visible way at an event to make important contacts with mutual interests.

Providing the Competitive Edge

Chances are if the employer enjoyed giving a speech and pitch to the audience you captured free of charge, your résumé will be flagged for the next job opening. Be sure to make a follow-up call within a week and each month thereafter for 12 to 18 months.

Sometimes the employer will give you the follow-up call to see whether you can arrange future speaking engagements, recommend potential clients, or otherwise perform a service for the company. This is the time to let the company know you appreciated its involvement in your event. Thank the speaker for the presentation, and ask for a job as soon as one opens with the firm.

Networking Through Hidden Job Markets and Resources

Professional and technical computer associations have job hotlines with tape recordings announcing job openings 24 hours a day to members, directing members to positions that may be part of a hidden job market—positions they wouldn't have seen advertised in the classified sections of daily newspapers, where most people look first for a job. Nationwide, classified daily newspaper advertisements now only list 20 percent of all job openings in any one local area.

Eighty percent of the hidden jobs are advertised in trade magazines, in the publications of professional associations, or they're placed on recorded hotlines available only to association members. Many applicants are recruited from calls put in to hidden job market hotlines accessible to members of professional computer interest organizations or technical communication societies.

Jobs are advertised in business newspapers, in chamber of commerce newsletters, or posted on electronic bulletin boards accessed by people through computer modems. These people know the number to call because they belong to specific software user groups with professional interests in the computer industry (or related industries such as corporate animation, graphic design, drafting, video, or technical writing).

Job referrals are passed around on the backs of business cards or on "hot sheets" at business mixers and socials sponsored by local chambers of commerce. Jobs are also advertised in national employment publications.

Most job openings are posted on cork and electronic bulletin boards inside corporate and academic walls. There is less risk to hire from inside a company. The staffer, temporary clerk, or contingency professional has already solved problems, worked out well, and has become a familiar face. Usually it's when no one inside is available and qualified to fill a position that companies seek an employee on the outside. When corporations must go outside to hire, they frequently offer a bonus to any current employee who brings in a qualified colleague or friend to fill a job opening.

The hidden job market is a network of diverse people in different occupations serving and doing business with one another under the umbrella of a specific industry. What these people have in common is the desire to meet others who can solve their problems and who pose the least risk to employers. Employers hire the person who is the least risk· to the company's financial investment in salary, insurance, training, and other benefits.

Does your résumé position and market you as the least possible financial risk to an employer?

Where and When Can Résumés Be Circulated?

Most job applicants give up a search too early. Several jobs open approximately every 12 to 18 months in the average computer firm. Industrial buying patterns also cycle in 12 to 18 month periods. Companies tend to hire in rhythmic cycles.

Therefore, coordinate résumé mailings with industrial buying cycles. To find out the cycles, call the purchasing department. Then compare those dates to hiring patterns by calling the personnel department.

For example, corporate desktop animation hiring peaks every February. That is the same time animated toy commercials and new Saturday morning cartoons (made the preceding February) air on television.

Research Hiring Cycles

Résumés are sought in cycles and by categories during the computer industry's spring cleaning cycle. A great many résumés are requested by employers whom job applicants meet by networking within professional and trade associations. You won't find the job you want by limiting your search to classified ads in daily general newspapers.

Communicate Your Interest in Computers

Frequently résumés are requested in classified or display advertisements or articles in computer business, professional, and trade journals. Your résumé can be tagged by those companies who ran the ads for the next job opening if you show the company how you can solve a problem it has or give the company some favorable free publicity.

One way that those applying for jobs as technical writers or public relations personnel can stand out from the crowd is to write company approved, freelance how-to articles or software reviews for public relations directors of computer firms or trade journals. This works well if the job you want is in marketing communications or training, too. It's useful if you aspire to those hidden creative expression jobs in the computer industry.

Even if your business depends on repairing computer equipment for clients, writing articles on your experience with computers is not a waste of time. It gives you visibility and opens doors when you share your knowledge with the newspapers, magazines, and trade journals of the computer industry, or newsletters of computer user groups. If you are selling anything, especially your mechanical ability to repair, keep your name in the papers.

Adopt a Company and Learn All About It

Writing about a company is great if your career aspirations are in corporate communications. However, freelance writing for trade journals about how a company solves its problems may backfire if you don't have professional writing and interviewing skills. If writing and publicizing a company is not your niche, then adopt a company and learn everything you can about it.

Letting a company know you have thoroughly researched it (or adopted it) is something to communicate by phone, or during your interview, or in your cover and follow-up letters. If you are interested in freelance writing about a company, it pays to adopt the firm and learn all about it.

Keep a record of the success strategies of the company that you adopt, the financial impact the company has made on the computer industry, and the problems the company has solved. Read the trade journals.

IDENTIFYING RESUME DATABASES

Your résumé has a good chance of ending up stored in a computer database, filed under the category of work you do or the skills and training you have. If you send your résumé to a national outplacement agency or employment service that specializes in electronic résumé transfer, your résumé could make its way anywhere in the nation or even overseas if you specify that you would be willing to work anywhere.

As needed, the database of job applicants is searched, and the applicants are called for interviews. Some software firms have turned into electronic employment agencies. They refer applicants to jobs without the applicant coming in personally by sending the scanned résumé by fax or modem across the country or internationally to an employer.

Résumé Screening Services

Electronic personnel referral agencies specialize in putting résumés on computer disk for the purpose of screening them for employers too busy to interview applicants in person. Outplacement and national computer employment recruiting agencies scan your résumé onto their databases.

Your so-called confidential résumé may be placed on a database. Employment referral, outplacement, screening, and résumé consulting agencies may download your résumé from databases directly to employers all over the country (or the world) through linkage with a computerized recruiting service (and more narrowly focused databases), or corporations on mailing lists. In a national chain of agencies and outplacement services, your résumé could be accessed by any of the local branches of such services.

Once on disk, your résumé could end up in market research and advertising agencies or with employment trend forecasting businesses. Once mailed out, a résumé is like a note in a bottle floating on the sea.

It's important to realize that the purpose of most in-house corporate personnel departments is to screen résumés out. Therefore, you may get faster and better results if you send your résumé directly to the supervisor of the department you want to work for in the company of your choice.

Some colleges also keep a computerized database of teachers and technical trainers who specialize in certain types of software in use by the institution.

You don't always know whether your résumé is being handled as confidential or is being scanned onto a disk, accessible to anyone on an electronic mailing list. Most outplacement agencies will not let résumés out of their offices and do promise confidentiality. Always ask first what will happen to your résumé over time before you send it anywhere.

Résumé-Producing Software

Inexpensive commercial or public domain software is easily obtainable to create résumés for you in a variety of formats. You key in the details of your previous employment and education. Out prints a completely organized résumé in the style you select. The résumé business itself is now computerized, but there are still consultants who write résumés for you by hand and then put the information on computer disk.

Résumé Consultants

Résumé writing companies charge a fee to create your résumé and cover letter on a computer. Civil service résumés are put on a special, detailed résumé form called the Civil Service (SF 171). (For more information on SF 171 forms, see Chapter 7.) Many retiring military personnel and others applying for government jobs use these official job applications in place of personal résumés.

Many résumé-writing agencies double as job search specialists or consultants. They identify your unique capabilities and interests and put them into a résumé package. Some of these job search specialists use job search organizer software to help you set your goals. The purpose of the software and the consultants is to get you to plan your career and organize the details on software or in a workbook.

There are numerous successful national electronic résumé networks linking thousands of companies nationwide. The résumé industry itself has become computerized—all because employers want candidates matched to specific jobs. Employers are flooded with stylized, look-alike, formula-written résumés. By casting your résumé on the computerized waters, you hope a job can find you. The résumé-writing and job search assistance services electronically notify these companies of your career interests and qualifications. Each service is different and is designed to make your résumé stand out from the crowd within the electronic networking systems.

RESUME WRITING: WHAT TO DO

Control Your Job Search

What all job seekers would like most is to take control of a job search. You want to know exactly what stands between you and a career. You want to know an employer's reasons for choosing an applicant to fill an opening. You need a tool to provide the competitive edge that shows you mean business.

What you want most is to be in control. To give you more control over your job search, you prepare a résumé that offers filtered information. You may feel powerless with only a one-page résumé to represent a lifetime of training and experience.

One strategy can put you in charge of your career destination: Customize your résumé to target different employers.

Job hunting in any one of the emerging niches requires a customized résumé. Send your résumés only to employers who are looking for someone with your skills, training, experience, and habits.

How Résumés Are Slanted

Résumés are slanted (with honesty) to fit the "qualifications needed" description for each job. Act as if your qualifications will be checked and verified. You don't know when questions will come up requiring a reference or transcript check.

The systems analyst's résumé will emphasize a track record of increasingly responsible problem-solving consultant work with contract requirements. The résumé focus will be on moving company operations into "intelligent systems" that are easier to use in a change-oriented environment.

Systems analysts want to change the way the public shops, plays, and learns by teaming up with software and hardware engineers. They want to make these changes within the fastest growing industry.

Work Preferences on Your Résumé

Let's look at how work preferences guide you into a specific type of résumé and computer job. Some job titles (like hypertext writer) are so new that no one has much experience in them, so an employer must scan your résumé to find out your work preferences as indicators of whether they should hire you.

An employer sees your résumé as a business plan. Persons who state they are destined to gravitate to the top levels of computer firms as executives will have résumés that look different from systems analysts who want to solve research problems in software design by making software easier to use.

One main difference between these two résumés is that the executive's résumé will emphasize sales based on consumer needs.

The executive's goal is to profit by filling a void in the market with the best or most popular products. Those sales-oriented administrators who rise to the top of computer firms may not be the most creative, but they will have managed the best marketing staff.

Responding to Change

Your résumé shows how you respond to change. In the computer world, a résumé must reflect how you respond to changes in spur-of-the-moment job scheduling, for example, or how you can change horses in midstream without hesitation.

Your biggest asset to spotlight on a résumé is that you work well under pressure, which is common in the technostressed computer industry.[1]

Show that in situations where employees must find spontaneous solutions to problems and challenges, you can do the unexpected with computers and thrive on it. Résumés in this field should show that change challenges you, and that you can grow on the job and continually learn new skills.

Your Résumé Should State Your Profit-Making Abilities

Every company wants to know how much money you brought in for your former firm last year and how much you expect to bring in for the new employer this year.

The bottom line is profit. Leave qualifiers out of your résumé. Only state the facts using dramatic, action verbs that emphasize achievements that brought a company profit.

Profit is a hidden factor in fields such as academia, research, and human resources. In academia, if a college course is not popular, fewer students will pay to register for it, and profit for the institution will be lowered. If you are in one of these fields it's still possible to show how you and your work profited an institution—even if you can't put it in exact dollar terms.

For example, profit is hidden inside grant proposals that use direct marketing techniques to compete for what money is available from the government or from private organizations. Profit is also hidden inside fundraising events and campaigns.

Profit results from getting the public to donate money in return for a benefit. Profit is obtained by creating visibility through public relations efforts for nonprofit organizations. Public relations includes placing news stories in the media to persuade people to spend money on an organization's technology, courses, and conferences.

---

[1]The computer industry, psychologists, and physicians treating stress symptoms of computer personnel applied the word technostressed to computer industry workers in the early 1980s. In the late 1970s, the word had been used by engineers, systems analysts, and programmers to describe mainframe computers worn out by too much number crunching.

Beware of Conveyor-Belt Résumé Styles

It's ironic that many of today's résumés appear so similar, considering the variety of jobs that exist in the computer industry. A person applying for a job as a word-processing secretary sends in a résumé of the same size, appearance, and format as a person applying for a job as a software engineer.

The only difference is in the degree listed under the education heading and in the job experience section. After reading hundreds of résumés a week, they all begin to look alike to many interviewers. What makes your résumé stand out from the crowd?

The Power Résumé

Your résumé is a map of your presentation strategy. Find out what is important to the company you choose to receive your presentation. You want to anticipate problems or questions.

You want your résumé to be powerful; but a résumé is an original product that is an authentic expression of your inner voice. The challenge is to fit your inner voice into a company's business plan. You would like to be at ease in a job that works for you and reap benefits from the multiplying number of computer industry niches.

Research Before You Write

Before you even sit down to organize details, sort facts, and begin to write your résumé, do some detective work concerning the computer companies to which you plan to send your résumés. Adopt a company and learn all you can about it. Find out how applicants are chosen to fill jobs.

Seven steps are required to find a job:

1. Show a company how you can solve problems. Identify employers for which you can solve problems.
2. Show a company why you will be the least possible risk if you are hired.
3. Motivate an employer. Computer firms always have their own reasons for hiring you.
4. List ten of the company's reasons why they might want to hire you.
5. Tell your prospective employer how you can serve the firm.
6. Sell your benefits as if your résumé were a personal direct mail marketing campaign.
7. Use the rule of a dozen.

Marketers have a rule of a dozen, by which they send out direct mail flyers 12 times a year to target the same potential customers. Treat your résumé as if it were a direct mail flyer and start a direct mail campaign.

Impress the Reader in 20 Seconds

The résumé is like a flash card vision of your achievements that must imprint itself on the brain of the person who skims the page. Treat it like a well-written and attractively designed advertisement. Use bold headings, plenty of white space between sections, and bullets to direct the reader's attention. The impression your résumé makes will determine the action an employer will take.

Changing Résumé Formats

A résumé format showing diversification is preferred by employers. Résumé formats do change as technology evolves. Employers today are searching less for number crunchers and more for user-friendly types—both in computers and personnel.

A strong résumé emphasizes job satisfaction through innovation and change. As your experience pushes you up the career ladder, you also need to grow laterally and learn broader applications in your specialty.

Itemize breadth and diversity in your past jobs. If you don't have relevant experience, emphasize how you can transfer your creative, technical, people, or general skills to the new job.

ASSESSING YOURSELF

Slow Down as You Write Your Résumé

Writing a résumé allows you to address your emotions and to reappraise your employment situation. As you outline your competencies (before you write your résumé), it's helpful to write down your feelings about being terminated or switching careers. Negative emotions should be worked through now, not during a job interview. Slow down as you write the final draft of your résumé. Reflect on your past job satisfaction.

Carefully writing a résumé may prevent you from sabotaging yourself in an interview. By the time you finish writing your résumé, you'll have less need to justify why you are changing jobs. You'll feel less impatient and more comfortable networking with colleagues.

Where Are You Going?

When someone asks where you are going or what your career mission is, you may respond in the manner of a visioning company or a benchmarking company. Your résumé emphasizes either visioning or benchmarking experiences, skills, training, job preferences, and career goals. Your résumé, like an organization, has a character of its own.

THE CHANGING COMPUTER INDUSTRY

Identifying Diversity

Today, new technology offers hundreds more enterprising, instructional, creative, inventive, financial, marketing, and people-oriented computer careers within niches in the computer industry that include the following fields: virtual reality, artificial intelligence, computer security, computer law, computer medicine, software talent management, preschool software product design, sales management, CD-ROM, interactive learning machines and software, desktop computer animation special effects for the corporate world, hypermedia (interactive communications and entertainment), multimedia communications, fiber optics design, optical disk design, computer presentation graphics, electronic publishing, wireless telecommunications, robotics, financial forecasting (using applied artificial intelligence software), neural networks and fuzzy logic, technical training, instructional technology and courseware design, documentation analysis, software manual writing and editing, the computer trade press magazines, the electronic and book publishing industry for journalists, computer-aided design and drafting (engineering graphics or architectural drafting), computer-aided manufacturing, numeric control, beta testing of new software for errors, software review, and desktop video for cable television and advertising agencies.

Jobs exist for database managers, managers of information systems, local area networks (LAN) and wide area networks (WAN) technicians and managers, communications technicians in utilities firms, computerized accountants, systems analysts, software designers, computer video game designers, software engineers, repair technicians, telecommunications technicians, satellite technicians and wireless telecommunications technicians, teleconferencing personnel, telecommuters, support staff—such as word processors and supervisors, data entry clericals, and computer operators.

The computer industry grows more diversified each day.

Changing Job Titles

Each year, many more job titles are invented that didn't exist the year before. Résumés reflect the traits required to succeed in each of these ever-changing jobs.

New upgraded software enters the market every six months, far ahead of annually upgraded hardware. New job titles and spinoffs from emerging jobs form every few months.

These jobs have titles such as the following: virtual reality designer, multimedia scriptwriter, corporate desktop animator-special effects, CD-Interactive hardware and software designer, computer security psychologist, fuzzy logic neural networks analyst, and applied artificial intelligence investments planner. These are only a few examples of the hundreds of new job titles created to meet the needs of continually upgraded technology. Nevertheless, new and emerging jobs still require certain traditional traits such as objectivity, punctuality, and accountability to support production and profit.

Objective, dependable people whose skills offer an employer concrete benefits are most likely to rise quickly to the top. Computers are shedding weight, and so are résumés. They are becoming more focused. Electronic job searching is popular.

Changing Needs

Two kinds of people work in the computer industry: number crunchers and multimedia user-friendlies. Two different résumé formats are used for these opposite types of jobs.

Computer industry needs are changing rapidly from the number-crunching machines and the logistics people who operated them in the 1980s to multimedia, user-friendly, interactive teaching, communications, and entertainment consoles and the ingenious courseware design people who create more personal ways to use computers today.

A decade ago, most workers in the computer industry were programmers, systems analysts, word processors, database managers, or computerized accountants who mailed out stylized, almost similar résumés.

What Would You Rather Be Doing?

Hundreds of different computer industry jobs exist. Some deal with service to people, some are highly technical and oriented to machines. Still other jobs are for full-time illustrators, animators, drafters, musicians, special effects persons, virtual reality designers, and video producers.

The computer press industry hires reporters, publicists, technical writers, and software reviewers. The CD-ROM industry hires novelists and instructional designers.

Do you want the flexible time schedule of a video game designer? There are sales jobs and engineering jobs, careers for the artistic, ingenious, practical, or imaginative.

There is an ever-expanding need for computer-aided software engineers, systems analysts, database managers, accountants and financial analysts, local area network managers, satellite technicians, multimedia producers, and computer specialists of every type. Programmers are less in demand now than software engineers, software designers, and systems analysts.

Would you rather be the person who designs virtual reality simulated models of the inside of the human body to train student surgeons? Perhaps you enjoy using your computer to design three-dimensional architectural models to present to architects so they can see how a neighborhood will look before building it.

Would you rather be a technical trainer? Do you teach courses in annually upgraded versions of the same word-processing software program year after year in a community college?

Does your résumé position you as an electronic publishing specialist? These examples are only a few of the hundreds of opportunities that the computer industry offers.

More than 650 small businesses exist for writers or artists using a computer full time. Such businesses include but are not limited to technical journalism about virtual reality developments, infomercial writing and production, software user manual publishing, color separation desktop publishing, hypermedia fiction writing, computer game design and illustration, desktop video scriptwriting, corporate animation, CD-ROM book production, interactive multimedia entertainment, and training materials production, design, or writing.

Due to the variety of jobs in the computer industry, many employers can scan résumés onto disks and store them in computer files of job applicants. The file may then be sorted into niches or job categories such as programmer, word processor, systems analyst, desktop publisher, or database manager.

Sometimes these files are given to professional screeners who may interview and select job applicants for corporations that don't do interviewing.

What you put on paper is important, especially when your résumé is scanned onto disks and made permanent. In the next chapter, you will learn what goes into a memorable résumé.

2
WHAT GOES INTO A RESUME?

CONTENTS AND FORMAT OF A RESUME

Résumés identify you and highlight your work history in one page. A cover letter can supplement this information. The contents of a one-page résumé includes the following.

- Your name, address, home phone, work phone, or message phone.
- A concrete, specific, targeted description of your work history highlights. Leave out early job descriptions that would definitely not apply to the current job or to the computer industry. For example, skip the years you worked as a cook, hairdresser, factory assembler, babysitter, cashier, or retail sales clerk, unless the work applies to the computer industry. Include the volunteer work you did for the computer industry user groups, publications, training or tutoring, customer service, commission sales, writing, speaking, interviewing, editing, college computer and robot clubs, or anything relevant to the future job.
- All software and hardware you can use. If you have reviewed software free for trade newspapers, include that experience. Any computers and software, or machines related to spinoffs of the computer industry such as wireless telecommunications, video, or multimedia you have worked on in the past should be included. Include computer camp counseling work and any training or designing experience. Currently, computer presentation graphics, multimedia, video production, virtual reality, simulation, CD-ROM interactive software and hardware, applied artificial intelligence, neural networks/fuzzy logic, computer camps, vacations and resorts, and computerized advertising design are burgeoning new fields with future potential. So include these related fields, now that video technologies, telephones, and computers can be linked by new spin-off equipment.
- Your education and training. Include all degrees, diplomas, certificates, credentials, and special seminars that trained you in the use of specific software and hardware. If you are self-trained, include what software or hardware you

use and which training manuals you have used. If you are a self-trained computer repair technician, include how you learned your trade. It's important to mention job-related associations you belong to that present continuing education, correspondence courses, seminars, conferences, or workshops.

- Work related honors, awards, and other certificates of outstanding work evaluation.
- Professional associations you have joined for networking.
- Security clearance level.
- Civil service level, if relevant.
- Publications, articles, books authored, if relevant.

This information should fill a one-page résumé. If you are a recent graduate, military retiree, midlife career switcher, or are changing occupations at any age, include optional information, if space permits, after the primary information has been listed. The optional information may include the following.

- Your career goal.
- Computer courses taken. Your prior training might be in a nonrelated field such as the humanities, nursing, or design. Include lifelong, continuous training, conferences, convention courses, seminars, workshops—any continuing education credits or certificates given by professional associations or schools.
- A brief summary of your transferable life skills or volunteer history. Using action verbs to list transferable skills is especially recommended for military retirees entering an entirely new field and mature displaced homemakers without prior paid work experience outside the home. Action verbs include words like: designed, wrote, edited, sold, repaired, trained, managed, solved, created, illustrated, organized, publicized, researched, audited, interviewed, distributed, purchased, programmed, analyzed, presented, spoke, raised (funds), coordinated, marketed, published, and produced—to name a few. Two examples of volunteer computer experience follow.

> *Designed and wrote the church newsletter using Ventura desktop publishing software on an IBM 486 with Ventura AdPro 1.1 for Windows and WordPerfect 6.0.*

> *Trained in adult continuing education in medical terminology and transcription and volunteered to process medical records at ABC Hospital's medical records department using medical transcription software and WordPerfect 6.0.*

If you have worked as a troubleshooter in any capacity, it shows you are interested in finding out what's broken and fixing it. If you trained anyone to use software, it shows an interest in sharing and communicating technical information to the public.

- Memberships in any organizations where you networked with computer industry personnel. Include your professional organizations, computer user groups, student chapters of national computer-related organizations, intellectual organizations, and related industry organizations. Examples include associations of trainers in the computer field, computer press associations, and computer graphic artists organizations. The Association for Computing Machinery is also an umbrella for many special interest groups. (See Appendix B at the back of this book.) Consult the *Encyclopedia of Associations* in your public or university library. This book lists thousands of associations and organizations you may join in every professional, trade, and social field imaginable. Each one of these associations has its own publication and often a job referral service, résumé databank, or recorded telephone job hotline for members.
- Foreign languages spoken, foreign software used. Bilingual skills are a plus in the computer industry. The fields of import and export of software and hardware, peripherals, and computer publishing are linked by global networking through modem, fax, and telecommunications equipment from satellites to phones.
- Diverse computer-related hobbies or hobbies that are work-related or especially creative, analytical, ingenious, or focused on problem-solving.
- Military service, if any.
- Magazines you subscribe to that show your reading preferences. Computer magazines, trade journals, scientific or creative magazines, or job-relevant publications may be listed. Don't stop at subscribing. Offer articles on a freelance basis; it's a great way to obtain informational interviews with people for whom you want to work.

A Résumé Is Your Greatest Marketing Tool

The first paragraph of your résumé should be able to "close the sale" and get you the job in the first few seconds the employer reads it. The face-to-face interview that follows should only serve to verify the employer's decision.

How does that first paragraph on your résumé close the sale? Begin by clearly stating what benefits you will offer and how you will serve the company's needs in less than two sentences in the first paragraph. Use action verbs and keep the sentences under ten words long. Next, tell the employer exactly what you're after.

Job applicants are sometimes turned down because their résumés fall apart in front of the powerful. Employers describe a résumé that falls apart as one that looks like you don't know what you want. One way to ensure that your résumé is remembered is to send a follow-up letter to the person who interviewed you. Keep reminding the employer and interviewer of your interest.

What Never to Include in a Resume

- Leave out your age, marital status, children's ages and babysitting arrangements, marital problems, divorce information, and anything from your home life. Don't include the fact that you were just divorced or are a single parent, a victim of job discrimination, an abused spouse, or were housebound with agoraphobia for the past several years. You would be surprised at how many résumés flood into employers with this type of private information.

- Don't include your physical challenges. An employer will not hire you out of sympathy because you're "handi-capable," disabled, homeless, a victim, a survivor, or because you're housebound and need telecommuting work. "Telecommuting /home-based computer work preferred" is all right to state on your résumé. If you are deaf, blind, invisibly disabled, or in a wheelchair and need to know whether the building is accessible or on a bus route, call ahead and discuss it with personnel before you send your résumé.

- Exclude any details that put you down. Keep negative self-talk out of your résumé. Employers are surprised by the number of résumés that start out with the statement "I dare you to hire me," or "I never worked for anyone before because I always ran my own business."

- Don't deal with past salaries and present salary demands. It's better to negotiate a job contract and salary at the final interview or when you are hired. You will have more bargaining power at that point. Salaries don't belong on résumés because they either drag you down to your former pay or price you out of the new employer's market. High salary requirements of older, experienced workers are what drives budget-cutting employers to seek younger, less experienced workers at lower pay or from overseas.

- Do not include your height, weight, or photo—unless it's requested. If you are asked to submit a photo, have it professionally taken and touched up to give a business appearance. It might end up being printed in an employee newspaper or house organ.

- Omit names of family members.

- Leave out the reference letters or names of references. If requested, you can provide letters of reference later when you're actually hired or are about to be hired. Some employers put names of references into a database and automatically add them to their mailing lists.

- Don't mention how you commute. If driving is the primary requirement of the job, such as a computer delivery truck driver, state only what is legally required for commercial vehicle operation.

HOW YOUR RESUME PERSUADES: THE RULE OF THE DYNAMIC DOZEN TRAITS

The most effective résumé will persuade an employer that you're all of the following and more:

- affordable
- adaptable
- accurate
- accessible
- creative
- efficient
- analytical
- dependable
- decisive
- prompt
- energetic
- retrainable

YOUR RESUME STYLE

This section examines four main résumé styles. Choose the style that best displays your work history. The four styles follow.

1. chronological work history
2. abilities
3. expanded
4. creative

If you have no paid work experience, the chronological style may not fill enough space. Or if you don't want to reveal your young or old age, an abilities or creative style works better.

The unpaid volunteer may wish to use an expanded, amplified résumé to emphasize with action verbs the duties carried out in the volunteer work. A creative résumé is right for the applicant who has created many imaginative projects, such as the following.

- computer illustration and graphics
- writing computer books
- writing freelance articles
- temporary technical editing
- hourly teaching/training

Organizing Your Résumé

An employer wants only the bare bones in your résumé. There are three ways to create a terse résumé: by arranging the order yourself; by hiring a résumé writer; or by purchasing résumé-organizing software. The software arranges your facts chronologically and prints out a standardized résumé based on the software's format.

If your goal is to write the most practical one-page résumé from scratch without having to spend extra money for software or a résumé-writing service to do it for you, how will you do it? Let's discuss the four résumé styles and their usefulness.

The Chronological Work History Résumé

You list your last job first. Information is presented in a sequence. It's practical and familiar if the job you're applying for requires sequential information processing as in programming, word processing, systems analysis, troubleshooting, accounting, training, research and development, and data entry. The *chronological résumé* is based on facts presented in reverse chronological sequence.

The less experience you have in the computer industry, the more likely you will list your education first. The chronological work history résumé begins with your name, address, and phone number listed at the top of the page. Omit the word résumé in the middle above your name. The personnel department's screener or an employer knows what it is and regards every piece of extraneous information as a time waster.

A résumé should look professionally printed. Some career consultants highly recommend using desktop publishing software such as Ventura for Windows, and Ventura's AdPro to lay out your résumé so it impresses the reader and makes you unforgettable in an absolutely professional, business-like manner. To an employer, your résumé is an advertisement that started with a unique concept.

The Chronological Résumé Is an Umbrella

Chronological résumés emphasize smooth transitions—bridges from one job to the next, or one period of time to the next. To an employer, your résumé is a creative concept. It's a basic framework used like an umbrella to tie all your different facts and categories together.

Without a creative concept umbrella or a framework, all your strengths and skills would hang like a string of different beads with nothing in common, no bridge to relate the fact that came before with the fact that lies ahead.

The purpose of an umbrella or creative concept in a chronological résumé is to hold the employer's attention. To find your umbrella, look for strengths—skills, talents, experiences, or training—that tell exactly what you can do for the future employer and what you did for past employers (or teachers if you are a recent graduate). These strengths are your smooth transitions. Employers hate gaps and jumps.

What are your benefits, advantages, and features? How will you meet the employer's needs? When writing a résumé, always consider the reader. Ask yourself, "What's in my résumé for the employer?"

Separate Your Skills

Before you write the final draft of your résumé, list each of your skills in its own category. If you are writing your résumé from the beginning by hand and polishing the final draft on your computer, begin by separating your skills.

Take a pack of index cards and write down one factual strength or skill per index card so you can sort the facts in a logical order. Sort your facts and organize your cards into categories.

Color-Code Your Categories

Use a handful of colored markers and assign a different color code to each of the categories. Put a different colored dot next to each category of strengths, skills, experience, and education.

As you color-code your index cards, identify each fact or strength with its proper category. Weed out what doesn't belong in that segment. Save what you've weeded out for a different area of the résumé. Categories can also be color-coded with stick-on colored dots.

Write down the name of each category at the top of a blank sheet of paper. Take your scraps of paper or cards with notes on them and staple together all of those in the same category.

Organize your categories in chronological order showing your entire work life, school, hobby, and volunteer experience. You can tell at a glance which activities relate most to the job in question. This is why it's best to work with hard copy for the organizational stage of preparing your résumé.

Employers prefer résumés that are orderly and that show chronological facts grouped in categories without gaps. The facts will impress employers if categories are tied together in a concrete manner with the most recent experience listed first, then the most recent training.

If you are just graduating and don't have any experience, list degrees and relevant credentials first. You may also try the abilities résumé instead or use the chronological résumé but list unpaid activities, internships, or training practice in a work-like setting. Use action verbs to make the best impression. Use all action verbs to describe related job experience, whether you worked for pay or volunteered for training or an internship. See page 35 for a sample chronological résumé format.

The Abilities Résumé

Names of employers, educational history, and dates are left out of an *abilities résumé,* which is designed to emphasize your qualifications. The abilities résumé rejects any chronological order.

The abilities résumé is excellent for freelancers, consultants, and temporary workers looking to switch from freelance to corporate or educational employment. Sometimes it accompanies a portfolio or list of publications. Use it if you don't want to reveal your age or lack of corporate experience, are seeking work after retirement, if you have worked as a consultant or independent contractor, are a homemaker or a house husband, or if you want to switch from owning your own firm to working for others. However, use the abilities résumé only as a last resort if you absolutely must leave out dates, names of employers, and educational material that would prejudice an employer at first glance. Most employers overwhelmingly prefer the chronological résumé.

What If You Have Gaps?

The abilities résumé is suited for persons with gaps in their work life. Perhaps you served in the military, spent time in prison, recuperated from health problems, became a perpetual student, took time out to rear children, volunteer, travel, or write books, decided to lead the life of a fine artist, or tried your hand at acting, and now you have decided that the computer industry is right for you.

You may have worked as a consultant or ran your own business for a time and then decided to moonlight part time or pull out and look for a full-time job. You may have stayed home raising children for a number of years. On your résumé, how do you account for large gaps in time when you weren't employed for someone else in a paying job?

The strategy for filling in time gaps is to use an abilities résumé. At the start of creating an abilities résumé, you'll find that your skills are fragmented into related categories of talents, skills, abilities, hobbies, or interests.

What you do each day shows your interests, who you are, and what you most wish you could do. The books you read generally fall into one or more categories that you prefer. Everyone has preference for tasks they do and would like to continue doing. Everyone also has a work temperament where some skills come more easily than others.

List Your Responsibilities

Your abilities, according to you, are really responsibilities to your future employer. So it's your responsibilities that would be listed on an abilities résumé. Certain responsibilities cross over to many different jobs; they are known as transferable skills. In an abilities résumé, you don't list a sequential job history. Instead, you emphasize your abilities and responsibilities in order of importance.

The reason your employers' names and dates of employment are left off of an abilities résumé is because you're emphasizing your expertise in a field. Expertise is gained during a lifetime of increasing responsibilities. These responsibilities accumulate from many different jobs, interests, life experiences, training, service, volunteerism, free-lancing, consulting, traveling, hobbies, and caregiving.

List Your Job Objectives

An abilities résumé is brief and limited to one page. It's concise and structured. Begin an abilities/responsibilities résumé with your name, address, and phone at the top, as with other résumés.

Below this, briefly state your specific job objective or a concrete employment goal. There should be no abstractions, ambiguity, or vagueness about your job objective.

Expertise or Involvement

Under the job objective, write the body of the résumé. The abilities résumé is only five paragraphs long. Each paragraph has a bold heading that stands out for each area of expertise.

If you don't think you have expertise in any one area, then list any involvement. To an employer involvement is expertise. Involvement suggests future expertise and present interest or preference. Most computer personnel find one area of the industry particularly appealing.

What's Your Payoff?

Ask yourself, "What's the payoff for my interest or involvement?" If you are involved in something, you'll soon become an expert if you are motivated to practice your skills. Is the involvement a labor of love or a love of the labor? Is your motivation the money you earn or the ego satisfaction? List any talents and skills you've developed. Think of the possibilities of what you're involved in now for what you'll be an expert in with continued experience.

If you have expertise in anything that can be applied to any facet of the computer industry, list it. Expertise in fashion design software sales or accounting systems database management are interests far apart but relevant to the computer industry.

If You Have No Experience

If you have no experience in any field related to the computer industry but would like volunteer experience in writing about computers and software, try writing reviews of new software and sending these brief articles to weekly and monthly computer industry newspapers and magazines. Thousands of new software programs in every category imaginable flood the market monthly.

Computer interest publications may print your reviews or articles. Some pay only in free copies of the publication. Information on new software is available from manufacturers.

Accumulate news clips of software reviews with your byline. These will impress an employer if the job for which you're applying requires expertise in technical communications or public relations. For persons seeking programming experience, try volunteering to work on computers at public or private schools or tutoring at business and technical schools.

The Function of an Abilities Résumé

The function of an abilities résumé is to outline how you turn your interests into involvement; how you turn involvement into responsibilities; and how you shape responsibilities into expertise.

Skills

Under your expertise paragraphs, group your skills by category in order of importance. List as your first skill the one that you use primarily in your present job or the skill you wish to use in your next career.

Typical headings for your skills paragraphs might be Desktop Publishing, Proofreading, Organization of Software User and Training Manuals, Support, Coordination of Documents, Documentation Analysis, and Word Processing. All of these skills show you have expertise with specific software that required training—either on the job, self-taught, or in a classroom.

Responsibilities

By grouping your skills as expertise, you tell an employer what responsibilities you handled on past jobs and what you are capable of handling in the next job. You want to show you can make a smooth transition between the software skills you used as a word processing secretary, for example, and the organizational and editorial skills you'll learn as you step up the ladder to a higher-paid job as a technical writer or editor.

You may be competing for a job against hundreds of applicants who have many years of experience as technical writers, instructional technologists, or courseware designers, as well as recent four-year college graduates with creative writing, English, journalism, education, computer information systems, and public relations majors and no work experience.

For example, suppose the job you want calls for someone to write/edit software user manuals so they're easy to understand. Who will the employer hire as the right person for the job? The former secretary who longs to be a technical writer, or the experienced technical writer with a programming background? Most often hired is the person who can make complex manuals easy to understand for beginners using the software for the first time.

Responsibility stands between you and the job you want. Responsibility is highlighted in the brief summary of your achievements, or qualifications. The brief summary of your responsibilities is one paragraph listed under each category of skills.

What Employers Don't Like About the Abilities Résumé
For most full-time in-house jobs, the abilities résumé arouses suspicion that the person with this type of résumé may be better off as an entrepreneur or independent contractor. Suspicious staff managers complain that the abilities résumé is frequently used to disguise job hoppers who've had many jobs for short periods of time.

Temporary Work
Temporary work should be listed as such. Make sure you're seen as a steady or long-term, loyal employee of a temporary employment service and not as a constant job changer. Many such services offer benefits to long-term workers who are sent out on many assignments over the years.

A dramatic increase in temporary desktop publishing and word-processing jobs have made temping an acceptable way of networking and presenting your computer skills until a company offers you a full-time or permanent job.

Drastic Career Change
If you feel that an abilities résumé might arouse suspicion about your work history, use the chronological résumé instead. However, when you make a drastic career change, the abilities résumé is excellent for showing a transfer of old skills to new job areas. Be sure to show how your experience in an unrelated field is relevant to the computer industry.

The Modified Abilities Résumé
The *modified abilities résumé* uses a concise chronological listing of job titles, employers, dates, and job descriptions. This abbreviated history follows your description of ability or function with the most recent employment listed first (reverse chronological order).

Military retirees switching to a totally different career field, former entrepreneurs, and mature homemakers re-entering the workplace after a long absence are comfortable with modified abilities résumés. They can show their entire work histories summarized in one page of work highlights.

The Expanded Résumé

On those rare occasions when you must have a two-page résumé, use the expanded résumé to include important information. For example, suppose you are a computer scientist working on highly classified material in a government job. You apply for a university teaching position or a research and development job in the corporate world using your scientific knowledge to develop special software. All of the relevant material may not fit on a one-page résumé.

Perhaps you are a writer who has never worked outside the home but would like to attach a list of your published books on computer careers and your published articles when you apply for a job as a documentation analyst. A video game artist's portfolio may also use an expanded résumé/portfolio package.

Stretch Detail and Simplify

The purpose of an expanded résumé is to use detail to stretch and simplify. The first page of an expanded résumé contains your name, address, phone number, and a brief summary of your work history. Include all the software and hardware you are familiar with and your job objective.

Names of employers and dates are included on the first page along with job titles, starting with the most recent job. Also list your training, education, degrees, and certificates in reverse chronological order.

The second page expands the job record and summarizes descriptions of duties performed using action verbs. Start sentences with verbs such as *programmed, designed, illustrated, animated, edited, wrote, coordinated, analyzed, managed, operated,* and so forth, stating whatever action you took on the project. Use the verb that best describes the duties you want to emphasize for each job.

The sentences should be brief—fewer than ten words each. Action verbs should be strong, dramatic, and show exactly what you did. Instead of writing, "Participated in the revision of a software manual," or "Helped coordinate the word-processing pool and the technical writers and illustrators in producing many iterations of a classified report on fire control for the military," simply state the following:

> *Dates: 1993–1994*
> *Job title: Documentation Analyst*
> *ABC Corporation*
> *123 Rex Drive*
> *Ararat, California   (619) 555-1234*
> *Duties: "Revised (name of software) manuals and classified reports on fire control according to military specifications. Re-wrote, edited, and proofread manuals, reports, training materials, and documents."*

Narration

A short narration expands your job titles into job descriptions on the second page of an expanded résumé. The responsibilities always encompass more than the job describes. The work history is long and detailed in an expanded résumé. The experience is often diverse. Sometimes each succeeding job is unrelated to the one that came before.

One employer received a résumé for a computer graphic designer's job that described a woman's 31-year work history of diverse, unrelated jobs such as bellydancer, nun, career counselor, programmer, computer-aided designer, corporate animator, and software manufacturer's representative. She had earned a master's degree in career counseling in the sixties, followed by an associate degree in computer science in the eighties, and a second A.S. degree in computer-aided design and animation in the nineties. A two-page résumé in this case served to emphasize how diverse skills could be combined to support the new job objective.

Disadvantages

The main disadvantage of a two-page résumé is that employers won't take the time to read it. The second page may be ignored. Many employers do not like an expansion of self-importance on a résumé. Once employed, however, employers may insist workers toot their own horn to show they have the self-esteem to turn hard work into advancement. See page 37 for a sample expanded résumé format.

The Creative Résumé

If you are applying for a highly creative job, then use a *creative résumé* to show how you relate your imagination to your work or to promote a company's character. For the majority of creative people in the computer industry who adapt imagination to reality, the creative résumé reveals the drive toward a creative expression.

Computer industry employers that receive creative résumés fall into some of the following niches: multimedia and presentation graphics; entertainment software and video game design; virtual reality; midi-synthesizer/computer music software design; special effects; corporate animation/desktop animation; desktop video; desktop publishing (electronic publishing); graphic design (commercial art); hardware architecture design; neural networks research; telecommunications; instructional software design; interactive fiction software production; corporate and entertainment scriptwriting; technical writing; fashion and textile design; interior or building architecture design with software; engineering graphics; computer-aided drafting; health care personnel training video production; robotics; children's programming; and applied artificial intelligence design.

Some of these niches, such as interior, textile, and fashion design, regularly use software to create their patterns and designs. The software is manufactured by computer firms but purchased by employers in the garment, textile, or interior decor industry. That's why portfolios are often part of a creative résumé package.

Portfolio With Résumé

If your job objective is creative, use a one-page résumé and attach a laser color photocopy portfolio of your work for art job objectives; or send a nonreturnable videotape for desktop video and virtual reality jobs, or slides for technical illustration. For writing jobs, attach photocopied, published clips or writing samples, and include a list of publications.

A creative résumé can be used for job objectives that emphasize imagination and analysis—especially for jobs with ad agencies or software design firms. In addition to art and writing, creative résumés can be used to show originality in programming or systems analysis, entertainment games design, software engineering, and the design of computer hardware architecture. (Hardware architecture design includes the engineering and design of hardware circuits, not the software.)

Artwork does not belong in the résumé itself. It should always be attached as a nonreturnable sample or shown in a portfolio. Use an 8½" by 11" sheet of good quality paper. Printed résumés are excellent as are quality photocopies on what some quick copy shops call résumé paper.

Cute résumés with teddy bears, scrolls, and résumés on computer disk and audiotape are all going to end up in the round file after the staff has a good laugh. If you use a creative résumé, keep it brief, serious, and business-like. Many employers now request faxed résumés in job advertisements. Therefore, it's acceptable, and may even be preferred, to fax your résumé. A mailed résumé can take from one to three days to get to an employer, whereas a faxed résumé takes only minutes to arrive.

Employers prefer computer artists to attach to the back of their résumés a nonreturnable portfolio of labeled artwork or slides accompanied by a table of contents. For interactive software and technical writers, employers ask to see a list of publications or published books and manuals and two writing samples or news clips of your published articles. Submit your best work, which should exemplify your creativity, imagination, and originality. In twenty seconds an employer will scan your résumé and samples for a quick first impression.

Persuasion

The creative résumé's purpose is to get you an interview. Creative résumés are fashioned after direct marketing letters. They are brief but powerful sales tools designed to convince companies to respond or to act. A creative résumé is like a marketing letter; it's written to be so interesting that a company buys the product—in this case, you. Direct marketing letters are often tracked to see whether they bring in sales. Track your résumé to see where it goes and who responds to it.

Training Shortages

You can design your creative résumé to address current training shortages in your field. Manufacturing employment in general is decreasing and downsizing in the United States. Yet ironically, training shortages exist in the field of computerized manufacturing in many cities. When it comes to computerized manufacturing, minimal awareness of this field causes job seekers to overlook the burgeoning jobs in numeric control technology.

A creative résumé can emphasize how you will fit into the expanding and understaffed field of numeric control, or how you will create visibility for companies using numeric control technology, for example. On such a résumé you could show all the benefits of computerizing manufacturing and how you will fit in.

Create Your Own Job Description

Create your own job and job description. In this way, a creative résumé is used to create your own niche or job in a new technology you could introduce to a computer company. The firm may not know how to create a job for you that doesn't exist.

Your cover letter could use terms like the following to point out benefits of the new technology you are introducing: "increased accuracy, greater repeatability, and faster production." For example, there is an explosive growth of numeric control machines in the marketplace, but American companies have fallen short of attracting new workers into the changing manufacturing industry.

A creative cover letter could show how you would attract new workers. You want to convince management that if you are hired, you will show them how numeric control can make changes for the company's benefit, production increase, and profit. These facts explained in your cover letter would also be summarized or detailed briefly on your résumé.

Create Bridges by Finding Out a Company's Needs

If you are switching careers, a creative résumé could act as your bridge between the trades and the professions. Your résumé may appeal to a worldwide market. The creative résumé can accommodate computer-aided design and manufacturing, thus showing an employer the potential of a company's investment in you.

A creative résumé lets an employer know that you don't intend to be used in rudimentary ways and it can show a company how to stop using computerized equipment in rudimentary ways. Creative résumés, like all résumés, show that you've done your homework and that you've researched a company and its needs before applying for a job.

On-The-Job Training

Creative résumés often focus on training objectives and are also effective if you are applying for a training position yourself. If you are competing for a job as a trainer, a training manager, or a training materials designer, the winning résumé would explain that buying software and machinery isn't all you would do.

On-the-job training looks great on a résumé because it shows you have had the challenge of being pressured to produce while focusing on learning as well. Classroom training outside of the work environment doesn't show the same challenge because you don't have the interruptions of the workplace.

You can also change careers faster through on-the-job training. For example, if you are a machinist who wants to enter the computer industry, perhaps as a robotics technician, the creative résumé can help you change careers and get an employer to retrain you at company expense.

Respond To Changes, Competition

A correctly written creative résumé makes you more competitive. Computerized manufacturers are no longer competing with one another in a closed market. Your creative résumé can reveal how you can aptly handle working and communicating in a worldwide market.

A creative résumé responds to changes. The computerized medical products industry, artificial intelligence, robotics, and computerized manufacturing are receptive to creative résumés. A creative résumé is practical but also has a vision for the future that compels the employer to call you back.

Response Is All That Matters

Your creative résumé is an honest ad. A résumé, similar to a direct mail ad, is a type of writing where the quality of the words can be measured precisely, accurately, and scientifically. The measurement is based on how many interviews each résumé generated before you're eventually hired. Your résumé is measured by how much profit it made for you—or how much money it lost.

You can test your résumé against one written by another person with the same qualifications. The best résumé is the one that produced the most solid job offers.

In résumé writing, response is everything. Changes are occurring in the places least conspicuous. For example, while urban daily newspapers are merging and decreasing in number, the computer industry press is growing in terms of job openings for creative people.

There are many more computer industry newspapers hiring creative personnel like reporters and desktop publishing designers than there are urban daily newspapers absorbing journalism school graduates. The bad news is that smaller periodicals often pay less. Creative people in the computer industry frequently find higher-paying jobs with publishers of computer books and software user manuals.

See page 39 for a sample creative résumé format.

PRESENTING AND SUPPORTING
YOUR OBJECTIVES

A résumé emphasizes your ability to do the job. Whichever format you choose, you'll highlight those qualifications that best support your objective. Most résumés today are hybrids. They are combinations of many components taken from chronological and abilities formats that most powerfully present your abilities.

The result of preparing an unforgettable, professional-looking résumé will be interviews. The résumé writing practice will prepare you for the interview, and the exercise in organizing your résumé will help you focus your knowledge, skills, and experience. Writing a résumé puts you in touch with where you are and where you want to go in your career.

If You Want to Get Hired, Help a Company Gain Recognition

Use your résumé when you join associations. Become an active member and get to know people with the authority to hire you. Sponsor awards or contests or scholarships to give others recognition and to help them grow in their jobs. This is the quickest way to gain recognition in the computer industry, even if you have no experience.

After you are hired, such activities will help your company gain recognition. As you further your image, you will be hired to continue similar activities to further your employer's image. However, as we will see later in this book, the first step in promoting your image is not always writing your résumé; it can also be writing a convincing cover letter.

Summarize Success

Your résumé is a summary of success (work history plus training). Résumé styles differ in the order and presentation of concrete work life details. The chronological work style is what most employers prefer because of its effectiveness and efficiency.

Summarize success. Be first. Reposition yourself.

Always Be First in an Employer's Mind

American businesses process 1.4 trillion sheets of paper annually. One sheet is your résumé. Many computer companies average 400 résumés for a job opening. Your résumé could be buried under towers of paper or software. In the computer industry, it's better to be a big fish in a microscopic pond. If you can't be first, reposition yourself. Enhance the image you have formulated by creating a niche.

In the next chapter, we'll explore how to create the visual appeal of cover and follow-up letters. We'll also discuss the six types of cover letters.

NAME
Street Address
City, State, Zip
Phone number with area code

JOB OBJECTIVE:

Use exact job title or specific statement indicating the type of position you want and type of organization selected.

HIGHLIGHTS OF QUALIFICATIONS:

Summarize your abilities, responsibilities, skills, qualifications, and achievements.

RELATED SKILLS:

Begin each skill with an action verb. List skills and accomplishments. Relate and transfer skills to the position preferred. Draw from all volunteer and paid experience. Group skills under subheadings.

**WORK HISTORY:
(DATES LISTED IN CHRONOLOGICAL ORDER)**

Begin with the most recent paid or unpaid work or activity, including computer related hobbies where you offer people training, how to advice, or share information within computer user special interest groups. Include any freelance article or promotional writing (e.g., public relations, press releases for trade journals, associations, or businesses).

**EDUCATION:
(LISTED IN CHRONOLOGICAL ORDER)**

List the most recent training first, name of school, degree earned, major area of study, or relevant coursework. Include workshops, GPA average of 3.5 or better. List any relevant seminars or work shops or continuing education in a computer-related field. List any licenses or teaching credentials.

MEMBERSHIPS IN ASSOCIATIONS:

List any memberships in business, educational, professional, or computer-related associations, and offices/jobs you held, such as organization newsletter editor, convention and events planner, speaker, membership chair, or job referral director.

REFERENCES:

Furnished upon request.

Name
Street Address
City, State, Zip
Phone number with area code

OVERVIEW
(Job title) utilizing (specific name) software or hardware

HIGHLIGHTS OF QUALIFICATIONS

- Knowledgeable in various applications of _____.
- Hardworking, dedicated, and dependable;
  can be counted on to get the job done.
- Easily develop good relationships with
  coworkers, staff, and students.
- Adjust well to new learning environments.

EDUCATION AND SPECIALIZED TRAINING

A.S., Office Information Systems
Microcomputer Professional Certificate
San Diego City College, San Diego, CA

DBase IV+	WordPerfect 6.0+	Database Management
Lotus 1-2-3	Ventura for Windows 4.1+	Spreadsheets
PageMaker	Microcomputer Installation	Computer Presentations
AdPro	Disk Operating Systems	Adobe Illustrator
Graphics	CorelDraw!	

RELATED EXPERIENCE AND ABILITIES

- Organized _____
- Coordinated _____
- Revised _____
- Proofed _____
- Determined _____
- Recorded _____
- Entered information
  from_____into_____
- Processed _____
- Drafted _____
- Prepared _____
- Maintained _____
- Performed _____
- Tracked _____
- Inventoried _____
- Answered _____

REFERENCES FURNISHED UPON REQUEST

NAME
Street Address
City, State, Zip
Phone number with area code

OBJECTIVE—To be responsible for_____ (use appropriate action verbs such as analyzing, solving problems, illustrating, designing, coordinating a specific department, writing/editing, researching, programming, troubleshooting, etc.).
To work with challenging projects with a leading provider of _____(insert the specific type of industry such as "a leading provider of clinical laboratory services").
To have an outstanding growth opportunity with an organization providing _____(e.g. data processing) services to _____(e.g. the federal government).

SUMMARY: More than _____ years' experience in _____. Expertise in _____ (use action verb such as designed or coordinated). In one brief sentence state whether you have authored related articles, or books, illustrated any published computer art, or designed animation.

POSITIONS HELD: List names of employers, job titles, and dates (in reverse chronological order).

EDUCATION: Names of institutions attended, training programs, degrees, and certificates.
(The next section expands your experience into action-oriented accomplishments.)

SOFTWARE EXPERIENCE: List all the software you know how to use and have had experience using. Indicate whether you install the software and design or modify it.

HARDWARE EXPERIENCE: List the models of computers you use, the hardware equipment, whether you are knowledgeable in networking, whether the computers are PCs or mainframe, Cray supercomputers, or any other relevant hardware information. Indicate whether you troubleshoot and repair the hardware.

PROFESSIONAL EXPERIENCE:

Dates:
(Most
recent dates
first)

Start with the most recent date and list your job title. Under the job title list what you did recently using action verbs. Which division of what department or team did you work with within the corporation or institution? Use action verbs similar to the samples listed below

- Analyzed _____.
- Ran _____ programs.
- Solved _____ problems.
- Reduced costs by $ _____ in _____ (year).
- Increased gross sales by $ _____ annually for corp.

37

NAME
page 2

- Made mathematical approximations.
- Interpreted _____.
- Established _____.
- Translated _____.
- Interfaced/interacted _____
- Produced documentation for_____.
- Met deadlines for _____.
- Published _____.
- Produced _____.
- Presented _____.
- Wrote _____.

TEACHING EXPERIENCE:
(Most recent dates first)

Date   NAME OF SCHOOL WHERE YOU WERE TEACHING
Job title (such as graduate assistant)
- Taught _____ to community college students.

Date   NAME OF SCHOOL
- Taught _____ to high school students as substitute and part-time hourly instructor.

Date   NAME OF SCHOOL
- Taught _____ to senior citizens at an intergenerational computer camp.

Date   •Lectured on _____ as a freelance public speaker.
(List places where you lectured or groups you spoke to.)

MILITARY SERVICE:
Dates   • BRANCH OF SERVICE, Job title.
(List job duties if related to your field now.)
State whether you were honorably discharged.

EDUCATION: Names of universities or technical schools.
Dates attended and degrees earned.

LANGUAGES: List any foreign languages you read and speak.

RECOGNITION IN PUBLICATIONS:
Set aside space on this second page to itemize a partial list of your published articles, books, or produced videos. If you have written many books or professional articles, attach a separate page entitled "List of Books and Articles Published."

REFERENCES AVAILABLE UPON REQUEST

NAME
Street Address
City, State, Zip
Phone number with area code

OBJECTIVE

Information Packager

SUMMARY OF QUALIFICATIONS

- Gather information.
- Reshape information.
- Sell information in a variety of formats.
- Design information to meet different needs.
- Information is my most valuable resource.

EDUCATION/TRAINING

Degree, Major, Minor
College, University, or School
Certificates or Specialized Training

RELATED SKILLS

(Action verbs)	BENEFITS TO ORGANIZATION
• Created _____	• _____
• Produced _____	• _____
• Operated _____	• _____
• Selected _____	• _____
• Announced _____	• _____
• Illustrated _____	• _____
• Designed _____	• _____
• Wrote _____	• _____
• Edited _____	• _____
• Proofread _____	• _____
• Researched _____	• _____
• Analyzed _____	• _____
• Prepared _____	• _____
• Delivered _____	• _____
• Coordinated _____	• _____
• Managed _____	• _____
• Trained _____	• _____
• Volunteered _____	• _____

WORK HISTORY

Dates   • Most recent job first

REFERENCES ON REQUEST

3
COVER AND FOLLOW-UP LETTERS

In this chapter, a format and tips for great cover letters are discussed. You will also learn how to use a cover letter to get your résumé noticed in a number of situations. Finally, follow-up letters that get you an interview are described.

THE COVER LETTER

The cover letter personalizes your résumé for each company. Before you sit down to organize your résumé, first write your cover letter. Your mind will be focused on the position as you begin to sort the many details that will form your résumé.

Your cover letter is really a direct marketing letter. Without it, an employer will have to wade through an entire résumé to find out how you will fit into the company. Your one-page cover letter introduces your résumé and communicates a specific message about your value to a company.

A great one-page cover letter begins by pitching (in the first sentence) exactly what position you want in a company. Define yourself as a specialist; today's job market belongs to the specialist rather than a generalist. A cover letter also serves as a powerful introduction to (or umbrella for) anything else included in the envelope and is a sample of your communication skills.

Hook Questions in Your Cover Letter

The first paragraph of your cover letter determines whether the reader will finish the letter. For your sales pitch, in the first brief sentence you need a positive hook. Introduce who you are, your skills, or services. Describe specifically how your skills will be used in the company. "Hook" the employer by stating how timely your services or skills are to the company. Or use a hook question such as, "What's the most powerful resource you have?"

Next, convince the employer to hire you. The simplest way is to give employers an observation they can verify themselves. The observation can be about their needs, or your skills. Computer companies are always searching for new ideas to plug holes or fill needs in the industry. Position your cover letter and résumé as a plug to fill a need.

Try using exclamatory hooks in the second paragraph of your cover letter. There are three types:

1. a fear hook—where you list a series of corporate fears and then tell how you'll solve the problems.
2. a story hook—where you briefly explain how you will provide benefits to the company, using professional expertise or media contacts.
3. an exclamatory hook or startling statistics—where you mention surprising numbers or statistics associated with your career that shock the employer in a positive way.

Finally, an imaginative cover letter closes by making you stand out from the crowd and get hired. (A résumé doesn't reflect the more action-oriented parts of your personality—it only states facts.) End the letter on a positive point. Show the employer how hiring you to apply your skills to the company's needs will bring positive results.

For further information on positioning yourself, read Al Ries and Jack Trout's book, *Positioning: The Battle for Your Mind,* Warner Books, NY, 1986. It provides advice about how to stand out from the crowd and win.

Cover Letter Tips

- Each time your résumé goes to an employer, it should be topped by a cover letter. The courtesy of a cover letter is held in such high esteem by employers that résumés coming in without them frequently are discarded.
- As your computer skills and experience expand, you will have to work hard to condense them in a one-page résumé or cover letter. Think of the entire computer industry as niches or areas of specialty. Your cover letter must be brief, but detailed enough to show your specialty or your unique qualities.
- Use your cover letter to personalize your communication and to establish a rapport with potential employers. Your hidden goal is to build a relationship with someone who has the authority to hire you. A résumé without a cover letter is too impersonal.
- The cover letter should express your enthusiasm and energy. It's your unique style, strength, and personality type that should shine through and move an employer to think of ways in which you could be profitable to the company.

Junk Mail or an Attention Grabber?

In the computer industry, thousands of résumés a year may pile up on someone's desk. These résumés begin to overwhelm an employer, and some may begin to see them as junk mail. These piles are given derogatory names like "the slush pile" in electronic publishing, "the stable" in information processing and technical communications firms, and "portfolio puss" in the corporate animation industry. How can you stand out? Only an action-oriented cover letter saves a résumé from the heap.

Your cover letter can emphasize that you're an award-winning computer illustrator or have recently completed an internship in data analysis or programming. Maybe your volunteer work has won you recognition, or your sales record is outstanding.

If nothing outstanding has happened to you in your work or educational life, then join a professional or trade association and learn all about the newest products of several companies. Act as a volunteer contributor to a local or national computer industry publication, or volunteer to do research or help out on a professional association's special task force or speakers' panel in your area of interest at the next convention.

Most employers who place classified newspaper advertisements request cover letters to accompany résumés. The format of your letter is important. A cover letter format is on page 43 followed by a sample cover letter.

SIX KINDS OF COVER LETTERS

You send a résumé and cover letter when:

1. answering an advertisement.
2. writing to a specific employer—the informational cover letter.
3. asking a friend for job-related information.
4. consulting an employment or outplacement agency.
5. networking with members of a professional or trade organization.
6. attending a trade show, exhibit, convention, or conference.

Answering an Advertisement

Clip ads from trade journals, national employment newspapers, professional organizations' newsletters, computer magazines, and the publications of computer user special interest groups. Write down phone numbers from the tape recorded phone messages of job hotlines for members of trade and professional organizations. Clip ads from your daily newspaper's Sunday help wanted section.

The hidden (not advertised) job market appears mainly in trade journals, those magazines and newspapers directed to readers interested in a particular industry. Most jobs advertise qualifications for the ideal candidate. If the ideal job applicant doesn't respond, often the employer will take what's available.

Send your cover letters and resumes to the widest variety of ads possible, even if you only have some of the qualifications. One reason for this is that company paid training is sometimes available after employment. On-the-job training is offered when the technology is so new that little training is available outside the company. When new software is designed, technical trainers are trained on the job so they can go out to other corporations and train the new software users.

In a classified or display help wanted ad, job requirements are listed according to their rank of importance, with the most important skills listed first. If you don't have all of the requirements, list what capabilities you do have and how those relate to the requirements.

Your Name
City, State, Zip
Phone number

Date of Letter

Name of person with the authority
to hire you in the department
in which you want to work
Title
Name of department
Company name
Street Address
City, State, Zip

Dear Mr./Ms._____:

Opening Paragraph—State the position you want. Tell why you want to work for that company. Make your sales pitch.

Middle Paragraph(s)—Mention your two best qualifications (related to the job in question). Explain how your skills and/or experience would benefit the company. Point out any specialized training or skills that relate to company plans. Sell your abilities. Document your sales pitch with startling statistics or statements showing evidence of your talents. Don't repeat yourself by listing what's on the résumé, however.

Closing Paragraph—Let the reader know that what's attached is your résumé or résumé and portfolio, list of publications, samples, or other itemized achievements. In the last sentence, let the employer know when you will call to set up an interview. (Don't wait for them to call you.) Your closing sentence should ask for a specific action from the company. Re-read the letter to make sure nothing is vague. Make every word concrete and practical enough to be remembered. Anything vague is quickly forgotten. There may be hundreds of competing cover letters on someone's desk.

Sincerely,

(Your handwritten signature in black or blue ink, *never* another color.)

Your Name Typed

Enclosure

SAMPLE COVER LETTER

Jamesa Kintle
123 Mt. Penn Lane
San Justa, CA 92104-7177
(619) 555-1234

July 1, 1993

Ms. Rayanne Hart
Director of Employment
Video Game Corporation
100 Prince Road
San Justa, CA 92104-7199

Dear Ms. Hart:

I want to serve Video Game Corporation. I create exciting, high profile Nintendo and Genesis games, working for the past year in the most fascinating industry possible. Your advertisement in the June 30 issue of the *San Diego Union-Tribune* for a video game artist matches perfectly my skills to your needs.

I understand Video Game Corporation is a fast-expanding San Justa company offering the challenge, environment, and opportunity I'm seeking as an experienced artist specializing in computer graphics, video game design, and corporate animation. I have the ability to draw and paint cartoons and comic book-like characters or background using CorelDraw! software on an IBM-compatible 486 model computer.

I also have illustration, desktop publishing, and desktop video production experience with IBM, Macintosh, and Amiga computers. I'm experienced with Ventura Publisher, PageMaker, and WordPerfect Presentations software.

As detailed in my résumé, my experience centers on video game design and illustration. As an award-winning team member, I gained an appreciation of the cooperation it takes in a large computer video game company to coordinate the art function with all the other areas.

My Special Studies A.S. degree in Computer Sciences and Fine Art from Grossmont College in El Cajon, California, included specific coursework in computer graphics design, presentation graphics, video production, animation, and fine art.

Thank you for your consideration. Enclosed is my résumé and photocopied samples portfolio. You may keep the portfolio. My salary requirements are negotiable. I look forward to meeting with you. I'll call you next Friday at 9:30 a.m. Or if you prefer, you may reach me at (619) 555-1234 after 3 p.m. weekdays to schedule an interview.

Sincerely,

Jamesa Kintle

Enclosure

State how you will be an asset to the company. Take out all extra words; only list strengths in your cover letter. Let's look at an advertisement and analyze how to compose a cover letter.

SOFTWARE SYSTEMS SPECIALIST

You will install user devices, diagnose hardware problems, load software maintenance releases, monitor system and subcontractor performance, maintain communications systems, assist customer end users, and perform other duties as assigned. Requirements include: a demonstrated knowledge of VAX/VMS or DSM operations, maintenance is a plus; a high school diploma/GED and five years directly related experience, or an AA in a related field and three years directly related experience. We offer a competitive compensation and benefits package. Please send your résumé and cover letter indicating department code for position of interest.

The actual ad appeared as a display in the Sunday section of a major urban daily newspaper. The company name and address were listed.

Your first step would be to call the company and find out the name of the person to whom you would direct your letter. You can also ask about new company information, such as new products. In your cover letter, this information can allow you to tell the employer how you could help the company reach its goals.

Some interviewers hold résumés a long time before getting back to you. To offset this waiting period, send a mailgram cover letter. Be assertive and courteous. Call the staff manager first, before you are called, and ask to set up an appointment for an interview. The cover letter on page 53 is a sample of an "answering-an-advertisement cover letter."

Blind Ads

How you respond to a blind newspaper ad is up to you. Some people never respond to blind ads (ads in which the hiring company is not identified). In a highly competitive industry, you may want to know in whose hands your résumé will fall, since it contains confidential information and your home address.

Thousands of companies use blind ads because they have economic reasons to remain anonymous. They may be placed by executive search firms on behalf of corporations. You must decide whether you want to discount potentially great opportunities by not responding to such ads.

WRITING TO A SPECIFIC EMPLOYER—THE INFORMATIONAL COVER LETTER

A different approach to your career search is to ask for information in your cover letter, rather than a job. Interview a department manager to make informed career decisions. This keeps you in touch with the company on a friendly, fact-seeking basis. Read the biographies of executives of major or fast-moving companies, which can usually be found in public libraries.

The department head for the area in which you want to work is the person who should receive your cover letter and with whom you should establish a rapport. Only the division specialist has the expertise in your area of interest, not the generalist in personnel. Address your fact-finding letters to the person who has the authority to hire you. Use a specific title such as Mr. Gene Wright, Manager of Information Systems, Day Computer Corporation, Inc.

Never send your letter to anyone without first calling and getting the correct spelling of the individual's name and title. Letters sent to the personnel or human resources department tend to get screened out. Often a personnel department's purpose is to weed out the unqualified.

You will have the best chance of getting hired if you send a mailgram cover letter and résumé with your business card. All job applicants should have business cards listing their three best skills and any degrees or technical school diplomas. Such a business card may look like this example.

TECHNICAL WRITER/SOFTWARE USER MANUALS
Dawn Whisper, M.A.
Public Relations, Training Materials,
Courseware Design
P.O. Box 123
San Diego, CA 92164
(619) 555-4321

Your database of employers may be gleaned from professional and computer journals, business publications, trade and professional associations, computer user groups, industrial directories, and the Yellow Pages. See Chapter 11 for additional resources.

Most of your research will be in finding out what type of software and hardware or applications systems are used in each company. Call the companies before you send them any letters or résumés and ask what systems they are currently using. Never waste your cover letters on unresearched companies.

You can also ask for a list of their suppliers and research those firms for possible job leads. For example, one salesperson didn't land a job at the company first applied to but found a great job with one of the company's material suppliers.

In addition to companies that supply computer corporations, there are other businesses that provide technical staff training with all of these companies. Networking expands the possibilities of finding jobs that match your skills. Employment agencies use this same kind of research to drum up job orders.

Keep in mind during your research that almost all corporations outside the computer industry use computers as tools. Most firms have information systems departments where data entry, word processing, and desktop publishing are accomplished. Also, corporate video production studios have computers connected to VCR machines and video cameras to create multimedia presentations, usually for training videos or product demonstrations called desktop video (DV) studios. Large corporations have management information systems (MIS) departments and computer operations divisions. Smaller companies have database management departments or data processing (DP) departments. Electronic publishing companies have desktop publishing departments and technical illustration or computer-aided design departments. Computer-aided manufacturing companies may use computer-controlled robots.

When you first telephone a company, ask for the director of computer operations or the manager of information systems. Either person can usually tell you which types of hardware and software are used by the firm. What you are seeking in your research are facts about a company's hardware and software, people, and job openings. Send out a dozen letters at a time to carefully targeted firms where you have already made verbal contact by phone or have interviewed directors of departments for company or product information.

Personalize all cover letters. Never send a form letter or a letter with a photocopied signature. End the letter with a question that makes it easy for the person to call you back with a product related or technical answer. By asking a technical question rather than asking for a job at first contact, you're seen as a potential customer. Emphasize how you can be of value to the business. This is a direct-mail campaign to show a company the specific advantages and benefits of your abilities.

See the sample cover letter to a specific employer on page 54.

ASKING A FRIEND FOR JOB-RELATED INFORMATION

This type of cover letter is used to gather job leads. Use it so that a copy of your résumé may be passed to people your friend meets at work or during meetings. You are not asking for a job in this letter. You only want information. Use the information to develop a profile of employers, companies, or job requirements.

Let your friend know you're looking for a certain type of job—maybe even with clients of your friend's company. Write an informal, friendly letter instead of a formal business cover letter, and have your friend pass the résumé only to personal friends and clients with authority to hire you. Sending three copies of your résumé with the letter is acceptable.

Ask for suggestions in the letter. Mention any plans for, or openness to, relocation. Let your friend know whether your correspondence is confidential. Leave out salary references. Human resources information is harder to obtain than product information. Some companies promote from within or pay a recruitment fee of several hundred dollars to any employee bringing in a qualified friend who fills a new job opening. Many new jobs aren't advertised to people outside the company until all employees are given a chance to apply. It pays to have a friend on the inside to pass around your résumé.

See page 55 for a sample personal cover letter asking a friend for job-related information.

CONSULTING AN EMPLOYMENT OR OUTPLACEMENT AGENCY

Target only those agencies that specialize in your field. For example, write to those agencies that specialize in placing military retirees, displaced homemakers, programmers, word processors and desktop publishers, database managers and systems analysts, accountants, software engineers, persons over age 55, recent college graduates, graphic designers, animators, drafters, technical writers or illustrators, temporary technical contract workers, or to outplacement services for displaced computer personnel or other specialized jobs.

You can also write to executive search and recruiting firms and job consultants who work within placement agencies. Address your letter to the director. The purpose of a cover letter sent to an employment agency is to set up a personal interview. Ask to have your résumé kept in the active file. Include in your cover letter when you'll call to set up an interview.

Keep the cover letter to an employment agency brief. Most executive recruiters will rewrite your résumé according to their own formats. Ask to see your résumé before they send it out. If you don't, you'll lose control of how they present you on paper.

Find out whether your résumé will be downloaded onto a disk and sent electronically to companies across the nation or added to mailing lists.

A sample cover letter to an employment or outplacement agency is on page 52.

NETWORKING WITH MEMBERS OF A PROFESSIONAL OR TRADE ORGANIZATION

You can use a professional organization three ways:

1. Use their letterhead when you write your cover letter to an employer.
2. Send your cover letter and résumé to the director of a trade organization for job referral or use of the job bank.
3. A cover letter and résumé directed to the job-referral officer or job hotline coordinator of a professional organization can be helpful if you do some homework. Work on the job bank for the trade organization, where you can develop a portfolio or database of details about the companies you solicit for job orders to go in the organization's job referral databank.

Volunteer to work with a professional or trade association, a regional or national organization of people interested in a specific area of computing. A list of these organizations appears in the Appendix of this book. Select the area of your interest and explore. Once you are in a professional organization, seek increased responsibility to establish contacts and relationships with other members and to show your talents. Volunteer to speak on panels at conventions.

Most of these computer professional or computer user societies have task forces or committees, user groups, or networks of people employed in the same or related areas of computing. There are public relations task forces, newsletters, fundraising committees, membership drives, speaker special interest groups (SIGs), and job bank listings. If you are looking for a job, try the professional computer groups and trade organizations first and then the hobby user groups.

Target the job bank SIG. If you are part of this SIG, focus on calling employers to get job listings for the recorded telephone job hotline for your members. Your job bank task force might work alongside a committee that arranges internships for students, or recent graduates or retirees re-entering the work force (often the student membership committee).

After you have established telephone rapport with a recruiter or department manager at several of the corporations, you can call for the hotline jobs and then send your own cover letter and résumé to recruiters with whom you've talked. Keep it brief, and mention your affiliation with the trade or professional organization.

You might ask your contacts to provide you with old job performance evaluations from former employees with jobs similar to yours. These evaluations will give you an idea of what people in the company thought of employees' skill levels. That way, you'll know what's expected of your performance on the job.

If your qualifications are appropriate for the job you want, include some of the job evaluation terminology in your cover letter to a prospective employer. At least knowing the details will help you fit in with the company on the same level of terminology.

Joining a professional or trade association demonstrates to employers two important facts about you:

1. What you can do as a volunteer and
2. How you handle responsibility.

Always include in your cover letter your volunteer association experience and the details of how you handle responsibility for your trade or professional association.

A sample cover letter used to network with members of a professional or trade association is shown on page 56.

ATTENDING A TRADE SHOW, EXHIBIT, CONVENTION, OR CONFERENCE

When you attend a convention or conference, visit the exhibit booths of each company. Ask the person at the booth the name of the department head, president, or person in charge of hiring for the department of your interest.

Write that person's name down on a sealed envelope containing your cover letter and résumé. Your cover letter would be addressed generically, for example, "Dear Exhibitor." Hand the envelope to the booth clerk.

If the person in charge of the booth or exhibit is the company president or employer, hand it over and start a conversation about the company's products, services, and personnel needs. Smile, chat, and leave a positive impression of yourself with whomever is representing the company at the exhibit booth.

If you know about a convention or trade show well in advance, volunteer to be on a panel or announce a workshop, even if you only introduce others or speak for five minutes. If you have experience, send your proposals to read a research paper, speak on a workshop panel, or give a seminar.

Many conventions have exhibitions of your state's task force in a specific field. Send your cover letter and résumé to your state advisory board on training and practice in your computer specialty. You might volunteer to join your state advisory committee board for drafting, or whatever your computer specialty is. For example, the Minnesota State Drafting Advisory Committee (MSDAC) is a task force located at the Department of Vocational and Technical Education of the University of Minnesota.

Consider handing out samples of your work with your cover letter and résumé at conventions and trade shows. If your job interest is in computer illustration or drafting, hand out nonreturnable samples in a miniportfolio to key representatives at trade shows. If you are a technical writer, include a list of publications and a published (or self-published) writing sample or news clipping with your cover letter and résumé.

A typical cover letter is on page 57, to be handed (with your résumé) to prominent speakers and company representatives at trade show exhibits, conferences, or conventions.

INTERVIEWS

Rarely will companies give first interviews at trade shows or conventions—unless the trade show is a job fair sponsored by several companies who are set up to recruit personnel at the gathering. Job fairs are usually sponsored by colleges or by professional and trade associations.

Some companies give only one interview. Others put you before several individuals from the personnel department. You then interview with the department manager. At a later date, you may be given a final group interview, before a board of subject experts who will decide whether to hire you. When each interview is over, send a different follow-up letter.

THE FOLLOW-UP LETTER FORMAT

A follow-up letter may be used at two different stages in the job hunt.

> 1. Right after every interview, send a follow-up letter of thanks to the interviewer.

2. You have sent your résumé with a cover letter. A few days later you made a follow-up phone call and still you were not called in for an interview. Now is the time to send a follow-up letter to seek the answer to the question "What stands between me and this job?"

The follow-up letter is more than a thank-you note or common courtesy. It's a reminder of your qualifications and continued interest in the company. The follow-up emphasizes to an employer that you want to work for the company, even if the job advertised isn't right for you this time around. If you didn't land the job for which you applied, another one will open.

Like the cover letter, the follow-up letter should be one page, usually three to six paragraphs. The format of a follow-up letter displayed on page 58 is followed by a sample letter.

Fannie Meghan
659 Starview Terrace
Broadview, New York 02113
(212) 555-1234

September 1, 1993

Miss Tricia Knowleton Price
Careers For Women Over Fifty, Inc.
909 Crestline Avenue
New York, NY 09124

Dear Miss Price:

Thank you for your exciting panel presentation on computer careers for workforce re-entry women over 50 at the Displaced Homemakers' Center. As I mentioned in Monday's phone conversation, I feel my strengths are in computer sales and software retailing. A copy of my résumé is enclosed detailing my software sales experience.

I have recently completed a course in sales given by the Broadview Chamber of Commerce. As a hobby, I collect software on database management. I own Paradox and DBase software and an IBM computer. I am a full-time volunteer at the Broadview Computer Society and president of the Senior Computer Users' Special Interest Group.

I've spent the last ten years involved in selling shareware software and presenting exhibits of various software to computer user and hobbyist association members.

I am particularly interested in working for database search companies, software libraries, and software location services, or selling software as a manufacturer's representative. I'm presently lecturing on Best Software for Screenwriters to the scriptwriting class of the Clarion Senior's Center. As a part-time software manufacturer's representative I often voluntarily promote the software as a sideline when I volunteer as public speaker, which is my hobby. So you see how easy it would be for me to slide into software sales and promotion as a paid job. I am a widow who is free to travel the country selling software wholesale or retail.

As you review my background and areas of interest, you'll see benefits I can offer a manufacturer as a software representative. I am open to relocation anywhere.

I'll call you next week for an interview. Perhaps we can have lunch.

Sincerely,

Fannie Meghan

Mary Ellen Kyle
1234 Grandview Terrace
Santa Rachel, CA 92104
(619) 555-5678

July 1, 1993

Mr. Leon August
Crest Computers
91011 Pacific Rim Gorge
Agua, CA 92105

Dear Mr. August:

In response to your advertisement in the *San Francisco Chronicle* of July 1, 1993, for a desktop publisher and desktop video producer, I'm enclosing my résumé.

I am deeply dedicated to both desktop publishing and desktop video. For the past two years I have been producing how-to computer videos as well as writing and publishing software user manuals for the latest version of Windows software. I work at home as a freelance producer and writer using an IBM compatible computer as well as an Amiga computer with Video Toaster hardware and a variety of multimedia software for a variety of software designers.

In the field of desktop publishing, I create software user manuals using WordPerfect software and Ventura for Windows as well as AdPro software. My self-published software manuals accompany my how-to videotape entitled "Everything You Want To Know About Windows." I also have an industrial broadcast quality video camera, Genlock equipment to interface my computer with my video camera, and a full range of videotape editing equipment. I am also able to produce minor special effects and animation in my desktop video productions.

I have the ability to handle all the requirements of your position in both desktop publishing and desktop video as well as multimedia presentations. I am interested in a staff job with Crest Computers handling all your desktop publishing and desktop video needs.

I am an award-winning desktop publisher and video producer who can make technical subjects easy and entertaining to learn; I can fill your needs. My background includes a master's degree in English literature and an associate degree in desktop publishing and desktop video. I will call on July 14 at 10 a.m. to answer any questions and to set up an appointment at your leisure. Thank you for considering me for the position.

Sincerely,

Mary Ellen Kyle

Enclosure

SAMPLE COVER LETTER: SPECIFIC EMPLOYER

James Vincent
2911 Hyatt Drive
Greensboro, N.C. 21434
(555) 555-1009

June 4, 1993

Mr. Barron Bettingsen III
Cosgrove Computer Corporation
1253 Wellington Court
Greensboro, N.C. 21444

Dear Mr. Bettingsen:

I know what to do with your clients who want a $1,000 project delivered on a $200 budget. I'm enclosing my résumé and portfolio to demonstrate how my award-winning computer designs impact all aspects of your current marketing program. The reason I'm applying for a position as a computer graphics designer at Cosgrove Computer Corporation is because I know you're looking for computer artists who can design on a tight budget. One of the most powerful marketing tools any company can wield is a cohesive design program.

I'm a computer artist and graphic designer specializing in editorial illustration. My design strategies keep very low-cost designs looking great because I know exactly what to exclude from the design process. If I'm hired, I can promise memorable, award-winning, interactive 3-D designs.

Your marketing department wants Cosgrove Computer Corporation to be noticed. I see an excellent fit between my computer art qualifications and your department's needs. I would appreciate the opportunity to discuss how I may contribute to your company's success. Please keep my portfolio on file to show your clients. I will call in two weeks to set up an appointment.

Sincerely,

James Vincent

(2) Enclosures

Aniba Merimdeh
1756 West Byrd Street
Las Vegas, NV 80028
(702) 555-5777

December 11, 1993

Dear Brian,

I met Karen Symmontree last summer while attending the Comdex convention in Las Vegas. She told me that you're using virtual reality technology at Laser Art Technologies to create special effects for the new television series, "The Time Hackers." She suggested that I get in touch with you.

I'll be finishing my desktop video internship in public relations at Blocks Cable Television in Las Vegas on December 23. (I wrote infomercial scripts and created press kits on an IBM 486 compatible.) On January 2, I will relocate to Los Angeles and job hunt there for about four weeks.

Since I saw you last, I've been writing freelance for *MIS* magazine and other computer trade journals and networking with friends in several computer industry professional associations as a volunteer newsletter editor.

Would you know of a way to get into an emerging technology like virtual reality and still make use of my B.A. in English? I'd really appreciate any information or job leads you can pass on to me that could be helpful in my job hunting.

I'd be happy to write a freelance article and publicize any aspect of your work or any aspects of Laser Art Technologies that would welcome visibility. I've enclosed three copies of my résumé. They can be circulated freely in the virtual reality industry or among virtual reality client and supplier businesses.

I'm housesitting your mother's condo while she's in Europe. I'm looking forward to seeing you.

Sincerely,

Aniba Merimdeh

Captain James Kendall, USAF (Ret.)
124 Coronado Court
Blakestown, MA 02154
(210) 555-1255

October 5, 1993

M. (Name of Current President)
Management of Data Special Interest Group (SIGMOD)
Association for Computing Machinery
P.O. Box 12114
Church Street Station
New York, NY 10257

Dear M. (Insert name of current president here):

I'm retiring from the U.S. Air Force on October 30, 1993. (Insert name of member used as reference here), a member of your Management of Data Special Interest Group, recently informed me of an opening in your organization for a volunteer position as director of membership recruitment. I'd like to apply for that position as I enjoy networking with colleagues interested in data management. I have enclosed seven copies of my résumé. I am seeking information and job leads in order to make a transition in my career from military to civilian life. My goal is to find a new career in data management.

For the past thirty years, my career in the Air Force as a recruiter centered on interviewing people and placing them in the right job. Now that I'm retiring from military service, I would like to devote the next twenty years or more of my work life to working with students interested in careers in data management. Last month I received my B.S. in Computer Information Systems (with an emphasis in data management) from National University, San Diego, and became a member of ACM.

Please feel free to pass my résumé to any member or to download it to disk for any electronic job referral databank system that members might know of in the field of information processing. I look forward to hearing from you in person.

Sincerely,

James Kendall

Agape Theodakis
900 Bathgate Ave.
Forensic Park, IL 20208
(303) 555-9898

September 16, 1993

Exhibitors and Key Speakers
1993 Comdex Convention
Las Vegas Convention Center
Las Vegas, NV 80798

Dear Exhibitor or Key Speaker:

I enjoyed networking with you at this year's Comdex Convention and electronic products trade show in Las Vegas. In January 1994, I will receive my B.S. degree in Computer Science (with a minor in accounting and finance) from the University of Illinois. I am interested in obtaining a programming position with a financial services corporation in February.

I have recent experience programming in FoxPro for CPA Associates in Chicago. During my five years at the University of Illinois, I worked part time during school and full time during the summers at CPA Associates. My experience is in a personal computer environment utilizing Novell Netware. I have a knowledge of hardware and software (Lotus, WordPerfect, and Windows). I am willing to relocate to any area of major growth.

My strongest areas are Novell Netware and Ethernet, 10 Base-T, and DBase. I have recent experience in network administration, PC installation, software installation, PC maintenance, network trouble shooting, and network performance analysis.

Thank you for your card and company literature. I look forward to speaking with you and will call you next week.

Sincerely,

Agape Theodakis

SAMPLE FOLLOW-UP LETTER FORMAT

Your Name
Your Street Address
City, State, Zip
Phone Number

Date of Letter

Interviewer's Name
Title
Company Name
Street Address
City, State, Zip

Dear Mr./Ms._____:

Opening Paragraph—Express sincere thanks for being given the opportunity of the interview. Mention the courtesies extended to you by anyone present. Indicate the job title, where and when the interview was given, and the date. Refresh the interviewer's mind with the most important part of the interview.

Middle Paragraph—Restate your reasons for wanting to join the organization. Use your best one sentence sales pitch to close the sale. In one sentence state that you want the job because you will offer the following benefits and advantages to the company. If you left anything important out of the personal interview, include it now. Finish the middle paragraph with any sentence that enhances your abilities. State any specific qualifications that fulfill an important company need.

Closing Paragraph—Offer to provide any information the company may want, such as reference letters, security clearance, or transcripts. Indicate when you're available for further interviewing at the company's convenience.

Sincerely,

(Your handwritten signature in black ink)

Your Name Typed

Jamesa Kintle
125 Mt. Penn Lane
San Justa, CA 92104-7177
(619) 555-1234

August 1, 1993

Ms. Rayanne Hart
Director of Employment
Dept. 300
Video Game Corporation
100 Prince Road
San Justa, CA 92104-7199

Dear Ms. Hart:

Thank you for the window of opportunity you provided. Interviewing for the position of computer video games artist was exciting. I look forward to joining Video Game Corporation and working with a dynamic manager like Anne Joan Levine.

As I mentioned during the special effects tour with Ms. Levine, I am familiar with all of the duties and responsibilities of the job. I spent the last year working in the special effects department of a video game design corporation and quickly learned the value of timely and original illustrations for the electronic game industry.

In addition to my experience in video game design, the knowledge I gained through courses in animation production and desktop video in my associate degree program will serve me well in fulfilling the requirements of the position. I can contribute significantly to your corporation with my award-winning illustrations and game designs.

Thank you again for the opportunity to interview with Video Game Corporation and for the fascinating company tour. I enjoyed our informative discussion, and the new animation was breathtaking. May I publicize your forthcoming video game by writing an article about it for the local weekly computer newspaper, *The Byter?* I volunteer each month to send them a column reviewing and recommending new software and computer video games. I look forward to hearing from you at your convenience.

Sincerely,

Jamesa Kintle

ORGANIZING SKILLS ON PAPER

Looking at the variety of cover or follow-up letters and résumé styles in the previous chapters showed you some formats employers may prefer. Now it's time to focus on simplicity. This chapter will give you the framework to write your résumé concisely. It will help you organize your résumé by using a simple plan.

THE RESUME PLANNER

Interviewers use résumés to screen out applicants. Résumé reading is seen by them as a negative process. Often only a chosen few are referred to an employer for a decision. Many résumés never get past the interviewer to the employer because the résumé isn't simple to grasp at first glance.

To keep your résumé simple, devise a plan to organize work-related information. Employers will notice clear, concise résumés.

The Organized Plan

You know an effective résumé unlocks doors, but how do you filter all the information about yourself and present it simply? You need an organized plan to refer to while you are creating a first draft of your résumé. Organizing this plan means first asking yourself to itemize what's important. Organize your plan for writing a résumé by filling in your own information in the following worksheets.

Résumé Plan Worksheets

Identification Worksheet

Pencil in the following information on this plan.

Name _____

Address _____

City _____

State _____ Zip _____

Home Phone _____

Business or Message Phone _____

Fax _____

Confidential? Yes _____ No _____

Skills Worksheet

Listing your skills is required whether you're changing careers, re-entering the civilian work force after military retirement, or re-entering the job market after being a full-time homemaker.

Employment Qualifications _____

_____

_____

_____

_____

_____

_____

_____

_____

_____

_____

_____

Are you changing careers? If yes, explain why briefly: _____

_____

_____

_____

_____

_____

_____

_____

Best Abilities Worksheet

_____
_____
_____
_____
_____
_____
_____
_____
_____
_____
_____
_____
_____
_____
_____
_____
_____
_____
_____
_____
_____
_____
_____
_____
_____
_____

Training Worksheet
List your training, like your work experience, in reverse chronological order: your most advanced training or most recent course, workshop, seminar, internship, apprenticeship, or on-the-job training is listed first. Be specific and concrete about details. Include all dates, certificates earned, schools attended, or pertinent training information.

Job-related Training:_____

Dates: _____

From (Year) _____ to (Year) _____

On-the-job training _____

Dates _____

Job-related continuing education _____

Dates _____ Where trained _____

Apprenticeships _____

Dates _____ Where served_____

Training Internships _____

Dates _____ Address of Internship _____

Computer training and coursework _____

_____

Hardware _____

Software _____

Repair _____

Troubleshooting _____

_____

_____

_____

_____

_____

General Education Worksheet

List your formal education in reverse chronological order with your most advanced degree first. This section is for persons who have formal education beyond high school, rather than job training. If you didn't attend an accredited university, four-year college, or two-year community college, it's appropriate to list your post-high school continuing education and technical school courses under TRAINING.

Educational history includes all college degrees, dates, majors and minors studied, and any licenses or teaching credentials. You may not have space on your résumé for this.

Advanced

degree(s):_____

From (Year) _____ to (Year) _____

Name of university _____

Address of university_____

_____

From (Year) _____ to (Year) _____

Name of university _____

Address of university _____

_____

Undergraduate

degree(s) _____

From (Year) _____ to _____

Majors _____

_____

Minors _____

_____

Name of university_____

Address of university_____

_____

Two-year college

degree(s) _____

From (Year) _____ to_____

Emphasis _____

_____

Name of two-year or community college

_____

Address of college or school _____

_____

Diplomas, Licenses,   From (Year) _____ to_____

or Certificates_____   Name of school or training course _____

_____

Address of school _____

_____

Computer-related courses: _____

_____

_____

_____

_____

_____

_____

_____

_____

_____

College-level internships served:_____

_____

_____

_____

_____

_____

Job Objective Worksheet

If you choose to include an objective, list the job-related responsibilities you want. Simplicity rules here. Keep your objectives concise, remembering that employers will toss résumés with complex, wordy job objectives because they're too time consuming to ponder.

Use the job objective segment of your résumé plan as a terse, personal, and powerful ad. Dramatize your résumé's selling message with excitement. Your résumé needs flair. Pretend you are running it in the daily newspaper classifieds and have to state your job objective in less than 20 words. Try several different styles.

Hardware and Software Worksheet

Computer Models: _____

Telecommunications Equipment: _____

Local Area Networks: _____

Operating Systems: _____

Modems and Faxes: _____

Computer Languages: _____

_____

Monitors and Access: _____

Databases: _____

Utility Packages: _____

Peripherals: _____

Telecommunications and Multimedia: _____

_____

Security Clearance: _____

_____

_____

Additional Information: _____

_____

_____

_____

_____

_____

_____

_____

Subject Expertise Worksheet

EMPHASIS: _____

_____

Electrical Engineering Background _____

_____

Computer Science Background _____

_____

Mathematics Background _____

_____

Other Scientific Background _____

_____

Other Engineering Background _____

_____

Writing _____

_____

Public Relations _____

_____

Art, animation, special effects _____

_____

_____

Data Processing _____

_____

Other: _____

_____

_____

_____

_____

_____

_____

_____

The Day-in-the-Work-Life Worksheet

If you are currently employed, highlight each feature of the systems and programs you work with in your computer specialty. Write down your job roles in chronological steps. Include each job description—summarized concretely with details.

Write "a day-in-the-work life" page that details on an hour-by-hour basis what you do at work during a typical day. To get your specifics flowing, you might record your typical hour-by-hour activities on a tape recorder at work and transcribe them later.

A DAY IN THE WORK LIFE OF _____ (YOUR NAME)

SAMPLE WORKSHEET.

9 a.m.   Arrive at work and begin (action verb) _____

10 a.m   Program _____

11 a.m.   Analyze _____

12 noon–1 p.m. lunch break

1 p.m.   Consult _____

2 p.m.   Sell _____

3 p.m.   Troubleshoot _____

4 p.m.   Demonstrate _____

5 p.m.   End of work day; or state whether you worked

                evenings, and describe your activities.

6–8 p.m.   Repaired systems on _____

Saturdays:

8 a.m.–1 p.m. Taught/trained/instructed _____

2 p.m.–4 p.m. Worked as a computer lab assistant at XYZ community

college _____

_____

_____

_____

_____

_____

_____

Chronological Employment History Worksheet

Once you have filled in these worksheets, you are ready to itemize and detail your chronological employment history. Keep in mind that in the interview, you'll be asked to discuss the features of the systems and programs you worked on in each job in your field of experience. The questions will be taken right out of your chronological employment history if you use a chronological résumé.

Don't make the employer search for specific information and dates. Don't leave unaccounted for gaps in your history. Show how your chronological work history relates to your career plan. Employers hire people who specifically choose a company because it's part of their plan.

Your employment history also summarizes your qualifications. It tells the reader at a glance what you can do and how many years you've been doing it.

List the job title, company name and location, and years employed. Also list your responsibilities as accomplishments using action verbs. (Example: Implemented audience tracking system that saved company $50,000.)

Use an employment history worksheet to explain the nature of your career briefly and concretely. Start with your most recent job first. Include every job you've had since high school that is related to the new job or show transferable skills.

Leave no gaps unfilled. Instead of leaving gaps in those years you didn't work, fill them in with volunteer duties you handled, so that all time is accounted for by job-related responsibility. Use separate worksheet pages to detail all your jobs if you had several jobs within the same firm.

Never include salary information or reasons for leaving a job on a résumé. However, you can put them on your worksheet to help you define what you like to do most and what made you dissatisfied in a former job.

Only part of the material on your worksheets will actually appear on the final draft of your résumé. Nevertheless, all the details you've sorted will ease you through an oral interview. Think about these details and practice answering questions about yourself in front of a mirror. List your work history in reverse chronological order.

Name of Company: _____

_____

Address of Company: _____

_____

_____

Job Title: _____

Dates from: _____ to: _____

Responsibilities:_____

_____

_____

_____

_____

_____

Name of Company: _____

_____

Address of Company: _____

_____

_____

Job Title: _____

Dates from: _____ to: _____

Responsibilities:_____

_____

_____

_____

_____

_____

Name of Company: _____

_____

Address of Company: _____

_____

_____

Job Title: _____

Dates from: _____ to: _____

Responsibilities: _____

_____

_____

_____

_____

Personal Requirements Worksheet

Willing to relocate: _____

Relocation areas desired: _____

Willing to travel: _____

Travel areas preferred: _____

Interests, hobbies, avocations: _____

Subjects or types of books read: _____

Types of magazines and newspapers preferred: _____

_____

Personality type, if determined through a personality test, such as the
Myers-Briggs Type Indicator (MBTI) _____

_____

Prefer to work alone or with constant activity and people

_____

_____

Introvert or extrovert? _____

Prefer usefulness/practical skills or imagination and learning for learning's sake? _____

Like flexible or fitted schedules? _____

_____

Highly organized person? _____

Prefer autonomy or supervision? _____

_____

Creative in your specialty? _____

_____

What conditions preferred at workspace? _____

_____

_____

Professional and trade association membership or volunteer work:

_____

_____

_____

_____

Publications, achievements, awards, productions, compositions, presentations, fellowships, scholarships, and kudos: _____

_____

_____

_____

_____

Foreign languages spoken or read, and ability: _____

_____

_____

Special skills: _____

_____

_____

_____

_____

_____

Military service: _____

_____

From _____ to _____ Branch of service _____

_____

Highest rank: _____

Service-related training or schools attended: _____

_____

_____

_____

_____

_____

_____

_____

_____

References Worksheet

Never print the names, home phone numbers, and home addresses of your references directly on your résumé. It's common courtesy to protect their privacy. When you are asked for names and addresses of references, get your referent's permission first and then use only a current business address and business phone number.

Keep the names of your references and, if your reference letters were written long ago, contact them and ask for current letters of reference. Employers want to see references dated within the current year.

You should be aware however, that former employers may be required by state law to report only the dates you worked for a particular firm, the job title, and a description of your job duties. Some states have privacy protection acts, information practices acts, and civil codes to protect confidentiality of information. Because state laws vary, check with your county law library to see which civil codes protect the privacy of employment, medical, and insurance records in your state. Your references may possibly no longer be allowed to comment on your job performance. For example, if an employer thinks Mary Jones did a wonderful job, but answers a request for references by merely confirming her job title, description of duties, and dates worked, it could be misinterpreted that something was wrong with her because the former employer held back comment on Ms. Jones's performance.

On an employment application, you will probably be asked to supply references from three people who know you professionally.

Name of reference: _____

_____

Job title: _____

_____

Organization: _____

_____

Business address: _____

_____

_____

Business phone number: _____ extension: _____

Name of reference: _____

_____

Job title: _____

_____

_____

Organization: _____

_____

Business address: _____

_____

_____

Business phone number: _____ extension: _____

Name of reference: _____

_____

Job title: _____

_____

Organization: _____

_____

Business address: _____

_____

_____

Business phone number: _____ extension: _____

Résumé Worksheet

Now that you have organized all your personal information on these worksheets, it's time to create a brief outline. From this outline, you will choose specific information to highlight and include in your final worksheet. This short outline is actually the first draft of your résumé.

Show exactly why you are qualified for the job in question. Choose only the job-relevant benefits, advantages, and practical information. Clarity is your goal. Now let's organize your outline further.

Pencil your information into the brief résumé worksheet that follows.

Name _____

Street address _____

_____

City, state, zip _____

Home phone _____ Business phone _____

OBJECTIVE (optional):

_____

_____

_____

_____

_____

_____

SUMMARY OF QUALIFICATIONS:

(Highlight your best skills and experience here.)

_____

_____

_____

_____

_____

EDUCATION AND TRAINING:

Institution

City _____ State _____

Degree/Certificate _____

or

Relevant computer coursework _____

Workshops/Seminars/Internships_____

_____

_____

Institution

City _____ State _____

Degree/Certificate _____

or

Relevant computer coursework _____

Workshops/Seminars/Internships_____

_____

_____

WORK EXPERIENCE:

Job title _____

Company name _____

City _____ State _____

Employed from _____ to _____

Major job responsibilities: _____

_____

_____

_____

_____

_____

_____

Special awards, assignments, achievements in this job _____

_____

_____

_____

_____

_____

_____

_____

Job title _____

Company name _____

City _____ State _____

Employed from _____ to _____

Major job responsibilities: _____

_____

_____

_____

_____

_____

_____

_____

Special awards, assignments, achievements in this job _____

_____

_____

_____

_____

_____

_____

_____

_____

Job title _____

Company name _____

City _____ State _____

Employed from _____ to _____

Major job responsibilities: _____

Special awards, assignments, achievements in this job _____

_____

_____

_____

_____

Job title _____

Company name _____

City _____ State _____

Employed from _____ to _____

Major job responsibilities: _____

_____

_____

_____

_____

_____

_____

_____

Special awards, assignments, achievements in this job _____

_____

_____

_____

_____

_____

_____

_____

_____

Job title _____

Company name _____

City _____ State _____

Employed from _____ to _____

Major job responsibilities: _____

_____

_____

_____

_____

_____

_____

Special awards, assignments, achievements in this job _____

_____

_____

_____

_____

_____

_____

Special computer skills:

Include your knowledge of specific software and hardware. List any computer language you use for programming or design. List skills such as the following: word processing, desktop publishing, software operation and knowledge of electronic publishing software, database operation, spreadsheets, programming, systems analysis, local area networks, computerized accounting skills, scientific programming, computer-aided design and drafting, technical illustration, technical writing, courseware design, instructional technology, computer troubleshooting, repair, teaching or training on software or hardware equipment, graphic design, animation, or any related computer skills you can use on the job as well as teach. Include any office information systems equipment and software you use daily in any capacity—from data entry to management of information systems.

_____

_____

_____

_____

_____

Licenses and teaching credentials/certification: _____

_____

_____

_____

Memberships in organizations:

List all associations in which you are involved that relate to the specific job you seek, such as computer associations, training organizations, creative organizations, or scholarly research groups.

_____

_____

_____

Awards, honors, scholarships, fellowships:
Include any special recognition you earned. _____

_____

_____

_____

_____

Publications and productions:
Include any books you wrote, articles published, videos produced, artwork exhibited or published. _____

_____

_____

_____

Computer language knowledge: _____

_____

_____

_____

Foreign language fluency: _____

_____

_____

REFERENCES: (Furnished upon request.)

Achievements Worksheet

Now that you've outlined the first draft of your résumé on this brief worksheet, you need to practice translating major job responsibilities into powerful phrases of achievement. Look at the list of action verbs at the end of this chapter. Instead of listing your accomplishments as duties, use these action verbs to make them as exciting, appealing, and forceful as a direct marketing advertisement designed to sell your qualifications.

The following examples demonstrate how powerful action verbs are used to describe a job applicant's achievements.

- Redesigned the entire computer room, changing the work flow of the office to meet ergonomic health standards, increasing output by 85 percent, and saving XYZ Corp. $200,000.
- Supervised the word-processing department's computers, valued at $1 million. Rerouted paperwork onto micro fiches, saving the company $86,000 in 1993 and 2,000 cubic feet of storage space.
- Sold 1 million ABC software programs for XXY Corp., earning the company $20 million in gross sales in 1993. Won the best sales staffer of the year award. Trained 900 salespersons at 12 sites across the nation in software operation in 1993.
- Created three new system upgrades for_____software.

Now it's your turn to briefly describe your accomplishments using the action verbs provided. When you're finished, use your verbs to make a customized list of achievements. Create action-oriented phrases to sell your skills to an employer with an exact job in mind.

Organized _____

Planned _____

Established _____

Trained _____

Developed _____

Coordinated _____

Improved _____

Supervised _____

Created _____

Wrote _____

Presented _____

Illustrated _____

Designed _____

Analyzed _____

Managed_____

Instigated _____

Revised _____

Planned _____

Decided _____

Sold _____

Budgeted _____

Communicated _____

Evaluated _____

Action Verbs Resource Sheet

Accelerated	Audited	Contracted
Accomplished	Augmented	Contributed
Accepted	Authored	Controlled
Accounted	Authorize	Cooperated
Accrued	Automated	Coordinated
Accumulated	Awarded	Corrected
Achieved	Bought	Correlated
Acquired	Brought	Counseled
Acted	Budgeted	Created
Activated	Built	Credited
Actualized	Calculated	Critiqued
Adapted	Catalogued	Cut
Adhered	Chaired	Dealt
Administered	Changed	Debriefed
Advertised	Charted	Debugged
Advised	Clarified	Decided
Affected	Coached	Deciphered
Affirmed	Coded	Decoded
Afforded	Collaborated	Decreased
Allocated	Collected	Defined
Analyzed	Commanded	Deflected
Animated	Communicated	Delegated
Announced	Compared	Deleted
Anticipated	Competed	Delivered
Antiqued	Compiled	Deregulated
Applied	Completed	Demonstrated
Appraised	Composed	Derived
Approved	Computed	Described
Arbitrated	Conceived	Designed
Arranged	Concentrated	Detailed
Ascertained	Conceptualized	Determined
Assembled	Conciliated	Developed
Assessed	Conducted	Devised
Assigned	Configured	Devoted
Assisted	Considered	Dialogued
Assumed	Constructed	Directed
Assured	Construed	Discovered
Attained	Consulted	Discussed

Dispersed	Graphed	Maintained
Displayed	Grew	Managed
Distributed	Guaranteed	Manipulated
Documented	Guided	Marketed
Drafted	Handled	Mastered
Edited	Headed	Measured
Educated	Healed	Mediated
Effected	Helped	Merchandised
Elaborated	Hired	Merged
Eliminated	Identified	Met
Emphasized	Illustrated	Micrographed
Employed	Implemented	Ministered
Encouraged	Improved	Moderated
Energized	Included	Modified
Engaged	Increased	Molded
Engineered	Indexed	Monitored
Enhanced	Influenced	Motivated
Enlarged	Informed	Multiplied
Enlisted	Initialized	Narrated
Ensured	Initiated	Navigated
Entered	Inspected	Negotiated
Entertained	Inspired	Networked
Established	Installed	Neutralized
Estimated	Instituted	Normalized
Evaluated	Instructed	Normed
Examined	Insured	Notified
Excelled	Integrated	Notaried
Exchanged	Interested	Obtained
Executed	Interfaced	Officiated
Exercised	Internalized	Opened
Expanded	Interpreted	Operated
Expedited	Interviewed	Orchestrated
Explained	Introduced	Ordered
Explored	Investigated	Organized
Exported	Invented	Oversaw
Exposed	Inventoried	Participated
Extended	Inverted	Perceived
Extrapolated	Involved	Performed
Facilitated	Issued	Persuaded
Faxed	Joined	Photocopied
Fixed	Judged	Photographed
Forecasted	Juried	Piloted
Formulated	Justified	Pinpointed
Forwarded	Keyboarded	Planned
Founded	Leased	Played
Functioned	Lectured	Posted
Furnished	Lessened	Practiced
Generated	Led	Predicted
Governed	Linked	Preempted
Graded	Loaded	Prepared
Granted	Mailed	Presented

Presided	Replaced	Structured
Pressed	Replenished	Styled
Processed	Reported	Subcontracted
Procured	Represented	Submitted
Produced	Required	Succeeded
Programmed	Requisitioned	Summarized
Projected	Researched	Supervised
Promoted	Resequenced	Supplied
Proposed	Reshaped	Supported
Proofread	Resolved	Surveyed
Protected	Responded to	Syndicated
Proved	Restored	Synthesized
Provided	Retained	Systematized
Publicized	Retired	Tabulated
Published	Retooled	Taught
Purchased	Retrained	Telecommuted
Qualified	Retrieved	Televised
Quantified	Returned	Terminated
Quickened	Revamped	Tested
Questioned	Reviewed	Traced
Raised	Revised	Tracked
Ran	Rewired	Trained
Reclaimed	Robotized	Transacted
Recognized	Routed	Transferred
Recommended	Scanned	Translated
Recreated	Scheduled	Transmitted
Reconciled	Scored	Treated
Reconstructed	Screened	Troubleshot
Recorded	Sculptured	Typed
Recouped	Selected	Typeset
Recovered	Sensed	Updated
Recreated	Served	Upgraded
Recruited	Set objectives	Underscored
Rectified	Set up	Used
Recycled	Shaped	Utilized
Redesigned	Simplified	Validated
Redecorated	Sold	Verified
Reduced	Solicited	Videographed
Re-entered	Solved	Videotaped
Registered	Sorted	Visualized
Regulated	Specified	Vocalized
Rehired	Spoke	Voiced
Reimbursed	Sponsored	Waited
Reinforced	Staffed	Waived
Related	Stabilized	Weighted
Released	Standardized	Won
Relocated	Starred	Word processed
Renewed	Stimulated	Wrote
Rented	Streamlined	Xerographed
Repaired	Strengthened	

EDIT THE RESUME

By now, you should have a good draft of your résumé. In this chapter, you will learn how to clarify the information in sample résumés and to use a checklist to edit your own résumé. You will learn to see and solve problems in résumés and find what works and what doesn't. You will soon be able to apply these strategies to your own résumé and enhance its job-getting appeal. Read the following résumés. Ask yourself if all time is accounted for, whether the information presented is appropriate to the position, and whether you'd hire these people.

Anne Joan Levine

OVERVIEW: Telecommuting job desired, writing software user manuals from my computer or yours.

EXPERIENCE:

1963–Present
Full-time freelance writer of home-based business books and newspaper columns on computer businesses.

1990–1991
Adult Education Teacher of Literature and Creative Writing
San Diego Community College District Continuing Adult Education

Taught novel writing to senior citizens at senior centers and in adult education classrooms during summer and fall semester 1990–1991, one day per week (until class closed due to low enrollment after 15 weeks).

1980–1981
Typist/Word Processor
Various clerical temporary employment agencies. (Type 50 words per minute.)

Typed medical report records for the psychiatry department at University of California at San Diego in temporary assignments for a variety of temporary agencies for two-week assignments.

Typed medical records and reports for Sharp Hospital, San Diego, for short assignments.

1976–1979
Substitute English Teacher and aide,
San Diego Unified School District, San Diego

Taught English to high school, junior high, and elementary school students, kindergarten to 12th grade as a part-time hourly substitute for various one-day assignments until 1978.

EDUCATION: Master of Arts in English, SDSU, San Diego, 1979.
Winner of 1st Sigma Delta Chi Scholarship

Bachelor of Science in English Education,
New York University, 1964.

REFERENCES: Available on request.

Anne Joan Levine

OVERVIEW: Writer of computer career books seeks a position as a courseware designer, instructional technologist, technical writer of software user manuals, training materials designer, or writer and editor of corporate or instructional video scripts.

EXPERIENCE:

1991–present: Scriptwriter, Instructional Videos, San Diego County Education Center, also wrote 500-page book for business services division at same site.

1987–1991: Independent Screenplay Author, Los Angeles, CA. Screenplays written for a variety of independent producers: Home video feature film scripts include: *Midnight Shift, Two Astronauts, Metalhead, Kiss Mommy, Playpen Hostages.* Animation: *The Amazon Hatchlings.* *Stage play: A Man's Woman.*

1985–1987: Instructional film/video scripts: "The Eric Computer System," 1976. "Elderly Abuse," 1987. "Self-Esteem," a video script, 1989. "International Child Abductions," 1990, budget feature film and television script. "How to Produce a Great Home Video," script. Plus two training film scripts written on distance education for independent educational film producers.

1980–1985: Typist/Word Processor:
Various clerical temporary employment agencies. (Type 50 words per minute.)

Typed medical report records part time for the psychiatry department at University of California, San Diego, in temporary assignments for a variety of temporary services.

Typed medical records and reports for Sharp Hospital, San Diego, for short assignments.

1976–1980: Grant Writer: San Diego Unified School District. Wrote grant proposal for Miramar Community School.

1975–1976: Chief Technical Writer/Editor: Creative Computer Sciences Corp., San Diego (rewrote Cobol manuals and scientific/technical reports.)

1973–1975: Speechwriter: Biomedical Media Planning, San Diego, CA. Wrote medical speeches for president of health planning organization contracted for public relations research.

SOFTWARE:

Desktop publishing skills:
WordPerfect 5.1 and Ventura Publisher software.

TEACHING EXPERIENCE:

1991–Present:

Grossmont College, El Cajon, CA.
Taught Creative Writing 126 two nights per week as part of
team teaching for five weeks of one semester with emphasis
on scriptwriting and drama.

1990–1991:

San Diego Community College District. Taught the following
Saturday continuing adult education, semester-long workshops
in creative writing:

San Diego Community College (part time). Creative Writing
Workshop for Older Adults Midway Center: Taught course in
composition, playwriting, autobiography writing. Taught "Home-
based Businesses for Freelance Illustrators and Writers." Freelance
business practices for animation script, comedy, writing feature films,
writing for desktop video/home video, and corporate scriptwriting
for instructional and industrial videos.

1973–1985:

San Diego City College. Taught evening business communications
course, Business Communications 119. Additional fiction workshops
include: videobiography and writing.

1968–1973:

Taught playwriting at North Shores Adult School, San Diego. Taught
course titled, "Writing the Inner Personal Journal." Taught "personality
type and writing style from both sides of the Brain." Taught "Writing
the Historical Action Novel."

1964–1968:

Substitute English teacher, secondary school, and kindergarten
Teacher's Aide, San Diego Unified School District. Taught hourly
and as an aide, helped teachers with secondary school English on
a temporary, hourly basis taking attendance, lecturing, and doing
clerical work for teachers as well as tutoring students in creative
writing. Helped design learning materials for curriculum for teachers,
worked with gifted students in creative writing workshops.

EDUCATION:

M.A. English, San Diego State University, San Diego, CA, 1979.
B.S. English Education/writing and psychology, New York University,
NY, 1964.

REFERENCES AND WRITING SAMPLES ON REQUEST.

ANALYSIS OF ANNE JOAN LEVINE'S RESUMES

Why Employers Rejected the Résumés

Ms. Levine's résumés aren't focused on any specific skill in either draft. Visually, they don't make an impact. The information is scattered between gaps of time when she was a homemaker and part-time worker, 1963–1972. Employers aren't going to spend time trying to make sense of the past 31 years of her life in this disorganized résumé. She has no obvious career goal.

The résumé must be reworked with emphasis on the transferability of her creative skills. To solve the problems in her résumé, her work history must first be simplified.

Practical Evaluation

Job Overview

Neither job overview is specific enough for the majority of employers to understand. Employers scan résumés for sequential facts and easy-to-follow format.

Experience

Work history in both drafts is unclear and not chronological. Too much emphasis is on issues not related to the job in question.

Education

The degrees are relevant to the job objective. There is no problem with the visual placement of the general education and degrees in the final draft. Rather than just list the majors, English and English education, in the first draft, Ms. Levine needs to specify the emphasis within her degrees: literature, linguistics, teaching, professional writing (non-fiction), or creative writing (fiction). An area of focus helps to fit the exact job title to the person's specialization or job responsibilities.

For example, suppose an employer is considering two applicants who majored in English for a job as an interactive fiction writer for a software game company manufacturing entertainment on CD-Interactive or CD-ROM. The person more likely to be hired would be the one whose English studies focused on creative fiction.

The writer more likely to be hired as a software user manual writer or software technical writer or editor would be a "professional writing" major (nonfiction), or a person who majored in English, technical writing, or technical journalism.

Overall

In the first draft, the sections aren't separated. Large gaps of unemployment exist. Also, superfluous experience is merged with important skills. In the second draft, her experience isn't sorted or organized into related segments that show how skills are transferred. Résumés need smooth transitions.

Anne Joan Levine

JOB TITLE: TECHNICAL WRITER/SOFTWARE MANUALS

SOFTWARE EXPERIENCE:

• <u>Wrote book on applications software uses</u> for home-based business owners, published by Simon & Schuster, 1985.

• <u>Weekly national newspaper columnist</u> for *The Business News* (for small business owners). Write business strategies advice columns. Write software reviews.

• <u>Wrote video script</u> training teachers in the operation of the Eric computer system for educational research, San Diego County Education Department, Media Center.

TRAINING EXPERIENCE:

• <u>Professional Writing Instructor</u>, San Diego Community College District, 1990–1991. Specialist in nonfiction. Adult Education.

• <u>English Instructor</u>, San Diego Unified School District San Diego, 1976–1978 (substitute teacher on assignment).

RELATED COMPUTER SOFTWARE EXPERIENCE:

<u>Writing</u>: Author of 23 published 100-page pamphlets on computer art careers and careers in graphic design.

<u>Word Processing and Desktop Publishing</u>: Owner of a private word processing, desktop publishing, and technical writing home-based business specializing in computer career information using WordPerfect, CorelDraw!, Ventura AdPro, and Ventura Publisher software on an IBM.

EDUCATION:

• Master of Arts in English (writing emphasis), San Diego State University, December 1979.
• Bachelor of Science in English Education, New York University, June 1964.

LIST OF PUBLISHED WORKS ATTACHED

REFERENCES ON REQUEST

ANALYSIS OF FINAL DRAFT OF ANNE JOAN LEVINE'S RESUME

Problems Solved

Ms. Levine's rewritten résumé is now focused on the targeted job title, that of a technical writer specializing in writing software user manuals. Although she has no experience in actually writing a software user manual, she has three related skills to emphasize, and she uses a bold visual appeal to display them:

1. Combined experience writing about software and the operation of home-based computer businesses.
2. Weekly newspaper business strategies column.
3. Prior teaching experience and education.

Related Jobs Using the Same Résumé

Ms. Levine could also apply for jobs writing, editing, or coordinating the publication of technical or literary training materials, developing curriculum materials, career books, and writing public relations literature for computer publishing companies or software manufacturing and design firms.

In the expanding field of electronic publishing, her knowledge of desktop publishing and word-processing software also qualifies her to write sales brochures and press kit materials for desktop publishing software firms. Desktop publishing skills are often used to obtain jobs as proofreaders, technical writers, or technical editors. One growth area is training materials courseware design for teachers of word processing or desktop publishing.

Practical Evaluation

Job Overview

The job overview has been eliminated. There is now the exact job title, "technical writer of software manuals." The employer can read under the experience cluster about Ms. Levine.

Emphasis on "telecommuting desired" was removed. At the end of the interview, she can ask whether telecommuting is permitted, or whether the hours are flexible.

Experience

In the final draft, experience is focused and strengthened. Experience is now organized into three clusters that make smooth transitions without holes in time or other noticeable gaps in employment and relate directly to the job title. Similar work is grouped together—writing with writing, teaching with teaching, and word processing with desktop publishing (listed under **Related Computer Software Experience**). With each **"Related Computer Software Experience"** specialty listed in a cluster, the job interest becomes more focused. To create visual appeal, she underlined the headlines of her specialty.

Employers can refer back to **"Software Experience"** to see that she reviews software in her weekly column for a national business newspaper. These facts in sequential order build up her credibility and qualifications for the job objective.

The chronological work history dates were subdued. She omitted from her résumé the time periods when she was on the "mommy track" from 1965 to 1973 and from 1981 to 1991.

Nor did she list her occasional temporary typing jobs, which spanned the years from 1959 to 1981 or her typing speed. Her typing speed was a hint to employers that she would accept a lower-paid clerical job instead of a professional, higher-paid job as a technical writer or editor. List your typing speed only if you're applying for a word processing, medical transcription, secretarial, court reporting, or data entry job where people are hired for their keyboarding speed.

Related Software Experience

Ms. Levine wanted to emphasize the importance of her familiarity with computers and software, even though she had never taken a computer or software course. She's entirely self-trained in several kinds of desktop publishing software and owns her own computer.

To de-emphasize her lack of formal training, she highlighted running her own home-based desktop publishing and word-processing business. She lists the software as well as the specialty. The types of projects her business dealt with showed her knowledge of, or interest in writing materials about, computer careers, specifically computer art.

Education

Ms. Levine's fine educational accomplishment, a master's degree, remains listed. Since she is not looking for a teaching job, professional writing is emphasized, especially the writing of nonfiction, computer-oriented educational and training materials.

Her degrees in English add to her qualifications for a job as a writer, whether in the software field, instructional design, or in education. It's often easier to train a writer in programming than it is to train a programmer to be a writer specializing in making the complex simpler.

List of Publications Attached

Instead of the usual "references on request," it's more credible for a creative person to attach a one-page list of their books, pamphlets, articles, art, videos, or interactive fiction—with dates of publication/production.

The final version of Ms. Levine's résumé is unforgettable, impressive, powerful, and competitive with the hundreds of résumés that her targeted company will receive. The revised résumé has a far better chance of being taken seriously than the original résumés that she used for two years without receiving a single interview.

Thor Tucker

OVERVIEW:	Applications Programmer, any field except finance.
EDUCATION:	
1985	A.S. Computer Science & Information Systems San Diego City College, San Diego 3.45 grade point average.
1977	Attended AT&T 4ESS Switching Machine School to learn how to repair 4ESS Switching Machine.
1962	B.A. Anthropology, American University, Washington, D.C. 3.0 grade point average
1963	18 graduate credits in Middle East Area Studies, American University, Washington, D.C.
HARDWARE:	4ESS, IBM 486, MAC, AMIGA, Video Toaster
SOFTWARE:	Microsoft Word, WordPerfect, DeLuxe Paint DBase IV+, Paradox, Lotus 1-2-3. Local area networks with Novell.
COMPUTER LANGUAGES:	Assembler, Pascal, C, C++, Basic.
EXPERIENCE: June 1977 to Aug. 1993	AT&T Corp, San Diego, CA 92103 COMMUNICATIONS TECHNICIAN & SWITCHMAN Personally responsible for maintenance and repair of a 4ESS switching machine. Worked on machine translations and also fixed carrier systems that go to different cities. Analyzed schematic diagrams and analyzed Assembly language of maintenance programs.
1963– 1977	AT&T Corp., Los Angeles, CA 90028 COMMUNICATIONS TECHNICIAN AND SWITCHMAN Repaired microwave and carrier systems and private line circuits.

References on request.

ANALYSIS OF THOR TUCKER'S RESUME

Why Employers Rejected the Résumé

Experience is subdued in the bottom third of the résumé. He has written it too generally without itemizing what he actually did for the past 30 years on a daily basis that is fully transferable to a programmer's job. He doesn't link his 30 years as a telephone company switchman to new areas of telecommunications.

Mr. Tucker briefly lists three tasks he repeated daily for three decades at the telephone company, but the details do little to convince an employer that he is a competitive programmer. Also, he asks to work in "any field except finance." Instead, he needs to focus on specific fields.

Practical Evaluation

Job Overview

Mr. Tucker wants to find an applications programmer's job in "any field except finance." But employers are looking for focus when they begin to scan a résumé. All we know is that he doesn't like the finance field.

He needs to replace his job objective with a more realistic job title, which would answer the question "In what field?" Several possibilities include:

> Applications programmer in telecommunications.
> Sales of applications software to telephone company spin-offs.
> Database management for telephone or telecommunications firms selling to corporations.
> Specialty items technology such as repair and installation of distance teaching telecommunications linkage equipment and related programming.
> Information systems technology or management.
> Local area networks (LAN) technology.
> Corporate telecommunications technology/repair, programming, or installation.

There's no emphasis on his 30-year outstanding performance as a telephone company communications technician/switchman.

Education

He has attended annual training at AT&T school to learn repair of the various telephone company machines but has left this off of his résumé, assuming that none of the skills are transferable to work outside the telephone company. Yet Mr. Tucker has had over 20 annual training sessions, lasting from two weeks to five months, at locations all over the nation.

His itemized liberal arts education in anthropology and Mideast area studies is irrelevant to his job goal as a programmer. It shouldn't have been given such prominence. He has overpowered his communications technician qualifications by emphasizing his early general education at the top of the résumé.

Experience

Mr. Tucker needs to show how his perceived narrow daily job experience, reading computer program errors in Assembler language code, transfers to wider fields outside the phone company. Emphasis on correcting errors in computer code serves as a bridge between the old communications technician job and a new job goal in applications programming.

Mr. Tucker needs to detail his knowledge of programming in C Language, Pascal, Basic, and local area networks using Novell, learned in his community college courses paid for by his employer. These are professional quality skills that can be transferred to the new goal as a programmer. His whole career is not bound to telephone company switching machine maintenance and circuit repair.

Mr. Tucker needs to position the most programming-relevant skills at the top of his résumé and make bold the most important competency titles. Only practical skills and experience that can be easily transferred to other companies needs to be emphasized.

In the cover letter, Thor Tucker can refer to his excellent work evaluations and attendance award and use them later as references.

References

There's no need to take up a line on the résumé with "references on request" for a person who has only worked at one company for 30 years. The prospective employer will know to call the phone company to verify the employment or ask for the name of Mr. Tucker's immediate supervisor.

Thor Tucker

APPLICATIONS PROGRAMMER: TELECOMMUNICATIONS

OVERVIEW: Communications technician and computer
software troubleshooter with 30 years
of maintenance and repair service experience
seeks programming position specializing
in machine translations, analysis
of Assembly language maintenance programs,
and analysis of schematic diagrams.

PROFESSIONAL SKILLS

COMPUTER LANGUAGE ANALYSIS:
- Assembler language (4ESS)
- Machine language translations

PROGRAMMING LANGUAGES:
- Assembler, Pascal, C, C++, Basic, Cobol, local area networks with Novell

DOCUMENT PREPARATION:
- Prepare reports and schematic diagrams. Use of word-processing software, advanced use of database packages and spreadsheets.

**EQUIPMENT REPAIR
AND MAINTENANCE:**
- 4ESS Switching Machines: Troubleshooting, maintenance, and repair of private line systems, microwave, fixed carrier systems, and telecommunications equipment that route to different cities.

EXPERIENCE

June 1963–
May 1993:

Communications Technician and Switchman
AT&T Corporation, San Diego, CA, and
Los Angeles, CA, centers.

EDUCATION AND TRAINING

Associate in Science (A.S.)
Computer Sciences and Information Systems
San Diego City College, San Diego, CA, 1985

AT&T company school training for repair of
4ESS switching machine, 1984.

Bachelor of Arts (B.A.), Anthropology
American University, Washington, DC, 1962.

ANALYSIS OF FINAL DRAFT OF
THOR TUCKER'S RESUME

Problems Solved

Mr. Tucker's résumé is now focused on his skills in the specific area of telecommunications. This industry reflects the marriage of computers to a vast network of corporate telephone systems.

The revised résumé applies his 30 years of craft level experience working for one telephone company to new technology opportunities with a wide variety of telecommunications firms that link telephone systems with computer equipment and peripherals. His unique combination of company training and employer-paid computer training in college courses has been shown prominently, highlighting his programming skills and technician experience.

The new résumé will help Mr. Tucker transfer his skills to a wider variety of businesses within the expanding telecommunications industry. He needed to show how his former job competencies and continuous retraining in new programming languages could be used outside of the phone company.

Related Jobs Using the Same Résumé

He is now prepared to apply in the burgeoning field of wireless telecommunications for job descriptions so new that no one has yet had time to get experience in them. He can choose to target telecommunication companies involved with the maintenance and repair or distribution of satellite, fax, and modem equipment used for global teleconferencing.

Mr. Tucker can apply for positions as a programmer or technician with local area networks, or a combination of both. Corporations receptive to an applicant with such skills include those in wireless telecommunications, manufacturers of equipment used for distance teaching, global video-conferencing, electronic mail, and telecommunications firms involved in information retrieval from databases.

Practical Evaluation

Job Overview

Mr. Tucker has clearly targeted the telecommunications industry. The revised résumé lists the specific job title as applications programmer, a title that uses all of his competencies rather than only his mid-career training in programming.

He clarifies his telephone company technician skills, showing his ability to link computer equipment with telephone and wireless systems.

Focus is now on a concrete specialty. Mr. Tucker implies that after 30 years in maintenance and repair with the phone company, he would like to transfer skills learned through continuous retraining and computer programming courses to a new company in the expanding telecommunications industry.

Professional Skills

Since Mr. Tucker desires an applications programmer's position, he emphasizes his competencies in computer language analysis, programming languages, and document preparation using advanced database packages, spreadsheets, and word-processing software packages. He lists his equipment repair and maintenance skills last, in spite of the fact that he's used these daily for three decades. It's obvious he wants a break in the routine and prefers to program. Overall, the order in which the professional skills are now listed shows how important they are in seeking a new position as a programmer.

Experience

He's worked at one company since his graduation. There's no need to list companies in the order of importance or break experience into subdivisions, as would be done if he had worked at numerous firms.

Education

Mr. Tucker's degrees are listed at the end of the résumé. His computer-related education leading to the Associate in Science degree in Computer Sciences and Information Systems is now listed first. It shows he spent two years in evening community college learning six new computer languages and specific technical competencies.

His general education is singled out and not mixed with job training. The general education B.A. degree he received in anthropology was listed last, only to show he completed a well-rounded education before starting his technical career.

His 30-year career with the telephone company presupposes that the corporation sent him to company school to learn how to maintain and repair the 4ESS switching machine he worked on full time.

YOUR RESUME CHECKLIST

Every employer or human resource manager in the computer industry has individual pointers for what's organizationally correct on a résumé. Visual appeal is subjective but all résumé readers prefer uncluttered résumés that spotlight job-related successes. Brevity and simplicity are important; redundancy will be noticed immediately.

Here are some commonly accepted do's and don'ts of résumé and cover letter writing. Use these tips as a checklist when editing your résumé and rewriting your cover and follow-up letters.

Do These Things!

1. Clarify skills valued by the employer in the job objective and overview section of your résumé.
2. Plan your résumé after you have learned everything you can about the job and the company.
3. Begin each sentence with action verbs that describe your competencies as you list concrete, specific, and job-transferable skills. Verbs should make statements positive yet not boastful.

4. Check and verify the facts on your résumé to make sure they're true before submitting it to an employer.

5. Be selective about your most important qualifications. Listing all your skills overwhelms the reader.

6. Simplify statements. Analyze your résumé for efficiency. Use sentences of ten words or less when possible.

7. Check for redundancies. Don't repeat the same idea in different ways on your résumé.

8. List your most important degree first. If you taught yourself about computers, then make it clear that you're a self starter.

9. Include your work permit type and your immigrant status if you're from another country.

10. Design your résumé like a story. All your experiences need to relate to your main plot. Stories can have sub-plots, but each must return to your main plot. Your résumé must stimulate a reaction in the reader.

11. Be specific and particular. State what you do best and what tasks you enjoy doing most in a job.

12. Track the responses to your résumé mailings until you are hired. Résumé tracking forms are located in Appendix A. Follow up the best prospects with letters each month for a year. Make monthly follow-up phone calls to see whether new jobs have opened and to check whether your résumé and follow-up letter are still active. Ask for referrals.

13. Put only required items on your résumé. List your licenses, teaching credentials, and security clearances only when requested.

14. Explain briefly how and why your education qualifies you to do the job.

15. Go with tradition. Appear conservative on your résumé when appropriate. Keep the tone or mood of the résumé objective and professional. Give practical reasons why an employer should hire you.

16. Show how you will apply your creativity to the company's needs.

17. Highlight your problem-solving skills.

18. Include temporary, part-time, job-sharing, home-based business, telecommuting, entrepreneurial, freelance, contingency professional, or independent contract work only as related to the skills or experience required.

19. List sales and marketing profits if you previously worked as a sales and marketing representative or for yourself.

20. List your accomplishments in terms of the company's profit, not your personal profit i.e., bonuses.

21. Show dedication to receiving a reply. In a follow-up letter, ask specifically what stands between you and the job.

22. Include dates for employment and education on all types of résumés as a reference point.

23. Provide your references' business phone number, not their home phone numbers.

24. Relate your military service to specific civilian job objectives. If you're retiring from the military, include what you did in the service as a bridge toward a specific career.

25. List memberships in only those professional associations and trade or business organizations that relate to the occupation. Include relevant volunteer work for professional associations.

26. Write with enthusiasm for your work and for the employer or job.

27. Place bold headings and bullets on important titles in your résumé. Itemize your skills and responsibilities in order of their importance.

28. Create visual impact by using large amounts of white space.

29. Desktop publish your résumé, preferably using the most current desktop publishing software. It has the best professional-looking appearance when laser printed.

30. Use the same fonts (type) for your résumé and cover letter. Make important headings bold to call attention to them.

31. Sell only what you can realistically offer an employer.

32. Proofread your résumé for errors three times on different days. Proofread after using a computer's spelling and grammar checker. Proofread your résumé again before having it duplicated for mailing.

33. Use 20-pound bond laser printer and duplicating paper, 100% cotton paper, or linen résumé paper to prevent smudging and tearing. The envelope and cover letter should be of the same color and weight.

34. Include experience that transfers general communication, organizational, or leadership skills to a variety of jobs. Track your growth with each new job.

Don't Do These Things!

1. Don't include personal information such as your religion, age, race, height, weight, marital status, child care provisions, ages of children, I.Q., GPA below 3.5, sexual preference, or any psychological testing results.

2. Don't include all former employers' names or staple old, handwritten reference letters to your résumé.

3. Don't list past salaries.

4. Don't send your photo.

5. Don't beg, plead, or manipulate an employer into hiring you out of pity because you're down on your luck.

6. Don't include odd-jobs experience that helped you pay your college tuition.

7. Don't complain—about anything.

8. Don't emphasize physical or emotional disabilities.

9. Don't exaggerate your achievements.

10. Don't describe yourself with a string of adjectives or passive verbs.

11. Don't complain about former employers or co-workers.

12. Don't let your overview overpower your entire résumé.

13. Don't proclaim ageism, sexism, racism, or any other discrimination, including jealousy or sexual harassment, as the reason you were fired from your last job.
14. Don't send unsolicited samples of your work and demand that your package be returned or held active in case a job opens.
15. Don't say that you'll gladly accept any job the company offers in any department—from sweeping the floor to the presidency.
16. Don't include your plan to someday open your own business after your employer has taught you the ropes and supplied you with a client list.
17. Don't emphasize how much more important your ideas are than production or profit.
18. Don't use the word résumé on your résumé.
19. Don't ask for tuition reimbursement for courses totally unrelated to the job.
20. Don't make it known that you have no time for lifelong learning and growth opportunities because you work so hard.
21. Don't advertise in your cover letter that you'll do anything illegal for a certain amount of money.
22. Don't give equal weight to each of your past jobs.
23. Don't ramble on about your military honors, travels, and experience unrelated to the job in question.
24. Don't tell your employer that you really don't need to work because your spouse pays the bills.
25. Don't label yourself with words that devalue you—such as "just a housewife for the past 30 years with a 1959 liberal arts degree seeking a creative job in the computer industry."
26. Don't demand to know where the company will be in five years and the role you'll play in it if you're hired.
27. Don't show how much you covet the power of the person with hiring authority or your prospective boss.
28. Don't include the fact that you can't drive and need to work near a bus line or telecommute.
29. Don't use your cover letter to ask employers to create nonexistent jobs in order to use your talents.
30. Don't crowd too much type onto one page.
31. Don't distract the reader with excessive use of italic, bold, and multiple fonts.
32. Don't type your résumé with a faded ribbon or send out unclear or flawed photocopies of it.
33. Don't use dark or bright-colored paper that cannot be photocopied by the employer or is hard to read.

NONTRADITIONAL RESUMES

In this chapter and the next, you will learn how to support your strengths with concrete evidence. You will learn how to write a nontraditional résumé so clearly that you can't be misunderstood. You will also gain advice on how to take your nontraditional computing career and make it more attractive to employers, both in the private and public sectors.

When You Need a Nontraditional Résumé

You need a nontraditional résumé in these circumstances:

- Taking a long time out for study (more than a year)
- Running a business
- Rearing children, or caring full-time for aged or disabled relatives in the home for more than one year
- Retirement from military service
- Unemployment of more than one year's duration
- Switching careers after retirement
- Working flexible hours in part-time or temporary work
- Immigrating from another country
- Applying for an internship or a cooperative work-study arrangement
- Seeking a work-travel assignment
- Working part time for more than a year or switching from full-time work to part time work
- Job sharing for more than a year
- Public speaking full time
- Many years' work as a freelancer, consultant, independent contractor, entrepreneur, or intrapreneur
- Temporary work, or assignments for a temporary employment agency
- Many years spent unemployed because of illness, disability, or confinement
- Work outside the country for more than a year
- Creative artist, computer midi synthesizer musician or composer, or staff writer entering the fields of software design, interactive education/entertainment, or instructional technology for the first time
- Switching from one career to an entirely new industry

Why You Need a Nontraditional Résumé

If you are a person who diverges from typical corporate personnel habits, you need to be especially convincing about your talents. Your résumé must be so persuasive that the employer will find your unique skills profitable. Nontraditional résumés break patterns.

Nontraditional résumés itemize specific benefits, offered in the order of their importance to the employer. Collect data about yourself on index cards. Ask yourself, "Which of my ideas are interesting and exciting?" Now be specific. Back up a few selected ideas with facts and details that clearly show benefits to the company. You need to retrieve the facts that gave you profitable ideas in the first place.

Show Your Team Spirit

If your career has not followed a traditional path, an employer may be wary of hiring you. A prospective employee with a history of autonomy and independence, for example, may not work well or be productive as a part of a team-approach to business. Nontraditional résumés need special drafting to earn respect by their presentation. Strengths need to be emphasized in such a way that the nontraditional job applicant appears attractive and competent, and able to join a team.

Ask yourself what generalizations can be made about your skills that would fulfill the job-related needs of the employer. How can you tie all the relevant facts to a specific part of the computer industry? You need to give meaning to all those facts about yourself on your résumé that will answer an employer's concerns.

If you find you really are not comfortable working on a team, perhaps you can fit into a company niche or fulfill a specific need. Target those needs or niches. By tying together your facts and connecting them to a specific need in the company, you could represent yourself as a resource for other teams or departments in a company or government office. For information on résumés and government jobs, read Chapter 7, Retirees and Others.

Setting Your Résumé Apart from the Competition

Do you know why most jobs are never advertised? Because employers prefer to hire from within the organization or from similar jobs in other, related companies. It limits the résumés they must read and the interviews they must conduct. For example, an advertisement for a manager of information systems (MIS) usually draws a national group of applicants who are already employed as managers in similar settings.

Additionally, as many corporations downsize or hire temporary employees and independent contractors as computer consultants, many middle managers are displaced or laid-off. These managers are competing with a large group of computer professionals who have not yet worked as managers, but who are applying in hopes of being hired.

Job applicants applying for the MIS position can include military retirees entering the civilian workplace after 20 to 30 years of logistics administrative work in the services. Other job applicants may be displaced homemakers carving out their own niches after recent retraining. Some job applicants are recent MIS graduate degree recipients looking for management trainee positions.

Applicants include former entrepreneurs seeking to be "intrapreneurs." (Intrapreneurs work inside a company as independent contractors.) Some are computer consultants who want to work for one company on staff. There are many systems analysts, software engineers, local area network specialists, and programmers who intend to move into management.

The days when one ad for a manager of information systems brought in only groups of employed managers who wanted to move laterally are gone. Today, many individuals are trying to get a foot in the door at the top to avoid the crowd at the bottom.

To open that door for you—at any level—you need to approach employers with advantages and benefits that set you apart from the competition. Let's discuss strategies for those with an interrupted work history and students. In the next chapter, we will target retirees, temporary employees, and immigrants.

JOB DISCONTINUITY STRATEGIES

If your career or jobs have been interrupted by time or switches, the following tips are for you.

TIP 1: SHOW TRANSFERABLE (LATERAL) COMPETENCIES

Your first task is to explain in positive terms the breaks in your employment or the reason for your career switch to a new field. Instead of climbing the ranks from clerk to president in one firm, you may have moved laterally through many careers, collecting transferable experience and skills that can be used equally well in many careers.

Job continuity is no longer promised. Technology changes. You move forward only by training continuously, adapting to and learning to use new products. If you can show that your skills are useful to many types of firms, you can transfer from one career to the next.

TIP 2: LIST MARKETABLE STRENGTHS

What strengths can you sell? What strengths can you use to persuade, motivate, and inspire an employer to hire you? Show the employer by showing exactly and concretely how your strengths are going to be used by the company.

If you are a displaced homemaker with no outside paid experience, sell your ability to inspire, motivate, and promote other people or products in the computer industry. You may be able to sell your ability to oversee and nurture a product from its inception through all stages of its growth. In short, you could tranfer your parenting skills from person to product.

Market the usefulness of your skills to an employer. Whether you get the job or not depends on your ability to express to the employer what's in it for them.

TIP 3: USE A NONTRADITIONAL ABILITIES OR CREATIVE RESUME

Don't use the chronological work history résumé if there are large gaps in time or breaks in the continuity of your work between graduation and the present. Instead, emphasize all your transferable skills. Additional information on an abilities-type résumé is in Chapter 2.

TIP 4: BEAT AGEISM

The computer industry is marketing to mature people, including senior citizens' computer clubs that network nationally. If you are a retiree returning to the workplace, show how you can promote computer information or products to the rising tide of "over age 48" baby boomers—millions of computer users. Computer interest among people over age 50 is rapidly increasing. Who is going to serve this market's needs with computer products from investment software to creative innovations?

In contrast, if you are young and less experienced, use the same strategy to appeal to the youth market. Children begin using computers in preschool and will use software through college. The computer industry is intergenerational.

TIP 5: SELL YOURSELF AS A CONSUMER

In the computer industry, feedback from consumers of computer products is coveted. Market yourself as a consumer of computer products. To show how active and vocal you are as a consumer, write software reviews and send them to newspapers, magazines, and computer user club newsletters.

Your common sense as a consumer of computers carries heavy weight in convincing a company to listen, improve products, and hire spokespersons or representatives. The computer world listens to consumers; that is why they use volunteer beta testers on new software.

TIP 6: ENROLL IN A COMPUTER-RELATED COURSE

Nobody networks better than working adult weekend/evening computer students with a course in common. Learn the latest technologies and software. Exchange business cards.

Find out about special fields and emerging trends, such as applied artificial intelligence used to forecast stock market trends. Learn the meaning of neural networks and fuzzy logic in the biotech industry. Take a course in local area networks and computer sharing, or global linking by modem. Join desktop computer animation enthusiasts, color desktop publishers, or graphic designers experimenting with new software at professional association seminars.

TIP 7: DO WHAT YOU ENJOY AND SHOW WHAT YOU CAN DO

Find out what feels comfortable in the world of work, what's easiest to do, and what skills come naturally. Take one of the personality questionnaires such as the Myers-Briggs Type Indicator (MBTI), the Keirsey Temperament Sorter, or the personality quiz in this book to find your type and temperament. The results may help you match yourself to the job and company that are right for you.

TIP 8: WHY SHOULD THEY HIRE YOU?

Make a list of all the positive reasons why an employer should hire you—from the employer's point of view. List these points on your abilities résumé plan and first draft. Then select a chosen few to include on your final, polished résumé.

Research the company you want to hire you. Then research the job there. If you have no experience, use practical examples of how you use your abilities, skills, or talents. Your summary or overview, placed after the job objective/title and before your competencies, contains the action you take. If you think you have few skills, then emphasize how you motivate and inspire people through your actions. For example, if you are a volunteer fundraiser for your local charity, use an action verb to describe the skill—raise funds. Stress the title "fundraiser," not "volunteer."

TIP 9: LOOK FOR LINKS TO EMPLOYER

Find activities that link you and the employer—working on professional association panels or committees together, doing volunteer work, or taking the same courses with company staff. To be hired, your résumé must become a list that links or matches a company's needs to your skills.

Try placing a classified ad under the heading "employment (or situation) wanted" in a trade journal. When you advertise the best you can offer, and link up your interests, chances are you'll get more responses from employers than if you had sent your résumé in response to a "help wanted" classified ad appearing in a general daily newspaper.

STUDENT STRATEGIES

You are a full-time student with no paid job experience and you wonder how you can find a job when all the jobs require experience. Should you only look for help wanted ads that begin with the words *management trainee* or simply *trainee?* No. There is a wealth of ways to connect with companies before you graduate.

Use the following student strategies as bridges. Select what's most comfortable for you, and then list the involvement on your résumé. These tips will connect your school experience to the work force.

TIP 1: USE PROFESSIONAL ASSOCIATIONS AS A BRIDGE TO EMPLOYMENT

Your first step is to connect with companies and begin relationships in capacities other than traditional employment. Look in the *Encyclopedia of Associations,* which you'll find in your public or school library. Choose several organizations or associations to join, at a reduced student membership cost, that are related to your field of interest.

In this book's Appendix is a list of computer associations that you can join at full-time student membership rates (lower than individual membership rates). Also look at the computer periodicals and publications listed and keep them in mind for making connections or networking.

Pick those associations that focus on your main interest in the computer field. For example, if you are interested in computer graphics, there are many different organizations dedicated to the use of computers for creating designs.

One example is SIGGRAPH, the computer graphics special interest group of the Association for Computing Machinery, or the American Institute of Graphic Art (AIGA) for commercial artists using computer illustration. If you are interested in technical writing, there is the Society for Technical Communication and the Association of Professional Writing Consultants. If you are looking forward to a career as a technical trainer or teacher of computer-related subjects, join national computer trainers' associations, like the Trainers Association of Southern California, or similar associations in your own state.

There is probably a national association to benefit almost any area of the computer industry. If there is no chapter or organization in your city, start one of your own. Ask your favorite employers to assist you in starting up a local chapter or to provide a meeting room at their company for after-hours seminars.

Ask several employers to volunteer as speakers for the local chapter meetings. Or plan an annual conference and invite those people you want to work for in the future.

Work on task forces, committees, and planning teams inside the special interest groups of national associations. If there is an annual convention, volunteer to be on the planning team. Offer to speak on a panel or to find experts to speak at conferences or meetings.

Publicize the professional association. Involve yourself in fundraising. Edit the newsletter for a year. Volunteer for take-charge activities that create visibility for you in the club. Leave the envelope stuffing and mailing chores to members who aren't looking for a job in a hurry.

Join Toastmasters and other public speaking groups that cater to a similar crowd of office workers, professionals, salespersons, business owners, etc., or start your own chapter of Toastmasters or related public speaking groups for computer personnel.

If speaking on panels or public speaking in general isn't your way of creating visibility, try writing. Become a reporter or editor for the group's newsletter and use that as a bridge to writing company newsletters or manuals. Use computer magazines, newspapers, and national periodicals to report on your national organization's research.

Summer and part-time jobs can come out of working on task forces and committees of professional associations. That's how you make business connections to use as a bridge between school and employment outside of your academic department's office.

TIP 2: TUTOR YOUR COMPUTER SKILLS

If you are interested in education or corporate technical training, offer to tutor in computer science, office information systems, technical writing/editing, or computer-aided design/graphics at special schools. Volunteer or apply for a job as an instructional aide in a school that uses many computers. Offer to train corporate staff in new software and hardware equipment use within your specialty.

Use what you learned in computer school to instruct workers who are being trained on the job. If your background is in the humanities, train workers with basic literacy problems in written communications.

Computer training programs sponsored by the government and private industry councils are offered to low-income students. These programs are offered to people over age 55, displaced homemakers, the homeless, and persons in recovery or recently released from prison. Opportunities exist to become involved as trainers, aides, tutors, fundraisers, grant proposal writers, or volunteers to share your computer skills with others. The people you meet in the training business can form solid business relationships when you graduate—especially if you want to become a technical trainer.

TIP 3: TEACH COMPUTER SKILLS TO THE DISABLED WORKER

Many community colleges have special programs in computer instruction for the physically challenged. Volunteer to help these students learn computer skills. Work with computer students with disabilities. Volunteer as a student aide or tutor, or work on a team that trains them in their homes or in adapted classrooms.

Computer programs for students with disabilities emphasize such fields as computer-aided drafting and design, word processing, programming, desktop publishing, circuit design, robotics, and software specialist training. You can become involved with teaching computer skills to the disabled while you're still a full-time student.

TIP 4: SHOW HOW MUCH YOU'RE INTERESTED IN THE JOB

Apply for summer or part-time work that leads directly into your preferred career track. Ask for an internship. Express more interest in the company than in the position, without putting the position down. Don't mention advancement yet. Instead, emphasize how much you're interested in the job in your cover letter—and how much you're interested in where the company's heading. To find out the firm's direction and position, in comparison to its competition, research the company in the library or call the firm's public relations director and ask for a press kit with an annual report. Find out the same information for several companies you wish to target and compare them with regard to their growth as well as your goals.

See Tips 5–8 for advice on how to write your cover letter and résumé.

TIP 5: WHEN YOU DO APPLY—THE COVER LETTER

In your cover letter, include positive statements about the firm. Emphasize how much you want hands-on experience, in contrast to the theory you learned in college. Point out how many good facts you've heard about the company at college. Give a few examples; state how good the company's reputation is in the computer industry, how durable or beneficial the products are, and how much they fill a need in the computer community market.

Sum up with how anxious you are to learn from the company if you are hired—even if it's only for temporary work.

TIP 6: STATE WHY YOU'RE QUALIFIED TO PERFORM THE DUTIES

Your résumé can't qualify you through a work history, so let it qualify you with concrete evidence of your skills. Briefly point out how your skills qualify you for each of the duties required in the job description.

Highlight your motivation for the job. If it leads to your career goal or is on your career track, mention that. Be honest and direct. All you are stating is what the job duties are, why you are qualified to perform those duties, and what motivates you to want to work for the company.

Indicate on your résumé or cover letter the date you will graduate. If the job is seasonal or temporary, or if it is strictly part time, note that you're willing to stay on if any full-time position opens within a reasonable time.

TIP 7: EVALUATE THE JOB EXPERIENCE

The focus of your résumé will be clearer if you are certain of the reasons underlying your choice. Ask yourself what value you will get from working for a certain company. Will it pay off your student loan? Will you learn more about computers? Is there any on-the-job training you can't find at college? Or, after evaluating a position, you find you have experience in a field totally unrelated to your career goal? By carefully considering the position you may apply for, you avoid confusing a potential employer with résumé information unrelated or unimportant to the job.

TIP 8: SUMMARIZE YOUR INTENTIONS IN YOUR OVERVIEW

Your résumé packages your strengths for a job. In a one-paragraph Job Overview, listed under your Job Objective, summarize your intentions. The Job Overview is useful for students and others without prior paid job experience.

Three sentences should accomplish the summary that will market your overall abilities. For example, your overview might look like this paragraph:

Job Overview:
Second year Computer Information Systems student completing a B.S. in Information Systems, School of Business Administration, New York University, applying for the summer position as Software Engineer. Exceptional skills with Windows, Macintosh, OS/2, Unix, and DOS working in C++, C, Assembler, Basic, Cobol, and Novell Netware. Commercial PC software development, file systems, compression, networking, and localization courses qualify me for the software engineering position and support my goal of future permanent work with C. C. Corp.

TIP 9: USE TELECOMMUTING OPPORTUNITIES

Full-time students may also work at home using their computers in a freelance capacity. You can contribute articles, cartoons, or illustrations to computer publications, index computer books, prepare databases, or do record keeping at home if your computer is hooked up by modem or fax machine to a company branch or headquarters. This work-at-home employment is called telecommuting. It's different from work you do at home in your own business because you're employed by the company and considered part of its staff.

Ask whether you can connect your home computer by modem to a school or company to help process information or research databases. Doctors and lawyers sometimes hire information brokers to search professional library databases by computer. These can be either freelance or staff employees.

The on-line field of information retrieval is called "the competitive intelligence industry." National clearinghouses of information and specialized as well as public libraries are linked to researchers through many private and government databases. Offer to use your own computer to assist a firm with data analysis or other research in your field.

TIP 10: USE WORK-STUDY PLANS OR COOPERATIVE EDUCATION

Create your own cooperative work-study plan focusing on companies most likely to hire you after graduation. Many colleges arrange paid internships or part-time work and study arrangements in the computer industry. Use these opportunities to create a link between school and the world of work.

Use a work-study situation to obtain increased perspective on the computer industry, the company, or your special focus. In your cover letter, explain how you will adapt your skills to the work-study environment. Let the employer know in your cover letter how you will manage your time, juggling school requirements and work responsibilities.

7

RETIREES AND OTHERS

RETIREE STRATEGIES

Employers are looking for seasoned job applicants, especially in the computer industry. If they can wear more than one hat, that's a big plus. Computer industry employers would prefer to save recruiter's fees and hire mature, experienced workers who come to them first. Some employers don't have the budget to pay an agency to recruit young computer professionals, so they turn to older workers.

With recent college graduates facing tough competition, the older worker can fall victim to ageism in the work force, however. If you're an older worker or military retiree, you need to have a selling point in your résumé and pitch a good closer at your interview that markets your experience and stability.

Therefore, to give yourself a competitive advantage and cut the time you may have to wait before finding your next job, begin your cover letter by showing your future employer how to reduce costs by hiring you.

In your résumé Job Overview (see Student Tip #8), state that you're not retired; you're in transition. You're moving between levels of responsibility. Stress commitment and enthusiasm on your résumé. Show how you have used a combination of practical skills, people management ability, and task-oriented qualifications at each level of your career, regardless of the type of company.

Keep dates off your résumé if you're worried about covert age discrimination. It's unlawful under the Federal Age Discrimination in Employment Act to be turned down for a job because of age. The law applies to anyone over 40. However, the law is hard to prove if employers give competency, experience, or personality-related reasons for not choosing you.

Civil Service Positions

Retirees may wish to consider applying for civil service positions, although these positions are open to any candidate. Many military retirees apply for civil service jobs where they can earn veteran's preference points on civil service exams. Government applications require Form 171 for government or civil service work. You answer the questions directly on the form instead of sending a résumé. Request a Form 171 from your local State Employment Office.

The U.S. Office of Personnel Management, Los Angeles Service Center, has specific instructions on completing an SF-171 on its form FL-216 (8/92), titled "How to Complete an SF-171 Application for Federal Employment." You can also obtain instructions on how to fill out the SF-171 from the federal Office of Personnel Management or from most community college student job placement offices.

Here's what the U.S. Office of Personnel Management's form titled "How to Complete an SF-171" states

Some Important Things to Keep in Mind Before You Start:

The SF-171 is the standard application form used by most Federal agencies. It is also a Federal employer's first impression of you. As with any other application, a completed SF-171 is not only a reflection of the experience and knowledge you possess, it is also an indicator of the kind of employee you would be.

When reviewers evaluate your SF-171, they assess the extent to which your experience and education will allow you to successfully perform the duties of the position for which you are applying. Although you may have described your educational background and work experience clearly, spelling errors, grammatical errors, and/or a sloppy appearance could give an employer a negative impression of your abilities as an employee.

An SF-171 that is neat, clear, and error free is to your benefit. It is extremely important that all the information you provide is factual. The SF-171 is a legal document: falsifying any portion could prevent you from being hired, lead to your dismissal, or be grounds for criminal prosecution.

How to Complete the Form:

First, read the front page of the SF-171 carefully. It explains how to describe your experience, how to claim veteran preference, and how to reproduce the form for your future use. The SF-171 may be photocopied. In addition, you may describe your experience on separate sheets of paper. Be sure to include your name, social security number, and all other information requested at the top of the experience blocks. Every SF-171, or photocopy, must have an original signature and date in order to be accepted.

Guidance on how to complete the SF-171 follows:

Availability:

You will only be considered for positions for which you have indicated willingness to accept the pay rate, working hours, and location. In most cases, the pay and job site are not negotiable. Please do not indicate that you are willing to work "anywhere." Indicate only those geographic locations where you are willing to work or are willing to relocate.

Military Service and Veteran Preference:

If you have never served in the U.S. military, answer "no" to question 17, and mark the "no preference" box in question 22. If you have served, be sure to read the "Veteran Preference in Hiring" section on the front of the SF-171 carefully. Item 21 is especially important to complete if you served in Operation Desert Storm and have earned a campaign badge or expeditionary medal.

Work Experience Blocks:

It is to your benefit to describe your work experience as clearly, concisely, and truthfully as possible. You will want to describe your experience in familiar, non-technical language. The initial reviewer of your application may not have direct knowledge of the positions you have held. Be sure not to use excessive abbreviations or technical references that only apply to specific projects. You will want to describe the actual duties that you have performed and indicate the percentage of time you spent performing each duty.

Provide the actual month, day, and year you started and left each position, and the number of hours per week you worked in the position. Do not include excerpts from formal descriptions of your duties. Instead, describe the actual activities you performed and your professional accomplishments. If possible, briefly describe how your level of responsibility for accomplishing specific tasks increased with the time you spent in each position.

All this information is used by reviewers to quantify the extent of your experience and to determine its relatedness to the position for which you are applying. Please claim any experience you have gained through volunteer work or hobbies, if this information is applicable to the position for which you are applying.

Education:

Indicate your baccalaureate and/or associate degree major on the first line of item number 29, and your graduate major on the first line of item

30. The "Number of Credit Hours Completed" is the number of total units you have completed. Only completed courses will be credited. Also, remember to enclose a photocopy of your transcript (or OPM Form 1170/17, List of College Courses and Certificate of Scholastic Achievement) for verification.

Special Skills, Accomplishments, and Awards:
This section gives you the opportunity to claim credit for special skills you have acquired, achievements you have made or honors you have earned that are not appropriate to mention in the course of describing your experience. This is the place to mention computer skills, public speaking skills, even personal developments that are pertinent to the position for which you are applying.

As with the experience blocks, attach additional sheets of paper if you need more space to describe your accomplishments. Items 33 through 35 ask you to claim your typing skills, licenses or certificates, and language proficiency.

References:
The references you list will be contacted. Include the full names, addresses, and phone numbers of individuals who can accurately attest to your character.

Background Information:
Answer questions 37 through 47 carefully and honestly. Be sure to review your responses in this section, and in all of the others. Re-read your SF-171 while imagining that you are the reviewer. **Each application must have your signature in ink, not photocopied, and a date.**

Your Past Jobs Are Platforms

All the strategies for military retiree résumés can be applied successfully to the résumés of persons retiring from any type of work or for those switching careers later in life. The computer industry contains niches new enough to absorb those with little or no experience as long as training is current. Your best selling points are the practical skills that can be transferred from one job to the next. You have only one career but many different jobs. Look at each of your past jobs as platforms, levels, or foundations within one career. Retirees who have spent twenty or thirty years in an industry or the service have a lifetime of stages or levels of skills and responsibilities to transfer to new jobs.

CIVILIAN AND MILITARY RETIREES

Tips and Strategies

TIP 1: EMPHASIZE ENERGY AND ENTHUSIASM

A long service record sells your commitment to service and loyalty to duty. What is left to market is your enthusiasm and practical skills with computers and people.

The use of action verbs gives your résumé the feeling that you are blazing with energy. Show how efficient you are by listing measurable achievements on your résumé. List ten transferable skills you're going to offer an employer.

TIP 2: ADMINISTRATIVE WORK: A NATURAL TRANSITION

Many retiring officers prefer to transfer to administrative work. One example would be working as a law office administrator for a computer industry legal firm or department. Your main responsibility would be to free lawyers from managing the office and staff administrative tasks.

Law office administrative work is similar to what many officers did during their career with the military service. However, to get such a job, you would be competing with experienced legal secretaries who want to rise to a career in law office administration.

TIP 3: WHEN TO USE A CHRONOLOGICAL WORK HISTORY RESUME

A lengthy career in one industry or a military career fits easily into a chronological work history résumé. Neither the expanded nor creative résumés can usually accommodate 10 or 30 years of service. An abilities résumé wouldn't show the length of your service. Since you are selling dependability in terms of concrete skills, loyalty, and military achievements, the chronological résumé is often the best, most traditional vehicle for your kind of track record.

TIP 4: WHEN TO USE AN ABILITIES RESUME

Retirees who are making a drastic career change could successfully use the abilities résumé. Mature people who are switching careers may use the abilities résumé to reflect a transition of skills rather than traditional, long-term service under one employer.

TIP 5: SHORT-LENGTH MILITARY SERVICE

If your military service was relatively short, simply state your branch and the highest rank you achieved, dates of service, and provide the date that you were honorably discharged. Stating your military service, even if it's unrelated to your job objective, avoids unaccounted for time gaps in your employment record.

TIP 6: TIE YOUR QUALIFICATIONS TOGETHER

Include in your résumé a continuity section that summarizes and ties together your qualifications. This could be a brief Job Overview paragraph at the top of your résumé.

List any computer training you received in the military service. Include any technical training that could be transferred to a new job in the computer industry.

TIP 7: WHEN TO USE AN EXPANDED TWO-PAGE RESUME

You may wish to use a two-page expanded résumé to explain your responsibilities. Don't use it merely to elaborate on your executive status rank or to dwell on how much control or power you wielded. Responsibility should never be confused with rigid control, but rather as an accumulation of abilities and knowledge.

TIP 8: UPDATE YOUR SKILLS

Keep your skills sharp and up to date. If you trained long ago, it's time to take technical courses, attend conventions, and even organize your own workshops and seminars. You could then invite volunteer guest speakers to sell their products to your captive audience.

Join computer user groups and professional associations. Act as a liaison between your association, schools, and corporations. It will keep you actively seeking contacts. Learn how to use the most recent equipment and the latest software associations.

Keep volunteering in those associations while you call upon companies. The advice provided earlier in this book on creating visibility works equally well for retirees, students, and those with no previous job experience. The idea is to make yourself as unforgettable in person as your résumé is on paper.

TIP 9: SELL WHAT MAKES YOU UNIQUE—ACTION AND ACCOMPLISHMENT

Older workers in the computer field, as elsewhere, undervalue themselves. They don't realize or express the value of maturity and business experience.

Don't just chronicle past job titles; highlight solutions based on experience. For example show how you helped to solve problems for your past employers and brought profit to the company, or tell how you increased production. Reveal exactly how you see a task through to completion. Emphasize commitment. Highlight the value of your work ethic.

List qualifications that give you a unique advantage over the rest of the computer industry workers. If you are a retiree from the computer industry or a related technology and want to get back in, evaluate only the skills you wish to transfer to a new job.

TIP 10: FREQUENCY OF INTERVIEWS

Some personnel managers who look at résumés all day reject older workers based on false stereotypes that they are inflexible and cost more in terms of health care insurance and salaries. Other personnel managers hire older workers specifically because of low absenteeism and high work ethics; these managers realize the older worker's dependability and respect for authority (especially true of retiring military senior enlisted personnel).

Your résumé could land on the desk of either of those types of managers. The more managers who interview you, the better your chances are of finding a job quickly. Two interviews a day is a good target to aim for.

TIP 11: THE BEST JOBS ARE FILLED BY WORD OF MOUTH

Older workers are most frequently hired by word of mouth, not through newspaper ads. Use your wide circle of business contacts, neighbors, and friends to recommend you.

Some older workers or retirees who travel find employment by building friendships during vacations that draw older people.

TIP 12: TEMPORARY OPTIONS

Consider working on a temporary or contingency basis. This is often a desirable route for retirees. Additional information on this job strategy is outlined in the next section.

TEMPORARY EMPLOYEES AND INDEPENDENT CONTRACTORS

Temporary Service Employment

A temporary worker may be a "contingency professional," a temporary technical worker, day laborer, or temporary clerical employee.

According to one temporary employment service owner, when referring to temporary work, the term agency is never used in conjunction with temporary employment. It's called a temporary service. Agency refers to an employment agency that places job seekers in permanent positions for a fee. Not all temporary services have employment agency divisions.

Computer personnel are often contingency professionals working on temporary jobs for long or short-term assignments, such as technical writers, desktop publishers, database managers, programmers, computer operators, and paraprofessionals. Contingency professional employment often means hiring persons on a continuing but temporary basis. A larger number of temporary workers are office staff replacements doing word processing, desktop publishing, retail store demonstrating, convention registering, or related clerical work. A smaller but rising number are technical professionals, computer programmers, software manual writers, or day laborers. College students often apply for temporary work during the summers to gain more experience.

According to workers, some temporary services charge the employer one fee per hour for a temporary clerical worker; for example, $15 per hour for a word-processing operator, and $30 per hour for a technical writer. The temporary service may pay the actual worker another fee, such as $10 per hour for word-processing specialists and $15 to $20 an hour or more for the technical writer working on contingency. The employee is never charged a placement fee for referral to a temporary job, regardless of the length of the assignment.

Temporary workers can cost the employer less than hiring full-time permanent employees. Insurance costs for the temporary employee, such as health benefits or pension plans, often are paid for by the temporary service. In contrast, independent contractors working solely on their own as freelancers must pay for their own health insurance and retirement plans.

Sometimes retirees return to contingency work within a year after retirement, asking for flexible or part-time hours. They may choose to work two or three full days per week or just during a season, in different parts of the country, or as a traveling temporary worker.

Temporary employees may work for many temporary employment services or only one. The temporary worker is sent to one or many businesses for each assignment of varying length, from one day to several months.

Temporary Work Is Increasing

Unlike contingency professionals, temporary clerical employees and certain paraprofessionals don't have the continuity of working for one service that leases out the worker to a company for many years. Temporary clerical workers and some technical paraprofessionals, such as desktop publishers and word-processing specialists get the feel of doing temporary work on short assignments to fill in for vacationing or sick staff employees.

Who's An Independent Contractor?

The independent contractor can be anyone who sells a service or product on an as-needed basis by contract with a client. The independent contractor may work alone as a freelancer or work with assistants or partners.

The client or customer can be an individual or a company. Independent contractors also may work as intrapreneurs, entrepreneurs, contingency professionals, temporary or part-time workers, and as permanent staff employees (moonlighting after work) at various times.

Examples of some independent contractors in the computer industry include the following occupational titles:

- animators
- beta testers
- human resource recruiters
- computer press: journalists
- programmers
- systems analysts
- technical and software user manual writers
- local area network (LAN) specialists
- graphic designers
- drafters
- technical illustrators
- architects
- engineering graphics specialists
- desktop publishers

- desktop video producers
- computer graphics presentation specialists
- computer trade show planners
- sales and marketing
- word-processing specialists
- computer technicians
- desktop videographers
- video game artists/designers
- special effects specialists
- multimedia specialists
- technical trainers
- managers of information systems
- documentation analysts
- computer-aided designers
- computer presentations graphics designers
- robotics and numerical control technicians
- designers
- software engineers/designers
- manufacturing technicians
- cable television/producers
- software reviewers
- software talent agents

Advantages to the Company

An employer doesn't have to pay any health insurance or benefits to an independent contractor. Independents don't receive worker's compensation from an employer. You may have to pay your own health insurance expenses as an intrapreneur, although some firms give perks that include insurance.

Financial responsibility to find clients, collect payments, and follow up leads rests with the independent contractor, not with the client or company hiring you. However, you take orders from the company that contracts with you to perform a service or supply a product.

Most clients won't contract with you based solely on your résumé or cover letter. In addition to a creative or abilities résumé and a business card, you'll probably need a brochure or flyer.

Written communication may get you into corporate or institutional offices for interviews. There, you bid to supply your service or product against competing businesses. Evaluate honestly what you will offer.

Independent contractors may be in bidding competition with foreign businesses that import and export computer peripherals, software, and services. There's a burgeoning foreign market for computer industry independent contractors and consultants (for example, foreign computer animators).

Tips and Strategies for the As-Needed Worker

TIP 1: TEMPORARY EMPLOYEES—WHICH RESUME?

If you are seeking temporary employment, use a chronological work history résumé. Skills are most important. The skills could be word processing, programming, accounting, desktop publishing, or software manual writing. List the computer languages and software you work with, and detail all hardware and software used. List speed of data entry if applicable, such as: "Word processing on an IBM 486 with WordPerfect 6.0 at 80 words per minute." List past employers and exact job duties as they apply to the skill you're selling.

If necessary, use an abilities résumé, an expanded résumé, or a creative résumé to focus on your abilities and responsibilities; special work history résumés are needed for approaching contingency professional employment services. Your résumé will highlight different areas of your unique skills and training background. Flexibility is emphasized. Many contingency professionals prefer flextime or flexible hours. If you customize your work or résumé to suit many individual employers (as an independent consultant would do), contingency employment could be for you. Often, contingency workers get two- or three-year leases to work for one employer. The employee may receive health benefits and possibly other perks but temporary work does not usually offer as many benefits to the short-term workers, and perks differ with each agency.

TIP 2: FLEXTIMERS MUST GROUP SKILLS

Group your skills and abilities. Can you name each job-related task you can perform? Every part-time or shared job consists of a series of competencies and practical skills used on an as-needed basis. If flextime is your goal, sell your qualifications to make that clear.

TIP 3: JOB SHARE

You can create and customize a job according to your individual preferences and share it with another person. Use an abilities or creative résumé to do this.

Pick someone in a situation similar to yours, maybe a person close to retirement or a double-income-with-small-children employee who wishes to work fewer hours. Job sharers, like flextimers, are looking for a chance to work flexible hours or to work on preferred days. Perhaps you prefer to work at home, part time; or you're retired and want to come back into the work force a few days a week. Perhaps you are going to school; or you want temporary work for a few years, not a few days.

Advertise in a business magazine or professional association newsletter for someone to job share. You are looking for an associate with a full-time job who wishes to cut back to two or three days a week or half-days. Offer to work the other half the week. Ensure that your skills and goals are compatible.

TIP 4: INDEPENDENT CONTRACTORS

Use a creative résumé as a brochure or flyer to offer your clients a healthy bottom line. Independent contractors prefer the creative or abilities résumé that is formatted to look like a business brochure to secure clients or customers. At the back of the résumé, attach a one-page list of clients, and services provided. If you are an artist or writer, include a miniportfolio or list of publications with your résumé.

RESUMES FOR NEWCOMERS IN A CULTURALLY DIVERSE WORKPLACE

Immigrants come to North America from all parts of the world seeking jobs, clients, or customers in the computer technology industry. What does a newcomer to the United States or Canada who seeks work put on a résumé?

Cultural diversity is prevalent in today's global computer industry. You will find software in most major languages sold in the United States, and computer products catering to the needs of people from around the world available in major U.S. cities.

Many computers continue to be built in the United States. The wide variety of software available is designed and manufactured primarily in the United States. Import and export of computer parts is a huge industry here. For example, most computer hard disks sold here are assembled in Asia.

Cultural diversity in the workplace includes the entertainment industry's use of computers for special effects. Most computer animation for the television and film industry is currently created by computer special effects in Europe and Asia. Corporate desktop animation and special effects for ad agencies are created mainly here through multimedia desktop video.

Despite the reality of growing cultural diversity, employers still look for work patterns and values familiar to U.S. corporations. Employers want information they can understand quickly when reading your résumé. What are the most important points an immigrant can emphasize in a résumé or cover letter?

TIP 1: CAN AN EMPLOYER TELL YOUR GENDER BY YOUR NAME?

If you are foreign to the the United States, as a courtesy you may want to state your gender in the Job Overview section on your résumé. The person reading your résumé may not know your gender by the spelling or sound of your name. Or, consider putting Ms. or Mr. with your name on your cover letter.

TIP 2: TRANSLATE YOUR SKILLS INTO COMPANY VALUES

Picking from among your many abilities is difficult, so list only those skills that are highly valued by the company. Research the company's labor needs at a library, or ask an employee what skills the company seeks. Look at the job description and briefly explain how your skills apply. Identify what you do best in terms of what the employer values most. Focus on an employer's greatest need. For example, explain how an employer will save time and money by hiring you. Qualify and quantify your reasons. Include company-valued details about your abilities and work performance on those past jobs of special interest to the new company.

TIP 3: TRANSLATE YOUR JOBS AND EDUCATION

Look for niches where your skills can best be used. Sort your experience into categories. Sort your educational courses or technical training into categories that are comparable to levels of education in your new country. Show similarities to the U.S. corporate workplace. Clarify and explain your education where needed.

Call a few employers or human resource managers and ask them what job descriptions and job responsibilities in your computer specialty sound most familiar to U.S. (or Canadian) employers.

If your English is not good, see a résumé writer or a teacher for advice, or take a course in résumé writing at a community college.

TIP 4: KNOW WHERE YOU WANT TO WORK

Travel to areas where you would like to live and work. Then decide whether there is enough computer industry growth in that area in your field. Send your résumés to appropriate companies in that area. It's best to attend a few professional conventions in your chosen geographic area to network with people in your specialty. By making business contacts you may find some good tips about working in that area.

TIP 5: MAKE YOUR RESUME CONVINCING

Convince the employer that your international skills translate into experience familiar and useful to U.S. corporations or institutions. Use statistics to verify how good your skills are. Quantify the skills in your résumé as in the following examples:

"Word-processing speed is 90 words per minute with zero errors. Specialize in statistical keyboarding and data entry on XYZ computer using ABC software."

"Two years' experience operating NMB computers in the biotech industry."

"One year's experience in database management using Paradox software on an IBM PC."

TIP 6: LIST YOUR IMMIGRATION STATUS

Let the employer know on your résumé whether your visa is that of a student or a resident alien, or whether you're waiting to become a citizen. It's important for them to know whether you are legally in the country and have a work permit or "green card," and how long you intend to remain here, if you're not a permanent resident.

List your status simply and briefly at the end of your résumé, without drawing undue attention to it. You can elaborate on it at the final interview or after you're hired.

TIP 7: LIST YOUR ENGLISH PROFICIENCY AND ANY COURSES TAKEN IN THE UNITED STATES

State your English language proficiency level. The employer wants to know that you understand and speak English well enough to handle the job. If you have a heavy accent, take some speech coaching to improve your English diction. List any English training or courses taken in the United States. Explain that at your former jobs here or elsewhere, fluency in spoken and written English was required, if this is true.

TIP 8: EXPECT TO WAIT LONGER TO FIND WORK

It may take a new immigrant longer to find a job than someone who has lived, studied, and worked in the United States for many years. You may be offered less pay if you're not yet a U.S. citizen. You may be rejected for a job because you don't have the right level of security clearance; you may seek redress in this area for some situations. However, your age, not your ethnicity, will often determine how many weeks you may spend trying to find employment.

Now that you have learned how to customize résumés and job search strategies, let's move on to customizing your career. In the next two chapters you will learn how to choose a computer career according to your special preferences and personality type. You will be able to use this information to focus your résumé and target the job that is right for you.

WHICH JOB
IS THE
RIGHT JOB?

This chapter is designed to increase your self-awareness and help you to find the job that is the right match for you.

If your résumés frequently elicit form letters that state, "Your credentials are impressive, but they don't fit our requirements at this time," perhaps you have not been applying to businesses that need what you do best. Maybe you are not writing your résumé according to your personality preferences.

Would you like more power to choose the job that works for you? The personality questionnaire, or preference classifier, which you are about to take in this chapter applies specifically to career choices within the computer industry.

The questions ask what types of work you feel most comfortable doing in the computer industry. Use the completed answer sheets to self-score the sixteen preference types and find your personality type. Then look under your personality type. There you will see a list of the job titles recommended for each.

The personality questionnaire is a tool for understanding normal differences in the way people organize skills. It may also help you understand and appreciate the differences between all types of people working in the computer industry.

What Interests and Skills Come Naturally?
Ask yourself what skills are most easy to learn and to practice. What comes naturally? What's harder to do—so hard that you become depressed, irritable, or stressed out and exhausted from doing it all day?

Which tasks would you rather be doing at work? Computer industry personnel differ in their work preferences as they do in their job tasks. Some like to analyze. Others are artistic. There are those who like to sell and talk. Some like to train or teach.

Do you like to work alone using the computer as a tool to express or reflect inner thinking or feeling? Would you prefer to use the computer as a tool to do other jobs—such as architectural drafting or industrial design?

Whether you are sending your résumé to a corporation or you already work in a paid job, employers are going to ask, "Do you mind doing things our way?" When you do mind, it's because your preferences are different from your employer's.

How Can You Use Your Personal Strengths to Improve Teamwork?

The preference classifier will reveal your personal strengths. You will learn how to apply these strengths to improve teamwork on your job.

You will come to appreciate the personality type difference of others in a variety of jobs. And you will learn how to apply your understanding of personality type, in a specific way—to selected computer industry job requirements.

What Are Your Real Preferences?

Your type, as determined by this preference classifier, reflects how you felt when you answered the questions.

Preferences can change under stress. Or you could be hiding your real type in order to pursue a career you want because of the security, status, or better pay. Your real preferences are those you feel when you aren't under pressure or aren't out to prove anything.

Understanding Others' Types

You need to apply your knowledge of personality type when your usual behavior no longer works on the job. Once you recognize your type, use it ethically. Don't let it prejudice you against coworkers with different types and different needs.

Use your knowledge of personality type to help your coworkers fit into their most comfortable niches at work and use their natural preferences. You will find people at work who get great pleasure out of filling in the details and grounding you in practicality. Other types may feel that their dreams for the future are being wasted by attention to details in the present.

Detail-oriented people are clear and precise; they look for common sense. You may wonder why employers so often give the creative, imaginative, and visionary work to people impatient with details, common sense, and usefulness. Detail-oriented people can be just as imaginative in practical ways.

People with a preference for sensing (using their five senses before using their imagination) might prefer to complete tasks step-by-step in sequence. They prefer practical, detail-oriented skills that rely on common sense.

In contrast, people with a preference for intuition (using their imagination before using their five senses) might feel more comfortable completing tasks by first using creative skills that express ideas or visions about the big picture. They are interested in the future and possibilities. They enjoy forecasting trends and predicting everything from the weather to jobs of the future.

Intuitive people may not want to write down step-by-step sequential plans for how they will implement the big picture at first conception. It's easier to examine ideas and visions about the finished plan before drawing up the details.

Thinkers in the Computer Industry

Analytical or technical "thinkers" like to design models and matrixes, or put ideas in categories and label them. They troubleshoot and repair computers or sell technical equipment to other businesses, or they invent, build, or research aspects of the computer industry. Such thinkers are found in great numbers in the computer industry. Their favorite niches include management, administration, design, engineering, systems analysis, robotics, and computer repair technology.

Artists who are thinking types may enjoy computer-aided drafting specializing in circuit design, architectural illustration, computer video game design, and engineering graphics. Thinkers frequently major or minor in courses using computer equipment to analyze and solve problems in science, technology, or design.

Feelers in the Computer Industry

"Feelers" in the computer industry are interested in creating software that is easy to use by people with more diverse interests and in various applications. Feelers may wish to use computers as tools to communicate with people and to package or disseminate information. They write computer books and software manuals, publicize and market ideas, people, and products.

Feelers run the electronic bulletin boards and databases that communicate or broadcast information to researchers (the information brokers). Frequently feelers work as trainers where they can share information. They are also found in educational sales, instructional technology, and courseware design. Feelers are eager to communicate how to use computer technology to make life easier. The term user-friendly may have been coined by a group of feelers who empathized with those wanting easy-to-learn software.

Feelers are frequently hired to make the language of complex operations clearer and simpler for beginners to understand. For them, making software easy to learn is as important as the software's function. A sizable number of feelers are English majors hired to simplify and clarify complex language in instructional brochures or manuals.

Feelers may major in nontechnical fields, taking several computer courses as electives to gain entry-level job skills or to switch careers. They often go into personnel work in the computer industry. Some focus on recruiting people for computer jobs. Many become human resource managers. They may also work with outplacement agencies or as career consultants for computer industry workers in transition.

Some feelers concentrate on imaginative, artistic expression. They enjoy creating illustrations and corporate animation using computer graphics. Others focus on crafts, such as computerized toy design and manufacturing, or desktop video and multimedia production (presentation graphics).

Feelers and Thinkers Decide Differently

Feelers tend to make decisions by asking questions that focus on emotion or inner values, such as: "Is this job worth my being so stressed out?" and "Why do I care so much?" Thinkers weigh the pros against the cons more scientifically or impersonally before making decisions.

Other Personality Tests

The personality test you are about to take is a tool to enhance your self-awareness, appreciate your coworkers' talents, and improve teamwork on computer-related jobs.

This preference classifier is not the classic Myers Briggs Type Indicator (MBTI®), one of the world's most popular personality tests. This classifier resembles other common questionnaires, inventories, sorters, and indicators of personality preferences that give you a four letter type. This type is based on the principles of the MBTI®, which is based on the theories of psychoanalyst C. G. Jung and is validated with statistical research.

If you want to take the MBTI® to find out your four-letter personality type without vocational preference questions about computer careers, or to take other popular vocational preference inventories, such as the Strong (formerly Strong-Campbell) Interest Inventory, write to Consulting Psychologists Press, Inc., 3803 E. Bayshore Road, Palo Alto, CA 94303, or call 1(800) 624-1765. Ask for their catalogue.

Most colleges and adult education counseling offices offer the MBTI® or other indicators and vocational inventories to the public at low cost, or sometimes at no cost to students. Counselors and consultants offer interpretation of the results and career counseling. You can also interpret these questionnaires on your own.

If you'd like to read more books and pamphlets on personality types, or temperament and the MBTI®, also write to Type Resources, Inc., 101 Chestnut Street, #135, Gaithersburg, MD 20877, or call (301) 963-1283 or 1(800) 456-6284. Other related books include *Introduction to Type and Careers*, and *New Directions in Career Planning and the Workplace*.

You may want to read the book *Do What You Are*, by Paul D. Tieger and Barbara Barron-Tieger, (Little, Brown & Co., Boston, 1992). The book includes a professional personality test.

To understand your temperament, see *Please Understand Me* by Dr. David Keirsey and Marilyn Bates, (Prometheus Nemesis Book Company, Del Mar, CA), a book that includes information about job choice based on temperament. It contains the Keirsey Temperament Sorter, an inventory of preferences, and it details four temperaments and sixteen types.

Where Do *You* Fit in the Computer Industry?

The preference classifier you are about to take is designed exclusively for computer personnel. Think about what kind of work environment you prefer. What tasks are easier to do? Before you look for a job in the computer industry, find out where you fit.

After you finish this questionnaire and score your preference type on the answer sheets provided, keep a record of your preferences or computer-related personality type (in the broadest sense). Then look at the list of jobs under each preference type to see what would feel most comfortable. The recommended job list follows the answer sheets.

All computer-related jobs have in common the use of different technical, clerical, analytical, artistic, or imaginative skills to solve problems. Like most jobs, all computer-related jobs also have in common the need to get along with people. The jobs suggested in this book are only a few of the many that exist in the computer industry. Any type can and does work in any job. How comfortable or satisfied individuals are with their jobs is another issue.

Increase Your Workplace Comfort Level
There are no right or wrong answers. Use the following Computer Career Preference Classifier to increase your own workplace comfort level—never hire or work with people on the basis of their type—which could be different on paper (theory) than in reality.

Do you often dwell on what you would like to be rather than what you are deep down? Were you ever afraid of revealing a core personality in your job that was too different from the job description—too free-spirited and entrepreneurial, or too practical and security-seeking?

Have you ever avoided revealing your real preferences on your résumé or on personality inventories? Were you told that the skills you prefer to use weren't practical, useful, or realistic for a particular job? Are you afraid that "the real you" won't fit in with a group at a particular company—or even in some segments of the computer industry in general?

There are economic reasons why people won't admit, even to themselves, the job they would really love to do if they knew they could get hired. They may never match their résumés to those companies that are looking for what they do best. Without exposing preferences (which are motivating and lead to further skill-building), there is no way to find companies that apply what you do best to technology, business, or training.

The Computer Career Preference Classifier clarifies which work situations are more comfortable for you. Now let's take the preference classifier.

COMPUTER CAREER PREFERENCE CLASSIFIER

Directions

The classifier contains 74 questions. Answer on the separate answer sheets that follow the questions. An extra blank answer sheet is provided in case you want to answer this questionnaire with a friend or take the classifier twice.

1. Read each of the work-related situations. Mark A or B next to the corresponding question number on the answer sheets provided at the end of the classifier. Note that the question numbers are not in exact sequence on the answer sheets but are divided between page 1 and page 2.

2. To score your answers, total columns A and B. Add the totals under each column in the boxes marked with a letter. Then circle the highest score in the lower boxes closest to the bottom of the page marked E or I, S or N, T or F, J or P. Finally, enter the four letters of your highest scores on the line marked "Your Type." (Your type on this classifier means your classified preferences based on your personality and level of comfort with your choices.) A sample self-scored answer sheet is provided after the two blank answer sheets so you can see what the completed, scored answer sheet looks like.

3. When you have found your four-letter type, look at the explanation and suggested job titles that follow in the next chapter.

1. You received a B.S. in Computer Science and Information Systems last month. This month you began an entry-level sales and marketing job with a major designer of computer video games and educational software. You would rather

   A. actively sell the CD-Interactive software to a wide variety of consumers by giving live presentations and demonstrations.
   B. work alone in a private office with the door closed to market the software by direct mail without face-to-face or phone contact with people.

2. Computers are your hobby. At work you have time to practice your hobby during your two-hour lunch break in your flexible-time job. You choose to:

   A. play computer virtual reality martial arts video games purely for entertainment.
   B. design programs for forecasting the weather daily for 100 years into the future.

3. You would enjoy a job that requires you to

   A. select from many details in corporate computer animation special effects and point out which details need improvement in shape or color, and keep accurate records of facts.

B. examine how artificial intelligence, neural networks, or fuzzy logic affect people's attitudes about the computer industry.

4. A large corporation has two openings. Which job would you take?

A. Financial database manager: where you will analyze stocks and stock market trends and apply artificial intelligence strategies to forecast upturn or downturn. You will also analyze computer systems.

B. Director of human resource development: where you will use your understanding of people to head the personnel department or research training and human relations in the corporation. Your main duty is to place the right people in the right jobs.

5. You are told to fire an employee for taking too long to come back after maternity/paternity leave. You

A. terminate the person as ordered, telling the employee that the company cannot afford the loss of productivity and profit directly attributed to the individual's absence.

B. refuse to terminate the person as ordered. You advise the employee to sue the company for family leave discrimination and side with the person because of circumstances.

6. When asked to take a day off to purchase a new computer for your firm, you

A. visit many different stores all day looking for exactly the right machine at the best price and quality.

B. impulsively buy the first computer you see that fills the boss's requirements for the make and model so you can take the rest of the afternoon off to have fun.

7. You paid $200 last month to reserve a nonrefundable ticket to attend a computer graphics convention five months from the present in Las Vegas. Today you found out there's a virtual reality convention on the same day in Egypt, which you find more exciting. You are

A. comfortable sticking to your original plans to attend the Las Vegas computer graphics convention because it doesn't require change.

B. feel deprived of a fascinating experience and wish you could afford to lose the $200 and take off for Egypt at a moment's notice instead.

8. To give yourself more visibility among colleagues you would

A. take a paid weekend job hosting a two-hour radio talk show, answering questions on the air about computers or software in your specialty.

B. take a two-hour weekend job writing a column for a computer industry newspaper about your own interests, reading, reflections, or research.

9. You would take an assignment in the computer industry in order to have

    A.   job security and a high salary to spend any way you please.

    B.   the chance to have your work made into a film and plenty of worldwide recognition at conventions, and receive only $1,500 for your work.

10. You'd rather take a job that uses your

    A.   realistic attitude and practical skills in logistics.

    B.   your imagination to create software that sells escape.

11. You wish you had majored in a subject at college that

    A.   would have allowed you to think logically and objectively so that now you could analyze strategies, map out models, or keep records to solve problems about production and profit at work.

    B.   would have helped you to understand what people value most about their careers.

12. On which three specialties would you focus within a college major in computer science and information systems and a minor in liberal arts, business, or education?

    A.   Systems analysis, programming, and math

    B.   Computer graphics illustration, professional writing, and technical human resource management

13. Your supervisor gives you an assignment to write an article for the company in-house employee newsletter on ten home-based businesses you can operate with your personal computer. You would prefer to

    A.   create a plan and outline first; follow it exactly to organize the article; then write the article.

    B.   write the article first, from whatever springs into your head at the moment and then weed out what doesn't belong when it's finished.

14. You're researching an international electronic database for a long list of articles and books on UFO abductions in Russia for an Ivy League university professor of psychiatry. You get a call from a Nobel-prize-winning astrophysicist asking you to stop your work immediately and tape record what he has to say before he leaves the country. You prefer to

    A.   finish your research for the psychiatrist and tell the astrophysicist you'll write to him later. It's annoying to have to stop in the middle of a project and switch to a new task.

    B.   drop what you're doing and look forward to the surprise, change in routine, and excitement of taping the astrophysicist's startling statistics on a different subject.

15. You meet many strangers of both genders at work who ask you whether you're married, what you majored in, what's your hobby, what you do for fun, and how old are you because they want to know you

better. All of you will be working as a team in your new job. You tell the strangers

    A.   everything you can think of about yourself. You reveal all that interests you. You ask all the strangers to lunch.

    B.   you are a private person and don't want to reveal personal information, but you'll gladly ask and answer questions about anything related to the job.

16. You want a high-paying, prestigious job in the computer industry that uses all you have to offer and that you'll be able to keep until

    A.   you retire in 40 years with major benefits such as health insurance, a paid-off home mortgage, and an adequate pension.

    B.   a better job offers you an opportunity to use your imagination for adventure, change, intellectual achievement and/or creative expression.

17. On Thursdays, your employer lets all employees out at four to attend personal enrichment classes. You have a choice of two workshops. Which one would you attend?

    A.   How to repair your personal computer.

    B.   How to write novels about the future of computers.

18. You are asked to evaluate an employee. You would first consider

    A.   the employee's productivity and profit to the firm.

    B.   the employee's warmth and personal service to customers.

19. You have a choice of working for two supervisors. You would prefer

    A.   the boss who talks to you straight about how to analyze a database system but uses harsh words and sarcasm to make you improve while keeping your relationship from getting too personal.

    B.   the gentle boss who tells polite lies to protect you from knowing why your work was rejected, then asks your immediate supervisor to reprimand you for errors.

20. Your job finishes at 5 p.m., but your department manager says you can leave early if you want or hang around and start tomorrow's work. You won't be paid extra or less either way. No one's left in the office to see you working. You

    A.   start tomorrow's work and leave exactly at five, according to your usual daily schedule. You'll know exactly which place to start again in the morning with no confusion.

    B.   drop everything in midstream, take off, and head for that new movie you're eager to see. Leave tomorrow's work for tomorrow, and have fun when you can.

21. Your computer work is always

    A.   completed and well organized long before the deadline.

    B.   finished exactly at deadline or just after. You enjoyed the exhilaration of rushing to complete it on time.

22. You are asked to train a group of visiting computer science students in systems analysis and advanced programming in machine language. You're more comfortable

    A.   giving an oral presentation and live hands-on demonstration to a large group in the company conference auditorium. You love talking face-to-face with large groups of people who share your interests in computers or related products.

    B.   distributing the latest software manual you wrote to the students. You wish they could learn independently on their own machines in school, at their own place of employment, or at home. You find giving an oral presentation to a group positively exhausting. You would rather train students by letting them read what you write (books, manuals, articles, or newsletters) as part of a correspondence course.

23. In the computer industry, you would be happier as a

    A.   business-focused logistics executive grounded in the present time and the real world who deals with troubleshooting and repair of computers or in the sorting and selection of details in accounting, database management, or financial programming.

    B.   future-looking professor who uses neural networks technology from the biotech industry to create new possibilities in programming, computer hardware, and robotics to mimic human life.

24. You bought a computer at the best price you could find. Three years later you

    A.   still use your computer as is. If it ain't broke, you don't need to fix it.

    B.   upgraded your computer to keep up with technology. Everything has room for improvement and change.

25. When asked what you think of the concept of time, you're most likely to say

    A.   the concept of time as a theory is impersonal.

    B.   you feel guilty if you don't use it to help people. Time is concrete.

26. There are two job openings. You have all the qualifications for both. You choose to

    A.   design software to track government legal cases and to merge databases with a secretly modified "back door" to allow intelligence agencies to access foreign computer systems for their own espionage purposes.

    B.   be a journalist who achieves visibility while investigating the software tracking program as well as banking and intelligence agencies' scandals.

27. You find it easier to

    A.   follow directions exactly as planned or told to you by others at work. You would rather do the company's thing.

    B.   break regulations and do the work your own way. You find it harder to follow someone else's plans to the letter because you can't get into the other guy's head to know what he wants, and there's no way you can please him.

28. You're better at

    A.   time management.

    B.   adapting to unexpected changes in schedule.

29. You are an unemployed and homeless typist down on your luck with a nickel in your jeans. An employment agency with a government grant pays for your training in word processing and sends you on two jobs. Both employers want to hire you with equal pay for similar firms near the same location. Which job would be least stressful?

    A.   receptionist guiding heavy traffic all day in and out of the office, answering constantly ringing phones while typing reports and running errands.

    B.   back office word-processing specialist in a quiet, one-person office where the boss is usually out and no one comes in or calls. You can have total solitude as you type one long software manual after the other.

30. You would prefer a job where most of the projects you deal with have these characteristics

    A.   common sense, practical, useful, direct, realistic, actual, down-to-earth, factual, specific, and traditional.

    B.   futuristic, conceptual, inspirational, motivational, random, possible, intellectual, imaginative, fantastic, theoretical, ingenius, generalized, nontraditional, and creative.

31. The computer firm where you are employed is adding a corporate animation department. You are offered a choice of two jobs. You decide to take the job as a

    A.   marketing and sales manager of computerized toys and video production of corporate animation.

    B.   designer and researcher of animated robot cartoon characters, and scriptwriter of cartoon commercials.

32. People who work around you usually say you would prefer to do what's

    A.   fair and truthful than do what will make people happy.

    B.   needed and valued to make people like you or to accommodate colleagues.

33. It's more important to you

    A.   to be right than liked.

    B.   to be liked than right.

34. You want a computer industry job where you can

    A.   thrive on order and know what your work day will be like.

B.   explore the unknown without being pinned down. You want to keep all work options open.

35. You prefer a job in the computer industry where you can

    A.   complete projects and get them out of the way by the end of each day.

    B.   turn your job into play. You believe if your work can't be fun, you won't work in that particular job.

36. A large software firm offers you a choice of two jobs handling their customer base of Fortune 500 accounts at the same pay and benefits. You ask to be placed

    A.   in the sales department to use your telephone skills.

    B.   as a computer operator working alone monitoring runs.

37. If you were promised the same salary and job security, you'd prefer to spend the next four decades as

    A.   a communications technician with the phone company reading assembly language code on the 4ESS switching machine, which makes use of your common sense to handle phone company breakdowns from inside the various computers. You prefer to deal with details instead of your imagination to fix what's broken on the job.

    B.   an investigative journalist and suspense novelist who writes about the connections between competing computer corporations. You prefer using imagination to absorb global impressions or create new ideas instead of checking, locating, or troubleshooting details for accuracy at work.

38. You would rather be a multimedia presentations specialist who

    A.   makes judgments based on past experience.

    B.   makes decisions based on gut-level guessing.

39. The type of people you wish you could be more like are

    A.   able to stay calm and objective when others panic.

    B.   able to walk ten miles in another's shoes.

40. If you could pick your mentor at work, that person would

    A.   welcome challenge, rebuttal, and confrontation, sacrificing harmony for clarity.

    B.   prefer harmony, even at the sake of sacrificing clarity to avoid conflict.

41. You prefer to associate with employees who

    A.   always want everything in its place.

    B.   don't plan to have a place for everything, because they'd rather wait and see what the job demands at different times.

42. You are hired to interview job applicants for the personnel department of an educational software manufacturer. You have plenty of time to spare. You would prefer that each job applicant

A. come only at the scheduled time of the interview.

B. walk in off the street when they felt like it and surprise you with their impressive credentials.

43. A major food processor has hired you to direct the internal management information systems department. You would prefer to manage

A. public relations and marketing to vendors, suppliers, internal users, and regulatory agencies, including managing the electronic data interchange program.

B. computer operations, telecommunications, and systems and applications programming where you'd get more of a chance to work alone without interruptions.

44. You find the future

A. best put off until it comes because it's too scary.

B. full of exciting possibilities.

45. In your computer classes you most enjoyed the courses that emphasized

A. hands-on practical skills leading to a comfortable job in the real world as quickly as possible.

B. theory about the futuristic possibilities computers might becapable of once microchips are enmeshed with human DNA molecules to form neural networks.

46. All the computers at work break down at the same time. Your first impulse would be to

A. keep things in perspective and push for precision and clarity when directing others to fix what's broken.

B. try to understand how human error impacts the people affected by the computer meltdown.

47. In a computer career, you would rather

A. solve analytical problems and increase efficiency.

B. express your creativity by improving communications or helping consumers.

48. You are asked to write a software user manual. You would rather

A. keep the original outline goal-oriented and reach a closure as soon as possible.

B. stay open-ended without goals because new information may come in by deadline.

49. As a documentation analyst, you are asked to manage the technical writing department. You would like to

A. hurry permanent decisions, turn solutions into action, and implement communications right into the word-processing department.

B. keep the staff from going with the first decision, keep offering better solutions, and hold communications until you've cleared it with the technical illustration department—before turning the current iteration over to the word-processing department.

50. You just graduated from college. Two employers are eager to hire you. Each offer equal benefits. You would rather

    A.   train many people, employees and students, in how to operate VAX hardware and use VMS (DCL) software and the VMS backup utility. Do lots of demonstrations for people.

    B.   be a VAX computer operator for a healthcare management firm monitoring production runs and performing backups of corporate data, working alone.

51. You prefer to work in a niche of the computer industry that deals mainly with

    A.   using practical, real, tangible, specific, common sense, hands-on troubleshooting skills based on practice, usefulness, and experience.

    B.   using your imagination to forecast trends that show others how to find hidden escape routes, back doors, advantages, alternatives, theories, and new ways of doing things.

52. If you were a salesperson in the computer industry, you'd rather sell

    A.   tangible products, like computers, modems, and peripherals, financial database software to accounting firms, or medical records technology and transcription software to hospitals.

    B.   ideas, like advertising, public relations, public speaking, logos, desktop video productions, technical writing, event planning, neural networks and fuzzy logic, artificial intelligence solutions, trend forecasting, interactive fiction, presentation graphics productions, and virtual reality games.

53. You're a person who has worked your way up through the ranks in the computer industry. Colleagues are most likely to call you

    A.   a tough-skinned, hard-headed employee who clawed your way to the top by your achievements, intelligence, persistence, and education.

    B.   an empathic, persuasive, self-made employee who always put the customer's needs first.

54. You're asked to give a presentation to fellow employees at a computer industry convention. You'd prefer to

    A.   convince the audience by logical analysis to clarify definitions, facts, or trends.

    B.   persuade the people by communicating to their values, sentiment, and identity with a stirring videotape or film.

55. When searching for a career, you

    A.   grab the first job you find so fast that you're disappointed later.

    B.   switch careers as frequently as you switched majors in college or tech school.

56. You want a good job in the computer industry that is

    A.   reliable, stable, serious, secure, unchanging, controllable, orderly, routine, familiar, scheduled, methodical, organized, and dependable.

    B.   flexible, adaptable, leisurely, playful, fun, spontaneous, changeable, open-ended, and creative.

57. Deep down, lots of people contact at work makes you feel

    A.   energized and eager to talk and share your life experiences. Your office door is kept open for the sounds of people networking.

    B.   sick, drained, exhausted, anxious, and bored by a continuous, crushing crowd on whom you wish you could close your office door.

58. A software company asks you to review their new database software or state-of-the-art paint and draw programs. As a gift, they say you can keep the expensive software you have reviewed for a computer magazine. You use the software to

    A.   produce a new product that will appreciate in value over the years, even when the software becomes outdated. Patent the new product and save the profits in your retirement plan.

    B.   have some fun teaching kids how to use it and then donate the software to an imagination-stretching computer camp high in the mountains of Aspen, Colorado. Afterwards, you enjoy a ski vacation as a guest of the computer camp.

59. You have a choice of two conferences to attend during the holiday season. You'd rather attend

    A.   a conference on improving your practical skills, which will allow you to pass a qualifying exam for a more secure job at a higher salary.

    B.   a conference on UFO abductions, advertising evidence presented by a distinguished military general, a Nobel prize-winning physicist, an Ivy League university professor of psychiatry, and three security guards who witnessed autopsies on space aliens at a secret military testing site's underground base.

60. When you read a software user manual, you are more apt to see

    A.   the errors of clarity and organization and how it can be improved or made more efficient. You want to critique and analyze it, or see how and where it went wrong. You welcome challenge and rebuttal. You want a software manual that remains objective and impersonal.

    B.   the way it motivates, inspires, and persuades you to understand the subject by its smooth-talking style. You praise it for simplicity and harmony.

61. You're hired to train advanced information systems students in programming the latest versions of C++ computer language. You let the students know that

    A.   you're more interested in the computer language capabilities than in the student's personal problems, learning needs, or motivation.

    B.   you're more interested in the student's personal needs and motivation, inspiration, and growth than you are in the programming language.

62. You'd rather take a job as a

    A.   tape librarian or computer operator where every minute of your workday is planned and scheduled, and you use a dayplanner (book or software). You wouldn't mind if your keystrokes were counted as you enter data into a computer. You don't mind following someone else's rules to the letter. You prefer to make lists.

    B.   multimedia presentation graphics producer where you have many hours of free time to see what spontaneous activities can be molded into video productions and computer graphics presentations without others requiring you to be an exacting, methodical perfectionist in detailed work, scheduling, and organizing. You would mind very much if your keystrokes were counted or you had close supervision. You hate to be evaluated on how closely you follow another person's plans.

63. On weekends you

    A.   make a list of every chore that needs to be done and every item you have to buy. You visit computer stores only when you need to buy a specific product on your list.

    B.   let whatever happens spontaneously take over the day, depending on your energy level, who calls, or what movie is playing. You dread working on your free time and prefer to see what fun just happens as the weekend progresses. You enjoy spending an afternoon browsing in computer stores, even if you don't need to buy anything.

64. On your résumé you would be certain to emphasize

    A.   your interest in giving presentations, speeches, or talks on your area of interest or experience.

    B.   your preference for communicating via the written word in memos to coworkers and doing as little face-to-face talking as possible.

65. You would rather take those thick software manuals and

    A.   review them for a practical, how-to, hands-on personal computer magazine.

    B.   turn them into spectacular 60-minute multimedia instructional videos for beginners.

66. You would rather repair

    A.   people's computers.
    B.   people's attitudes.

67. You want to duck out the door and take a break when

    A.   coworkers cry openly.
    B.   you say something negative that you really don't mean, but you believe it must be said because it is logical and fair.

68. You wish your résumé and cover letter could

    A.   analyze, challenge, and confront ageism with the truth.
    B.   deny that ageism exists in your specialty and convey optimism, energy, and enthusiasm for the job.

69. To start and finish a job, what you need most is

    A.   an agenda with handouts and flow charts.
    B.   room to move in all directions by self-pacing—a chance to change the agenda and diverge from the original plan.

70. You'd rather

    A.   do the best quality work you can on each project so you can be proud of yourself, even though no one else ever notices. (You may secretly keep records in a log book.)
    B.   have self-determination.

71. You are always willing to

    A.   share personal experiences at work by talking and expressing your opinions; volunteering to work on committees and attend meetings, functions, office parties or after-work cultural or sports events; and speaking on panels at conferences.
    B.   write a personal journal that involves research, reflection, meditation, and challenge—especially when a coworker interrupts you in mid-paragraph.

72. On your résumé, you would prefer to

    A.   list only those realistic, practical, useful, routine, hands-on skills or experiences that specifically fulfill the requirements of the job description.
    B.   express yourself by abilities or examples of creativity and persuade the employer to consider job possibilities that don't yet exist but that accommodate your ideas.

73. Your employer is giving you an "Employee of the Month" award. You'd prefer the prize to be

    A.   an award for successfully beating rival firms.
    B.   a psychology book on why women see competition as loss of self.

74. You spend too much time

    A.   rigidly impatient with exploring your career.
    B.   gathering information.

COMPUTER CAREER PREFERENCE CLASSIFIER

Answer Sheet: Page One

	A	B
1		
8		
15		
22		
29		
36		
43		
50		
57		
64		
71		

TOTAL

	A	B		A	B
2			3		
9			10		
16			17		
23			24		
30			31		
37			38		
44			45		
51			52		
58			59		
65			66		
			72		

TOTAL →

E   I

S   N

143

COMPUTER CAREER PREFERENCE CLASSIFIER

Answer Sheet: Page Two

	A	B		A	B
4			5		
11			12		
18			19		
25			26		
32			33		
39			40		
46			47		
53			54		
60			61		
67			68		
			73		

TOTAL

	A	B		A	B
6			7		
13			14		
20			21		
27			28		
34			35		
41			42		
48			49		
55			56		
62			63		
69			70		
			74		

TOTAL

T   F

J   P

YOUR PREFERENCES REVEAL YOUR TYPE ___ ___ ___ ___

COMPUTER CAREER PREFERENCE CLASSIFIER

Answer Sheet: Page One

	A	B
1		
8		
15		
22		
29		
36		
43		
50		
57		
64		
71		

TOTAL

	A	B		A	B
2			3		
9			10		
16			17		
23			24		
30			31		
37			38		
44			45		
51			52		
58			59		
65			66		
			72		

TOTAL →

E   I

S   N

COMPUTER CAREER PREFERENCE CLASSIFIER

Answer Sheet: Page Two

	A	B		A	B
4			5		
11			12		
18			19		
25			26		
32			33		
39			40		
46			47		
53			54		
60			61		
67			68		
			73		

TOTAL

	A	B		A	B
6			7		
13			14		
20			21		
27			28		
34			35		
41			42		
48			49		
55			56		
62			63		
69			70		
			74		

TOTAL

T   F

J   P

YOUR PREFERENCES REVEAL YOUR TYPE ___ ___ ___ ___

COMPUTER CAREER PREFERENCE CLASSIFIER

Sample Self-Scored Answer Sheet
Answer Sheet: Page One

	A	B
1	X	
8	X	
15	X	
22		X
29		X
36		X
43		X
50		X
57		X
64	X	
71		X

TOTAL

4	7

4	7
E	I

	A	B		A	B
2		X	3	X	
9		X	10	X	
16		X	17	X	
23	X		24	X	
30	X		31		X
37	X		38		X
44		X	45		X
51		X	52		X
58		X	59		X
65		X	66		X
	3	7	72		X

TOTAL →

3	7
4	7

7	14
S	N

147

COMPUTER CAREER PREFERENCE CLASSIFIER

Sample Self-Scored Answer Sheet
Answer Sheet: Page Two

	A	B		A	B
4		X	5		X
11		X	12	X	
18		X	19		X
25		X	26	X	
32		X	33		X
39		X	40		X
46	X		47		X
53	X		54		X
60	X		61	X	
67	X		68	X	
	4	6	73		X
		⟶		4	6
TOTAL			4	7

	A	B		A	B
6	X		7		X
13	X		14		X
20	X		21		X
27	X		28		X
34		X	35		X
41		X	42		X
48		X	49		X
55		X	56		X
62		X	63		X
69		X	70		X
	4	6	74	X	
		⟶		4	6
TOTAL			1	10

8	13
T	F

5	16
J	P

YOUR PREFERENCES REVEAL YOUR TYPE   <u>I N F P</u>

YOUR PREFERENCES AND TYPE

Now that you have your four-letter type, what do you do with it? Use it as a guide to achieve job satisfaction. A résumé balances your need for job satisfaction with a company's drive to control its production and profit.

To move the balance in your favor, your résumé must contain something measurable on it to make an impact and to position you first in the employer's mind. Your four-letter type can give you clues about what to put on your résumé that's measurable. How you have applied your personality preferences to skills, and skills to production and profit, is only part of the picture.

To understand how your preferences relate to job satisfaction, you need to know the characteristics of the four letters of your type. A list of suggested jobs follows the discussion of each letter. Let's discuss the differences between extroverts and introverts. Your first letter was either *E* or *I*.

ARE YOU PEOPLE ORIENTED?

E Is for Extrovert
About 70 percent of the people in the United States are extroverts. They get their energy from being around people and doing people-oriented activities.

If your first letter was *E*, you see yourself at this time as an extrovert. (It's also possible to be a closet extrovert, and list yourself as an introvert; or to be an introvert at your core and list yourself as an extrovert because that's what you would rather be to fit in.)

In résumé writing, you act as an extrovert when you talk about each part of your résumé with people you meet at professional associations and job fairs, with computer industry employees in your field, and people on job search committees. You are comfortable working around a steady flow of people and lots of people-processing activity.

Look for jobs that require you to be outgoing, sociable, interactive, and enterprising. Look for breadth of skills or job activities rather than depth of expertise and concentration.

You find it hard to maintain concentration on a solo activity if there is any interruption or distraction by people. Extroverts make excellent receptionists, customer relations persons, vendors, and teachers or trainers. About 49 percent of computer programmers are extroverts and nearly 52 percent are introverts.[1]

You need extensive contact with clients because people contact energizes you and being alone drains you. Attend events such as conventions, conferences, and meetings.

Involve yourself in planning events for the computer industry such as trade shows and exhibits. You are energized by talking, so volunteer to do public speaking on panels at conventions and meetings of professional associations. An ideal job in the computer industry would be where you can manage people, technology, or events.

If you are an extrovert, look for a job in the computer industry that allows you to do the following tasks:

- Run national associations of computer professionals.
- Do public speaking and presentation graphics work.
- Sell and market computer tangibles (products) or intangibles (ideas).
- Produce software videos.
- Train employees how to use software or hardware, or teach in a school.
- Open a computer matching service for business partners.
- Organize computer camps.
- Do many things at once.
- Work in an environment where there are many distractions.
- Work in the computer press arena as a journalist.
- Sell wireless telecommunications equipment and car phones.
- Do demonstrations for stores.
- Plan campus computer fairs.
- Direct marketing research and consumer tracking.
- Manage a large staff.
- Attend meetings and volunteer on committees.
- Put your opinion in the company newsletter; be a columnist so you can interview many supervisors and employees.
- Work in the public relations and marketing communications department of a computer firm.
- Create visibility for all your ideas, working with a partner who can help you make your ideas realities.
- Make audio or videotapes.
- Practice listening skills.
- Get daily feedback from coworkers and employers on how you're doing. Don't wait until job evaluation time.

---

[1]These statistics are from *Manual, a Guide to the Development and use of the Myers-Briggs Type Indicator* by Isabel Briggs Myers and Mary H. M. Caulley, Consulting Psychologists Press, Palo Alto, 1989, p. 245, "Ranking of Occupations by Preference for Extroversion/Introversion." (This percentage does not reflect a worldwide study, only the sample from the more than 250,000 MBTI® records at the Center for Applications of Psychological Type, Inc. in Gainesville, Florida.) Scoring in the *Manual* was done between 1971 and 1989.

I Is for Introvert

Approximately 30 percent of the U.S. population are introverts. Introverts are energized by introspection, concentration, and working alone. They prefer depth to breadth in job duties.

If your first letter was *I*, precision, vision, understanding, insight, analysis, objectivity, and reflection are your best skills. The more quiet time you have, the more creative you become. Market your precision in written communication.

Introverts need more time to think and reflect on questions before they speak. Many jobs in the computer industry fit the needs of introverts desiring solitary activities where they can think, analyze, or express their creativity for long hours at a time.

If you are an introvert, you are territorial. The job you can thrive in must allow you to concentrate on one long project at a time with the office door closed for privacy. Your skills focus in depth on one or two subjects. If the focus is too wide, you feel scattered. Target a niche. Become expert in what gives you energy. Your worse mistake would be to become a generalist or jack-of-all-trades. A second skill can be used as a backup when the first subject becomes obsolete or is no longer needed by employers.

You are drained by people. Find a job that will conserve your energy levels by allowing you enough time to work alone. Your work is going to be guided by your internal reactions and reflections on your subject of expertise. Working alone or with one or two other people on long projects requiring deep concentration, such as writing computer books, might satisfy you.

Introverts are complex people who usually don't show everything they are feeling without thinking about it first. In a live interview, introverts may keep their best points to themselves, preferring instead to put them in their résumé or cover letter.

Interviewers may not allow for different response times from candidates, and could confuse introversion with a lack of enthusiasm for the job. Résumés and cover letters of introverts can use direct mail marketing techniques to illustrate enthusiasm and circumvent this problem. If you have an "I," highlight the skills in your résumé, brochure, or cover letter by showing samples of your work and a list of your achievements.

If you are an introvert, look for a job in the computer industry that allows you to do the following tasks:

- Work alone as much as you need for recharging.
- Write or illustrate.
- Choose long projects, like books, to concentrate on with the office door closed for privacy.
- Deal with people through mail order or computer bulletin boards.
- Limit your public speaking commitments.

- Choose distance teaching and correspondence courses if you are a teacher.
- Conserve your energy.
- Travel less than an extrovert if you are in sales.
- Stop working when you are exhausted and take a break.
- Write what you have to say and reflect on it.
- Concentrate on creative or analytical work.
- Interview people one at a time with as few interruptions as possible.
- Work outdoors where you spend more time alone than directing people face to face.
- Telecommute or work in a home-based consulting business.
- Review software and books or tapes.
- Sell your listening skills.
- Hire a publicist to promote your ideas, talents.
- Do radio and TV interviews by telephone hook-up to your home.
- Develop your artistic talents with software.
- Restrict your telephone time.
- Communicate in writing and sell it.
- Design courseware and instructional technology.
- Perform computer technology and robotics repair. Customer interaction is minimal.
- Work alone at night.

HOW WE TAKE IN INFORMATION

Your second letter was either *N* or *S*. There are two ways we take in information, by intuition or sensing. Intuitives (N types) like to gather information holistically, under a theoretical umbrella. Sensors (S types) like to gather information factually, chronologically, sequentially, and specifically.

Misunderstanding or lack of communication at work or in the home often is due to the differences between those giving out information as sensors and those taking in the information as intuitives. Let's look at the differences between sensors and intuitives.

N Is for Intuitive

Intuitives are in the minority. Only about 30 percent of the world's population take in information using intuition. Therefore, it's going to be hard to do things your supervisor's way, unless you happen to match your type with the organization's character.

If you are an intuitive, your résumé needs to show how much you inspire and motivate people with your theories about the future. You deal in randomness and possibilities, rather than concrete logistics. Intuitives thrive on theory. Whether you are an introverted or extroverted intuitive, if your second letter is N your best skill is your ingenuity.

Intuitives Need Change and Diversity

You wouldn't be happy for long handling routine daily details, such as keeping records of accounts payable and accounts receivable or typing title insurance policy forms in the word-processing department. You need diversity and change on a job—many projects, ideas, and possibilities.

You would be happy working as a computer newspaper or magazine reporter writing a different article each week on a variety of subjects rather than teaching word processing each semester using an upgraded version of the same software.

Look for a job where your main skills would be to persuade, motivate, and inspire alternatives. Introverted intuitives are happy writing, programming, analyzing, and illustrating or designing courseware. Introverted intuitives would feel more comfortable selling by direct mail order catalogues or electronically, where constant face-to-face contact wouldn't occur. Extroverted intuitives are energized by being training managers, speaking in front of audiences, managing people at all levels, and creating marketing ideas. Extroverted intuitives could sell intangibles such as ideas to advertising agencies. They are also excellent at motivating and inspiring others to enter the computer industry.

Intuitives are catalysts who bring people together from different walks of life, and they make great event planners for computer conventions. As an intuitive, you would enjoy designing or writing a corporate video or managing a nonprofit organization that recycles used computers for use in schools.

Programming appeals to intuitives. Many combine diverse backgrounds, for example in health care or environmental sciences, with computer programming for research, design, or training.

Intuitives Need to Use Their Imaginations
Intuitives prefer to use fantasy and escape rather than facts to sell products or ideas. If you are intuitive, you may want to develop a skill for making all your good ideas reality and then selling them. Any personality type can be creative or imaginative, but intuitive types are more frequently creative in general and future-oriented ways. Sensor types are often imaginative in specific, present-oriented ways.

If you are an analytical intuitive, the best computer-related jobs lie in designing computer video games, selling your interactive fiction, teaching and training others in your specialty, and working in theoretical disciplines.

If you are not an analytical-type intuitive, try corporate animation, desktop video, desktop publishing, technical writing, computer press journalism, computer graphics, and the more creative aspects of computing. Many intuitives prefer to work at home as telecommuters with their computers hooked up to employers and others via modems, VCRs, and fax machines.

Intuitives Look for Alternatives
Use your intuition to study the possibilities in your résumé. Besides your ingenuity, your ability to look at alternatives and consider what else can be done is valuable.

Looking for alternatives energizes you. You could be an ideal resource person. You can find a thousand ways to market a product or service, or a hundred businesses that utilize one skill.

If you are an intuitive, look for a job in the computer industry that allows you to do the following tasks:

- Think of many things while working on one project.
- Work out alternate routes or new possibilities.
- Leave the details to sensors (sensing types).
- Work flexible hours—as late as you want.
- Analyze how computers work.
- Work with words and creative writing.
- Explore hidden meanings; create "back doors" in software.
- Find out how different things are connected.
- Question authority.
- Give general answers to specific questions without arousing anger in others.
- Work without always following others' directions.
- Sell escape fiction, such as games and stories of fantasy.
- Explore your creativity. (Desktop publishing/design and interactive, multimedia, desktop video are good fields for you.)
- Keep out of the accounting department, unless you're managing an accounting firm's public relations or personnel department.
- Perform analysis of complicated problems for research departments and think tanks.
- Do computer engineering, where the emphasis is on computer language analysis rather than on continuous sorting of sequential details.
- Look into new uses of computers, and virtual reality used in new ways. Look to international markets for new possibilities.
- Forecast trends.
- Use foreign language abilities to design translation software.
- Evaluate and analyze inventions or work with inventors and patent attorneys.
- Improve or develop new products that use old things in new ways.
- Use computer technology in psychotherapy or rehabilitation.

S Is for Sensing

Sensors like to gather information literally. The résumés of sensors reflect the perspiration more than the inspiration that drives their work. About 70 percent of the world's population are sensors.

The job most likely to be a comfortable fit for you will be direct, realistic, down-to-earth, steady, specific, and geared to the present. You would prefer to sell tangible products rather than ideas. You like to sell what you can touch, smell, hear, or see through your five senses.

Sensors want to see ideas applied to real solutions. To sensors, intuition means playing hunches, and hunches aren't backed up by concrete facts.

Sensors Are Literal

You are literal about data. You enjoy the tactile experiences of textures, videos, sounds, sights, and smells. Virtual reality is your stage. You want a job that uses your hands-on skills or troubleshooting ability. You are a master of facts or tools.

Your ideal job needs a here-and-now aspect to it, such as in analyzing or programming financial databases. You would prefer to leave the theorizing to physical scientists and mathematicians. You like computer courses in which the content is applied to real world problems. Sensors are comfortable in the business world.

If you are a sensor, look for a job in the computer industry that allows you to do the following tasks:

- Deal with details and specifics.
- Find solutions using common sense rather than theory.
- Explore computer security and computer law professions.
- Work with applied sciences. (Theory puts you to sleep.)
- Enjoy lots of physical activity at work. Move around. Walk.
- Troubleshoot and repair technology.
- Learn computer-aided drafting or engineering graphics.
- Deal with accounting or applied mathematics.
- Apply your financial knowledge to artificial intelligence.
- Create technical illustrations, typography, or applied art.
- Robotics technology and computer-aided manufacturing, which require your hands-on skills.
- Concentrate on one project at a time.
- Take jobs that offer immediate, tangible results. (You want to see where your efforts lead).
- Work at jobs that deal with the present. (Thinking too much of the future wastes your time.)
- Work with figures or facts. Routine is important.
- Choose programming specialties in financial database management or health care fields.
- Work sequentially and chronologically.
- Learn step by step and teach computer subjects the same way.
- Simplify the complex using facts and details.
- Supply exactness and not sweeping generalities.
- Give clear instructions and ask for the details immediately.
- Question authority before taking anything literally.
- Look for the trees, not the forest.
- Keep daily logs, dated memos, and records of your work environment and activities, or anything unusual that occurs.
- Instead of trying to fix what's not broken, ask an intuitive to show you all the ways something can be improved.
- Shop comparatively.
- Use software for fashion design.

HOW YOU MAKE DECISIONS

Your third letter was either *T* or *F*. There are both thinkers (T types) and feelers (F types) in the computer industry. Let's look first at thinkers, who are found in large numbers in programming, software engineering, scientific research, and systems analysis positions. Fifty percent of the world's population are thinkers. However, two thirds of the thinkers are male and one third of the thinkers are female.

T Is for Thinking

Thinking deals with how you make decisions. Here is where you focus your need to come to closure when you make decisions be it what to put on your résumé or where to work. Thinking means you reach conclusions through logical analysis. You often step back from becoming emotionally involved in a decision.

According to Otto Kroeger, management consultant and author of *Type Talk At Work, (How the 16 Personality Types Determine Your Success on the Job)* (Bantam, Doubleday, Dell, 1992), 96 percent of top corporate executives are thinking judgers (TJ types). Only four percent of corporate executives who have risen to the top CEO level are not thinking judgers.

For example, suppose you are a thinking, judging person. According to Kroeger, "As long as our system is profits and productivity driven, TJs will rise to the top." Profit is a key factor in determining how those who run the computer industry make their decisions. On a résumé, how much money you made for a company last year influences how desirable you are to employers.

So if you are a T or TJ, connect with organizations that have a similar character. (The same advice applies to the other preferences: connect what you are to where you work.)

Hard Heads and Firm Words

As a thinker, you will try to be logical, calm, and unemotional. Sometimes your clear-headedness will be perceived as hard-headedness. You will talk truthfully to others rather than make up polite lies to avoid hurt feelings. You believe there is always room for improvement in people's work, and you will evaluate and critique the work of others. You are best at analyzing the work of others and making it clearer and sharper.

Being natural skeptics, it's comfortable for a thinker to critique. They will question authority if the authority's conclusions aren't backed up by factual, scientific evidence. They may insist that the boss is wrong until the boss proves he or she is right. It's more important for a thinker to be right; if you are a thinker, you couldn't care less who likes you. You don't need harmony at work.

A thinker likes to organize either facts (if he or she is also a sensor) or ideas (if he or she is also an intuitive) into logical order. Thinkers hate redundancy. In the computer industry, many thinkers are business-like, brief, and curt in conversation. Thinkers are impressed with logic.

Thinkers enjoy solving the problems of machines, software, business, or technology more than solving the problems of people—unless they can administer or manage people without getting involved in emotional issues.

If you're a thinker, look for a job in the computer industry that allows you to do the following tasks:

- Settle disputes objectively.
- Analyze securities, facts, or computer systems.
- Troubleshoot and repair computers or peripherals.
- Sell technical instruments.
- Write technical software or hardware user manuals.
- Design software or hardware.
- Design and program computer games.
- Handle accounting problems.
- Manage financial databases.
- Invent more efficient computers.
- Sell cable television to telephone companies.
- Investigate computer security problems or crime.
- Practice computer, tax, or computer-related entertainment law.
- Design computers for military robotics.
- Write technical textbooks.
- Open an electronic university to teach computer sciences.
- Teach critical thinking to employees or college students.
- Make decisions.
- Become a computer consultant, solving problems.
- Work as a systems analyst.
- Be an expert witness or professional skeptic.
- Use computers for scientific, economic, or financial research.

Feeling Types

F stands for feeling types. About two thirds of all females and about one third of males in the United States are feeling types. Feelers seek rapport with co-workers, either through correspondence or in person. Feeling types avoid conflict and need harmony in the workplace and in the work task. Feelers like to give feedback, and consider the emotions of everyone around them before making a decision.

Although thinking types can be found in music, art, and literature, their verbal language and technical illustration tends to be complex and analytical. They seek to evaluate or critique. Feeling types, however, seek to praise rather than critique, evaluate, or analyze. They seek inner values leading to serenity in the project or work environment.

If you are a feeling type, a computer job or task may be both technical and creative. However, if the work can't be directly applied to helping people or enhancing people's lives, environment, imagination, or healing, you aren't too interested in it. You ask, "Is it worth working for?"

The Journey, not the Destination

You are process-oriented rather than task-oriented. Your overview and career goal is always centered on self-growth, service with a smile, or ensuring that there is value to your work.

Feelers can be found in everything from artificial intelligence and neural networks to nanotechnology and biotechnology. They are frequently found working as trainers, editors, public relations directors of software companies, writers, illustrators, and event planners.

You have a great need for affiliation and rapport with those around you at work, even if it's only through correspondence. You are loyal to your boss as long as the workplace needs for harmony and rapport aren't overlooked.

When you are under stress, rather than list the pros and cons to make a decision objectively, you'll ask yourself whether the outcome is worth it. What does the work mean to your growth and the growth of those around you who use the product, service, information, or idea? You trust your feelings.

The Feeler's Niche Is Communication

In the computer world, software is viewed as a tool for business and education, for learning through entertainment, or as creative arts therapy. Sell software that you feel upholds your values about work and life. Emphasize software as a tool to make communication easier and better. Your niche is probably in a communication field like one of the following: CD-Interactive courseware design, CD-ROM, virtual reality, animation, desktop video, desktop publishing, the computer press and journalism, public relations, human resource management, people-oriented research and personnel trend studies, electronic publishing, video production, psychology, multimedia, special effects, telecommunications, local and wide area networks, wireless communications, music and graphics design or illustration.

Feeling Types Frequently Design Software

Educational technology, designing or selling software as entertainment or education are areas where you do well. You would feel comfortable designing preschool software and games, helping people see value in computers, cable or phones linked to computers, or expressing yourself using computers as tools for an aesthetic, communicational, personal, or visual experience.

If you are a feeling type, look for a job in the computer industry that allows you to do the following tasks:

- Write articles or books about careers in the computer field.
- Design computer software to teach through entertainment, idealism, or service.
- Capitalize on your communication and interpersonal skills.
- Sell software to hospitals.
- Speak to sales groups.
- Direct public relations.
- Work as a journalist in the computer press.
- Design instructional courseware.
- Use computers to enhance the environment.
- Use computers in psychology and therapy.
- Animate corporate training films.
- Use computers and video in multimedia productions.
- Record information on CD-ROM.
- Use desktop publishing or desktop video to create books or ads.

- Write software user manuals to help people learn a skill.
- Manage the marketing communications department.
- Plan events, trade shows, and conventions.
- Publish a newsletter on ergonomics.
- Work as a computer illustrator or graphic designer.
- Teach computer skills to the physically challenged.
- Place employees in jobs.
- Work in outplacement for retiring personnel.
- Open a software talent management agency.
- Design computer games for the learning disabled.
- Teach creative writing using word-processing software.
- Teach computer-aided design and illustration.
- Use computer equipment to create music, work with sound and lights, or edit films.
- Create national clearinghouses for new databases.
- Start a business or professional association.
- Introduce computers and software training to a preschool or senior center.
- Bring together international businesses or groups for a common interest.
- Use computers for therapy in special education.
- Work as a documentation analyst.
- Train corporate managers.
- Telecommute so your time can be as flexible as possible.
- Combine sculpture and animation for 3-D technology and software.
- Operate an environmental information camp.

HOW DO YOU STRUCTURE YOUR LIFE?

Your fourth letter was either *J* or *P*. There are both judging types (J) and perceiving types (P) working in the computer industry.

Many times it's the judging or perceiving preference that is the reason some employees are terminated for "not fitting into the group." They are competent but are matched with people of the opposite preference in a particular work situation.

In fact, the J or P preference may cause all types of conflict, tension, hostility, and arguments at work—from tardiness to disorder, from rigidity to delays.

Why does judging or perceiving cause so much conflict? The J or P preference deals with the way you structure your environment. The judger wants order. The perceiver wants flexibility. The need for structure opposes the need for spontaneity.

If you are a P type, your résumé reflects someone who needs a flexible working environment with flexible hours. You can adapt to many types of work situations on demand. As a spontaneous, creative person, you can meet unexpected needs as they arise.

When you send your P type résumé to a J type employer, it may get tossed in the round file. The J type employer is looking for an applicant who is productive and comfortable in a routine. The person in the employer's mind must be decisive, orderly, deliberate, and work well under pressure during certain hours. If you diverge from the J character of the employer, you will feel there's a wrong fit.

As a P type, you want to keep your mind open for new information. The J type wants quick closure that makes sense. Judgers will want advance notice of changes instead of adapting themselves to the constantly changing information. When a judger is staying on a predetermined course in the face of change, and a perceiver is adapting to change instead, there is conflict. The perceiver may feel exploited and reactive.

J Is for Judging

About 55 percent of the world's population, and 90 percent of top level executives, are judgers. Judgers seek structure in everything—"the planned life," as Isabel Briggs Myers writes in her book, *Gifts Differing*. Everything has a place in your system of order.

If you are a J, you are a natural leader, a person who likes routine, stability, security; you may work for the same company many years. You are a saver rather than a spender; relaxation does not come easily.

In your career, you seek closure. You want everything at work decided on as quickly as possible, and you want to make the decisions. You are traditional in many ways and need to belong to a group. This structure-seeking behavior shows on your résumé.

You are methodical, scheduled, and organized. There is a definiteness about the way you organize your résumé. It's usually chronological, organized, and exact. You use a plan for everything, from writing your cover letter to the last follow-up call, entered in your computer.

You make use of day planners and clocks and are a master of time and records. You like to count, measure, and control. You hate constantly changing information. The biggest problem with writing your résumé is revising it. J types have a harder time relaxing than P types.

In a job, you need to seek balance and moderation. Instead of becoming angry at P types for taking too long, look to them to provide alternative routes to the same goal. Look to the spontaneity of the P to teach you how to enjoy work more.

P types see you as an authoritarian figure to be feared. Perceivers see you as the girdle into which they are squeezed whenever their self-determination grows. You see yourself as the parent scolding a P type child, instead of equals at work.

If you are a judger (J type), look for a job in the computer industry that allows you to work in the following areas:

- Records management
- Executive level or junior executive trainee work in computers
- Programming
- Accounting
- Systems analysis

- Financial database management
- Applied artificial intelligence
- Software engineering
- Clerical supervision or clerical work
- Word processing
- Desktop publishing
- Computer security
- Drafting
- Robotics technology, computer-aided manufacturing
- Numerical control
- Electronic mail processing
- Manage multiple projects, objectives, and deadlines

P Is for Perceiving

About 45 percent of the world's population are perceivers. Tight schedules cramp your style if you are a P type. You like to wait and see what happens. Surprises are welcome.

You wish to create your own deadlines and work whenever you feel the inspiration or motivation to do your thing. You won't work to meet anyone else's deadline unless the recognition of your creativity or your entire financial security depends on it. You are "laid back." However, you often do your work too near ther deadline, cramming everything into the short time you allowed yourself. You may thrive on the adrenaline. As a stress avoider, you also may avoid work if it makes you tense—or get it out of the way early so you can have fun.

Your work must be fun or you won't do it. If you adapt yourself to a J type's rigid schedule or plan, your health could be affected. Your spontaneity would make you a good police officer on a foot patrol—or the equivalent in the computer security field. Your résumé will change its slant many times as you work at temporary jobs in different fields.

P types are free-spirited intrapreneurs, entrepreneurs, independent contractors, and freelancers who often work for someone else if there's autonomy and flexibility on the job. Above all, a job must offer you a chance to move freely. Express your creativity, need for movement, and change on your résumé, and explore the more innovative areas of the computer industry. Stay away from records management jobs where you have to organize and file facts all day.

If you are a perceiver (P type), look for a job in the computer industry that allows you to do the following tasks:

- Explore new uses of computer technology.
- Allow spontaneity to dominate your work life.
- Learn all you can about your employer or your job.
- Choose a job where you'll know what others are doing.
- Start up many different new businesses.
- Work with alternatives and possibilities for change.
- Sell software.
- Research, working with think tanks where you can design your own models—especially if you're also a thinker/intuitive.
- Design video games.

- Seek variety in your work assignments.
- Explore the relationship between computers and robots and the needs of the physically challenged.
- Keep technical writing options open.
- Design robots.
- Write interactive fiction for CD-Interactive and CD-ROM laser discs.
- Plan computer industry conventions and trade shows.
- Learn skills that are transferable from one career to the next.
- Use computer rather than paper files.
- Use loose-leaf notebooks where you can add or remove pages.
- Expand your job search internationally.
- Depend on last-minute spurts of energy.
- Think on your feet.

Now that you have some understanding of the personality preferences, you can see how they may combine to form 16 personality types. These are based on the principles of the Myers-Briggs Type Indicator (MBTI®). The 16 types are as follows:

ISTJ	ISFJ	INFJ	INTJ
ISTP	ISFP	INFP	INTP
ESTP	ESFP	ENFP	ENTP
ESTJ	ESFJ	ENFJ	ENTJ

WHAT THE LETTERS STAND FOR: THE 16 PERSONALITY TYPES

ISTJ	introverted, sensing, thinking, judging
ISTP	introverted, sensing, thinking, perceiving
ESTP	extroverted, sensing, thinking, perceiving
ESTJ	extroverted, sensing, thinking, judging
ISFJ	introverted, sensing, feeling, judging
ISFP	introverted, sensing, feeling, perceiving
ESFP	extroverted, sensing, feeling, perceiving
ESFJ	extroverted, sensing, feeling, judging
INFJ	introverted, intuitive, feeling, judging
INFP	introverted, intuitive, feeling, perceiving
ENFP	extroverted, intuitive, feeling, perceiving
ENFJ	extroverted, intuitive, feeling, judging
INTJ	introverted, intuitive, thinking, judging
INTP	introverted, intuitive, thinking, perceiving
ENTP	extroverted, intuitive, thinking, perceiving
ENTJ	extroverted, intuitive, thinking, judging

These 16 personality types are found among all people in the world, according to the principles of the MBTI®. A brief description of the action needs of each type follows.

Type	Action Verb	Job and Skills to Emphasize
ISTJ	Systematize	Organize businesses or accounts.
ISTP	Troubleshoot	Hands-on activity with tools.
ESTP	Promote	Excitement and variety bringing computer use to the airwaves.
ESTJ	Administer	Manage an organization or be an administrator using applied sciences. Computer security and law is your niche. Teach time management.
ISFJ	Organize	Work in data communications in large corporations (e.g. the phone company or a hospital.) Work with medical records software as a traveling salesperson and manufacturer's representative.
ISFP	Compose	Compose computer music on a midi synthesizer. Extract sounds. Put music on software. Design fashions using software. Ensure the well-being of many. Work with color and texture. Illustrate software ads in an art studio, sign shop, or computer store. Sell crafted pop-up books.
ESFP	Demonstrate	Entertain or perform using computers. Help the disabled use computers. Use computers for sports or games. Sales and marketing. Make computers fun to use in computer camp. Software talent agent.
ESFJ	Transcribe	Give customer service with a smile and manage an office using word processing, records management, and desktop publishing. Run the sales department with an eye to meeting customers' needs and handling customers' complaints. Work with medical records transcription software. Law office administrator.
INFJ	Consult	Teach how computers are used in health care and medicine. Write software user manuals. Use a computer to illustrate ads or to create corporate animation and desktop video special effects. Teach instructional technology.
INFP	Write	Write interactive fiction. Autobiographical software designer and writer. Subjective writing specialist. Work for the computer press as a columnist and catalyst. Write career books and design newsletters. Use a computer for editorial design. Run quality circles for computer personnel. Do technical writing. Write software video scripts. Recruit computer personnel and do career consulting for outplacement agencies that place technical professionals. Research ageism and job discrimination issues in computer firms.
ENFP	Counsel	Train employees and managers in how to use computers and instructional technology to solve human resource problems. Teach new uses of computers to rescue people. Help computer people in therapy for technostress. Write career books about computers. Produce software video scripts, infomercials and animation/special effects. Manage human resources.
ENFJ	Train	Public speaking. Sell ideas and intangibles. To train and persuade. Train executives in conflict management.
INTJ	Structure	Systems analyst, scientist, or scientific programmer. Explore artificial intelligence, neural networks, fuzzy logic, electrical and software engineering. Solve problems globally.
INTP	Analyze	Analyze securities. Apply artificial intelligence to global database management. Create computer models to predict the environmental changes well into the future. Design categories. Use programming in more flexible ways. Define and map matrices. Design art using special computer effects or math fractals. Theorize, differentiate, evaluate, and critique. Design new software or invent better hardware.
ENTP	Market	Sell ideas and other intangibles. Run a technical marketing company. Produce videos. Sell computers globally. Import and export. Use computers for travel adventures. Make multimedia adaptable for video conferencing. Create networks for computer sharing. Invent new ways of using computers to network with people. Link telephones, cable TV, and computers. Report on new computer technology. Run a technical publishing company. Invent a better modem. Systems analysis.
ENTJ	Lead	Lead computer firms into new ventures. Practice computer law. Raise venture capital as an investment banker or broker. Manage or be an administrator in a company that combines computer systems with education. Seek closure.

RECOMMENDED COMPUTER JOBS FOR EACH TYPE

The job recommendations below represent only a fraction of the jobs that exist in the computer industry. New jobs are created each year whose titles never before existed.

ISTJ
Accountant, data manager, computer security investigator, auditor, software engineer, attorney, economist, career military and civil service computer administrator, business information technologist, numerical control specialist, comptroller of financial databases, law office administrator, paralegal, medical software transcriptionist, medical records technician, software manufacturer's representative, applied mathematician, financial operations manager.

ISTP
Computer-aided drafter, computer-aided manufacturing specialist, robotics technician, computer repair technician, business computing programmer, applied systems analyst, systems engineer, astronaut, virtual reality specialist, defense and weapons computer simulations instructor, traveling computer security specialist, information systems consultant, defense weapons vendor or designer.

ESTP
Real estate software sales, computer program radio talk show host, computer marketing personnel, peripheral retailer, wholesaler, importer of computer products, design automation publicist, auditor, traveling software distributor, cable TV multimedia producer, wireless telecommunications manufacturer's representative, promotor of new hardware and software products.

ESTJ
Law office administrator, paralegal, computer security specialist, computer lawyer, investigator, manager, business information technologist, data communications engineer, programmer, information retrieval specialist, database manager, records manager, numerical control manager, robotics engineer or technician, accountant, financial programmer, marketing manager, banking programmer or systems analyst, insurance database specialist, wholesaler, international database manager, executive recruiter, broadcasting multimedia executive, hospital and health services administrator, computer science and information systems instructor, production and operations manager, public administrator, logistics specialist, insurance investigation, systems engineer.

ISFJ
Local area network (LAN) specialist, telecommunications equipment technician, organizer, word processor, desktop publisher, teacher, librarian, medical software technology designer, telephone company craftsperson, communications technicians, switching machine operator, computer operator, data-entry clerk, secretary, paralegal, applied computing programmer, applied computing specialist, records manager, court reporter, wireless telecommunications equipment technician,

nurse practitioner, health care software transcriptionist, medical records administrator, data communications specialist, telecommunications technologist, computer science education specialist.

ISFP

Medical transcriptionists and health care computing operator, word processor, secretary, bookkeeper, computer illustrator, crafts person, computer software fashion designer, computer repairer, computer peripheral retail sales clerk or manager, medical records technologist, medical records, software manufacturer's sales representative, desktop publisher, mail-order customer service manager, preschool computer specialists (games for teaching preschool), computer midi synthesizer music composer or vendor, exhibit designer.

ESFP

Software talent agent, computer laser light show performer, sports computing specialist, manufacturer's software representative, retail computer store sales clerk, virtual reality entertainment retailer, computerized theatrical production specialist, software video producer, computer animation advertising agency representative, public relations account executive, traveling computer sales, computer music (midi synthesizer and special effects) performer, physical therapy and rehabilitation computer trainer or sales representative, software fashion designer, merchandiser, nurse practitioner and trainer, vendor, computer camp counselor, travel agent.

ESFJ

Database manager, medical secretary or transcriptionist, medical records software technician, programmer, computer store retail manager, sales and customer representative, communications technician with phone company, telecommunications sales representative, computer animation advertising account executive, publicist, professional associations convention planner, computer professional association national organizer, special events planner, Peace Corps organizer, trainer, nurse trainer, business education teacher, office information systems manager.

INFJ

Computer illustrator and designer, animator, technical writer, software user manual writer, teacher, courseware designer, instructional technologist, on-line librarian, tape librarian, ergonomics designer and researcher, biomedical computing specialist, interactive fiction writer for CD-Interactive/CD-ROM, electronic publishing consultant and color desktop publishing specialist, mediator, human resource manager, outplacement director, personnel consultant, recruiter, exhibit designer.

INFP

Freelance writer, freelance editorial illustrator, computer press columnist/journalist, grant proposal writer, software user manual writer, computer career book author, cartoonist, desktop animator, desktop video script writer, courseware designer, newsletter designer, writing teacher, consultant, computer camp counselor, organizational development specialist, electronic publisher.

ENFP

Counselor, computer camp resort recruiter, "technostress" psychologist, computer personnel researcher, computers for the physically handicapped trainer, vendor, ergonomics vendor, professional speaker, career book writer, computer press journalist/columnist, temporary agency recruiter, organizational development specialist, outplacement interviewer, convention and event planner, publicist, trade show and exhibit manager, cruise ship computer room director, courseware designer, personnel agency manager, small business opportunities, publisher, corporate training video producer, animator.

ENFJ

Public speaker, trainer, teacher, computerized job bank counselor, retail salesperson, manufacturer's representative, interactive multimedia producer, audience tracker, organizational development consultant, office manager, recruiter, human resource development manager, event planner, computers and society researcher, computers and human interaction researcher, traveling seminar specialist, public relations account executive, video producer, computer graphics presentations designer, total quality management trainer, traveling salesperson and manufacturer's representative, computer personnel researcher, computer uses in education trainer.

INTJ

Allied health fields researcher, automata and computability theorist, biomedical computing programmer and systems analyst, computer architect, design automation specialist, documentation analyst, symbolic computing and mathematics researcher, software engineer, biotech computer specialist, biomedical engineer, information broker, competitive intelligence specialist, computer security investigator, software manufacturer and designer, object-oriented programmer, financial analyst, applied artificial intelligence financial forecaster, trend forecaster, economist, computer science educator, neural networks and fuzzy logic programmer/designer, electronic publishing vendor, molecular biology software developer.

INTP

Computer architect, numerical mathematician, robotics engineer, measurement and evaluation computing specialist, simulation specialist, software engineer, computational linguistics researcher, educational researcher, securities analyst, systems analyst, programmer, scientific programmer, operating systems specialist, programming languages designer, microprogramming researcher, software designer, computer game programmer, biomedical computing programmer, automata and computability theory researcher, trend forecaster, atmospheric and environmental forecaster, satellite technician or tracker, mathematician, educational researcher, biostatistician, numerical control robotics researcher, inventor, electronic engineer, technical writer/science writer, graphics designer.

ENTP

Instructional technologist, marketing research manager, labor trends forecaster, economist, inventor, software engineer, designer, multimedia and presentation graphics designer/producer, electronic publisher, wireless communications developer, telecommunications network engineer, technical public speaker, organizational development specialist, outplacement consultant, entrepreneur, intrapreneur, manufacturer's representative, traveling salesperson, computer camp owner, computerized photographer, special effects designer, corporate animator, public relations account executive, advertising agency account executive, promotion director, data communications vendor, documentary/training films filmmaker, programming languages designer, hardware, peripherals, and robotics designer, virtual reality designer, computer and video games programmer/designer, systems analyst, physician's training video producer, independent contractor, computer marketing consultant.

ENTJ
Data manager, organizational development researcher, general manager, entrepreneur, operating systems director, career military officer, lawyer, computer security director, design automation researcher, programmer, systems analyst, entrepreneur, intrapreneur, organizer, planning director, time management trainer, software developer, hardware importer/exporter, computerized genetics researcher, environmental investigator, electronic engineer, software engineer, venture capital broker/banker, executive recruiter, analog/digital circuit engineer, fundraiser, marketing analyst, wireless electronic security wholesaler, weapons systems specialist, public speaker, hardware design engineer, network switching software engineer.

The following chart describes the computer industry niches that fit the various types most comfortably:

Computer Software/Hardware Research, Design, Invention, Analysis	INTJ, ENTJ, INTP, ENTP
Software, Hardware, Courseware Development	ENFJ, ENTJ, ENTP, ENFP
Technical Services, Programming, Administration	ESTJ, ISTJ, ESTP, ISTP
Troubleshooting, Computer Repair and Debugging	ESTP, ISTP
Database Management, Manager of Information Systems, Production	ESTJ, ESFJ, ISTJ, ISFJ
Telecommunications Technician	ISFJ, ISTJ
Sales of Computer Products	ESFJ, ESFP
Sales of Ideas, Advertising, Public Relations, Abstract Concepts	ENFJ, ENFP
Public Speakers, Sales Trainers	ENFJ, ESFJ, ENFP, ESTJ, ENTJ
Secretarial, Guy Friday	ISFJ
Medical Transcription or Medical Records Technology, Software Manufacturer's Representative	ISTJ, ISFJ, ESFJ
Clerical and Customer Service With Direct People Contact	ESFJ, ISFJ
Clerical with Machines Transcribing Equipment	ISTJ, ESTJ
Administration, Organization	ESTJ, ENTJ
Inventions (Hardware) and Robotics	ENTP, INTP, ISTP
Software Design	INTP, INTJ
Art, Educational, Design Writing Software	INFP, INFJ
Accounting	ISTJ, ISFJ

Personnel, Interviewing, Human Resource Management	INFP, INFJ
Art, Illustration, Computer Animation/Design, (Including Preschool Software Design)	INFP, ISFP, ENFP
Interactive Fiction/Learning With CD-I and CD-ROM Scripts, Training Films, Software For Education Design, Product Publicity, Technical Advertising Copywriting	INFP, INFJ, ENFP
Systems Analysis	INTJ, INTP, ISTP, ISTJ
User Friendly Software/Hardware Design	ENTP, ENFP, INFP
Video Producers, Multimedia, News Cable Producers	ENTJ, ENTP, ENFJ, ENFP
The Computer Press	INTJ, INFJ, INFP, ENFP, ENTP
Midi Music Synthesizer Composition, Special Effects	INTP, INFP, ISFP, ESFP, ENTP, INFJ
Corporate Animators, Special Effects Designers	INTP, INFP, INFJ, ISFP, ENFP, ESFP

By this point, you have probably learned how to match your personality type with the character of the organization for whom you choose to work. Select those action verbs and preferences that emphasize your best qualifications. Finally, use words in your résumé or cover letter that describe your personality type strengths to direct attention to the job you want.

Writing résumés is all about packaging yourself as information. People seek work for a variety of reasons, but if you are insightful, introspective, or reflective, you know intuitively that it takes as strong an ego to turn down a promotion so you can be happy in your career as it does to climb the ladder. It's hard to resist a promotion or the offer of a prestigious job, even when you know you would be happier doing what excites you. Status is valued by society, but you may place more value on freedom in your job.

10

SAMPLE RESUMES

In this chapter, there are 53 résumés to guide you as your write your own résumé. They are classified by each category found in the computer industry to help you observe details that target different niches. Compare them to your own résumé details.

The job applicants' names, addresses, and company names in the résumés are fictitious. However, the job descriptions, titles, duties, and responsibilities are real employment requirements in the computer industry. It's important to study the job duties in the résumés.

The golden strategy of résumé writing is "do unto employers as they would have you do unto them." Value their company's needs. Observe how qualifications listed on the sample résumés match the needs of the position. When you send your own résumé out, keep in mind the character of the company. Does it match your preferences?

At the end of this chapter, you will find record-keeping pages to help you track your résumés so you can follow up as new openings occur in any company. The 53 sample résumés in this chapter apply to the following areas of the computer industry.

- artificial intelligence
- biotech computing
- biotech medical writer
- communications analyst
- computer-aided design
- computer convention/events
- computer graphics
- computer journalism
- computer law
- computer operations
- computer security
- computer technology/repair
- database management
- data entry operations
- desktop/electronic publishing
- desktop video/animation/special effects
- digital special effects/image manipulation
- document production manager
- drafting/medical
- drafting/engineering
- fashion design/software
- information services systems analyst

- interactive design
- interactive fiction writing
- marketing communications
- marketing management
- medical records technology
- medical transcription
- multimedia
- network systems engineering
- neural networks
- numerical control
- personnel management
- programming
- quality/regulatory assurance
- robotics technology
- sales and marketing
- scientific programming
- software engineering
- software talent agenting
- software test manager
- software writing
- systems analysis
- systems engineering
- tape librarian
- technical illustration
- technical writing
- technical training
- video computer games design
- videoconferencing
- virtual reality
- wireless communications
- word processing

MICHAEL B. CHIFTELESEN

89 Setton Lane
Manchester, IL 60603
(303) 555-1999

JOB OVERVIEW

Permanent employment as an applied artificial intelligence financial database manager specifically in stock market trend forecasting. Seek to become part of a growing software development company.

SOFTWARE/HARDWARE

C++, C, Pascal, Basic, Novell, Unix kernel, GUI, SCSI interface development in C, on IBM AS 400 hardware, and IBM PC.

EDUCATION

B.A. in Economics with applied mathematics minor, University of Chicago, December 1992. Second minor in computer science and information systems.

SOFTWARE EXPERIENCE

December 1992 - Present
MEREET INVESTMENT SOFTWARE DESIGN, INC., Chicago, IL
Database Manager, Software Designer, and Programmer
Identified a particular stock market situation and environment as one that resembled a known period in history. Applied artificial intelligence tools to stock market forecasting. Designed forecasting software. Produced videos and gave seminars.

RESPONSIBILITIES

- Automated investment advisory service.
- Developed software within a closed network.
- Created an end product of presentation software.
- Designed and developed data management software.
- Coordinated with national database services to obtain current quotes.
- Developed an array of artificial intelligence technology including the following:
  - Statistical processes.
  - Extrapolation and trend analysis.
  - Pattern matching to historical development of indicators.
  - Neural networks expertise system and heuristics.
  - Measured breaks in stock market prices for changes in direction.

References on Request.

Amyra C. Cohen
49 Rowbrook Blvd.
Sinclair, CA 92000
(714) 555-1212

JOB OVERVIEW

Clinical documentation specialist. Responsible for document control and archives to meet government requirements for clinical studies within a biopharmaceutical company developing innovative products in medicine.

SOFTWARE/HARDWARE

Lotus 1-2-3, dBase, Paradox, Excel, WordPerfect, PowerPoint.
IBM-compatible PC.

DOCUMENT CONTROL EXPERIENCE

October 1979–1993   LOMBOCHE PHARMACEUTICALS, INC., Pendleton, CA

Clinical Documentation Specialist
- Responsible for document control for clinical studies.
- Maintained department archives to meet FDA requirements.
- Tracked and reported study status.
- Maintained all pharmaceutical documentation in databases using a variety of dBase and spreadsheet software.
- Prepared pharmaceutical documentation for FDA audits.
- Utilized medical terminology extensively.
- Administrative support activities included heavy use of word-processing software and spreadsheets.

June 1974–October 1979   ST. MICHAEL'S HOSPITAL, Oceanside, CA

Medical Records Technician and Transcriptionist
- Coded medical records and transcribed medical terminology in medical records department of an acute care hospital.
- Operated IBM 129 computer.

EDUCATION

B.S. in Business Administration
with minor in health sciences, San Diego State University, June 1979.
A.S. Medical Records Technology
Mesa College, San Diego, 1973.
Certificate in Medical Transcription and Medical Office Administration
Mesa College, San Diego, June 1972.

References available upon request.

Anne Jeanne Smith
4455 Texas Street
Wilmington, DE 20304
(302) 555-7895

OBJECTIVE

A permanent staff position as an advertising medical writer with a health care company, medical advertising agency, or computer corporation specializing in medical software, video, and multimedia presentation technologies.

SUMMARY OF QUALIFICATIONS

· Gather information.
· Reshape information.
· Sell information in a variety of formats.
· Design information to meet different needs.

RELATED SKILLS

· Interpreted complex clinical research and development data into simple-to-understand marketing support materials.
· Interpreted, wrote, and edited: monographs, presentations, video scripts, sales aid layouts, and clinical/marketing research claims support materials.
· Managed projects from inception to completion.
· Authored three self-help and nutrition books published by major New York publishers.
· Wrote many multimedia computer presentation graphics scripts.
· Wrote medical advertising copy for a variety of advertising agencies for Fortune 500 international health care firms.

EXPERIENCE
1964–Present:

Independent contract medical writer,
A.J. Smith Medical Writing Productions,
(self-employed), Wilmington, DE.

EDUCATION/TRAINING

B.S., English Education
New York University, NY, 1964
Continuing Education in Medical Writing
American Medical Writer's Association
Continuing Education Seminars, 1992

REFERENCES
Upon Request

Wanda Barston

1756 Eastwell Drive, Borne, MN 30324

(217) 555-1678

GOAL

A permanent position as a communications analyst in a large-scale LAN/WAN information systems and services department managing and troubleshooting network projects.

OVERVIEW

- Six years' of LAN/WAN experience with an in-depth knowledge of interconnect technologies.
- Technical and working knowledge of synchronous/asynchronous protocols, TCP/IP and SNA network methodologies.
- Three years' hands-on experience with bridges, routers, 10base T cabling systems, modems, MUXes, and telephone company services (T1, 56k).
- Six years' experience with network test equipment (LanAlyzer, Firebird).

SOFTWARE

Knowledge of Microsoft, LAN Manager, Novell, Unix, DOS, and E-mail.

EXPERIENCE

January 1987–Present:

Communication Analyst, Able Data, Inc., Bloomington, MN.
Managed the Information Systems and Services Department of a large-scale LAN/WAN corporation. Troubleshooter on network projects.

EDUCATION

B.S., Information Systems; Certificate in Telecommunications
Borne Computer College, Bloomington, MN, 1986
A.S., Computer Science and Information Systems
Bloomington Community College, 1983

REFERENCES

On request.

Robert Vine
2394 Crestview Ridge
Brooklyn, NY 11230
(212) 555-9007

OVERVIEW
Eight years of experience, with increasing responsibilities, as a technical illustrator, with in-depth exposure to AUTOCAD engineering graphics, design, and drafting. Focus on blueprint reading, dimensioning, tolerancing, assembly drawing, and airbrush illustration. Four years' experience designing special effects. Seek a position as a computer-aided designer in industrial design.

ABILITIES
- Detailed drawing of complex concepts in engineering graphics.
- Assembly drawing and cutaways.
- Airbrushing.
- Presentation graphics design on Macintosh computers focusing on multimedia and video.
- Computer applications on Cadds 4x computers.
- Technical illustrations in Freehand and Illustrator software.
- Computer tracing from originals.
- Macintosh production and traffic management.
- Desktop publishing with PageMaker and Ventura Publisher software, specializing in color separations.
- Strong design using AUTOCAD software.
- Computer illustration with Coreldraw! on IBM-compatible computers. Finished designs using line or airbrush.
- Corporate computer animation, special effects, and desktop video using the Amiga computer, Video Toaster, and camera.

ACHIEVEMENTS
- Developed detailed, cutaway drawings of computer hardware.
- Designed drafting blueprints of hardware using AUTOCAD software.
- Illustrated parts brochures with Adobe software on the Macintosh.
- Created three award-winning corporate animation videos using the Amiga computer and Video Toaster, focusing on special effects.

EMPLOYMENT
June 1985–Present: Technical Graphics Artist and Computer-Aided Designer/Drafter, Creative Media Technical Advertising Agency, Brooklyn, NY.

EDUCATION
Associate in Applied Science
Technical Illustration and Desktop Video
Brooklyn Community College, 1985

References available upon request.

FRANCINE SHOEMAKER
9 Mae Lee Drive
Hagarstown, MD 30389
(217) 555-7855

OBJECTIVE

Experienced computer and electronics events planner seeks affiliation with convention, trade show, and exhibit planning agency or national association of computer professionals.

ABILITIES

- Computer trade show, exhibit, and convention planner with Mann Computer College Annual Job Fair.
- Knowledge of exhibit design and booth sales.
- Public relations, tours, and press conference planning.
- Site selection and budgeting.
- Coordination and organization from inception to completion of computer and electronic trade shows, exhibits, conventions, conferences, meetings, seminars, workshops, and job fairs with institutional and hotel sales and catering managers.
- Sold 250 booths at annual Computer Equipment Dealer's convention.
- Personnel interviewing, screening, and hiring of exhibit designer's crew and carpenters.

EXPERIENCE

June 1992–September 1993: Sales Manager, convention and conference space, Mann Computer College, Hagarstown, MD.
June 1987–May 1992: Exhibits Designer and Events Planner, Glentackie Technical Events Planning Agency, Chevy Chase, MD.

VOLUME

Average annual exhibit booth sales of $600,000 1992–1993.
Average annual exhibit booth sales of $350,000 1987–1992.

EDUCATION

Certificate in Events Planning
Certificate in Desktop Publishing
Baltimore Community College,
Adult Continuing Education Division
Baltimore, MD, 1987

References on request.

THERA SANDOR
4494 Rest Ridge
San Diego, CA 92104
(619) 555-1387

EDUCATION
Associate in Applied Science
Commercial Art
San Diego City College, 1980

OVERVIEW
Thirteen years of experience, with increasing responsibilities, as an ad agency staff graphic designer. Focus on heavy advertising, agency brochure, print, greeting card, calendar, and electronic design. Seek a position as a staff illustrator in the advertising department of a large corporation, or as a staff illustrator/graphic designer/desktop publisher or desktop video producer with a major advertising agency.

ABILITIES
- Detailed drawing of complex concepts in advertising design.
- Illustration of children's books, and editorial design.
- Airbrush illustration.
- In-depth experience with CorelDraw! software, Ventura Publisher, and
        Ventura AdPro in graphic design for IBM-compatible computers.
- Design multimedia presentation graphics on Macintosh computers using
        QuarkXPress, Adobe Illustrator, PhotoShop, and Freehand software.
- Computer tracing from original art.
- Ad agency traffic management, routing, and media buying.
- Desktop publishing with PageMaker software on both the Mac and IBM.
- Specialist in computerized color separations.
- Corporate computer animation, special effects, and desktop video using the
        Amiga computer, Video Toaster, and video camera.

ACHIEVEMENTS
- Designed 4-color editorial illustrations for newspaper ads, for ad agency.
- Illustrated ads for brochures with Adobe software on the Macintosh and
        CorelDraw! on the IBM.
- Created an award-winning animated corporate training video on health tips for
        truckers, using the Amiga computer and Video Toaster. Included special effects.

EMPLOYMENT
June 1980–Present:
Graphic Designer (Staff Artist/Illustrator),
Barnett Public Relations and Advertising, San Diego, CA.

References on request.

Amida Browne
54 Orange Terrace
Kansas City, MO 64106
(816) 555-4542

JOB OBJECTIVE:
Journalist covering the computer industry seeks a senior editorial position on a trade publication. Experienced in Macintosh computers using QuarkXPress.

EDITING EMPLOYMENT:

1988–Present:	Managing Editor of *Technical Education,* a national computer trade journal for trainers.
1983–1988:	Senior Acquisitions Editor, *Computer Investor,* a monthly national trade magazine.
1981–1983:	Associate Editor of *Telecommunications and Computers,* a national weekly business newspaper for the computer industry.

INVESTIGATIVE REPORTING:

1981 - Present:	Developed computer industry sources. Published investigative reports in periodicals for owners of desktop publishing businesses. Wrote a weekly investigative reporting column on electronic publishing.

CITY REPORTING:

1980–1981:	Reporter, *The Daily Kansas News.* Covered local business news for an urban daily newspaper with a circulation of 300,000 in a city of 750,000.

FREELANCE WRITING:

1963–1980:	Full-time freelance reporter: national magazines. Wrote over 300 business articles.

PROFESSIONAL ASSOCIATIONS:
* Computer Press Association.
* Society for Professional Journalists.

EDUCATION:

Bachelor of Arts in Journalism
New York University, NY, 1963

REFERENCES ON REQUEST.

Phillip Treston

5699 Grand Terrace
Vista View, OR 95984
(402) 555-3444

JOB TITLE:
PARALEGAL/LEGAL RESEARCHER: COMPUTER OR PATENT LAW

CASEWORK:
- Interview and discovery interrogation and background research work for computer law cases pending before the courts.
- Researched state and federal computer and patent laws, judicial decisions. Wrote briefs for attorneys.
- Prepared preliminary arguments and pleadings in computer law.
- Obtained affidavits.

COMPUTER LAW DOCUMENT DRAFTING:
- Drafted contracts under supervision of attorney.
- Prepared separation agreements, tax returns, incorporations, computer security statements, patent filings, and trust agreements.
- Prepare reports and schematic diagrams.

LEGAL SUPPORT:
- Assisted computer law specialists in preparing hardware and software patents, contracts, applications, shareholder agreements, benefits plans, loan documents, software development documents, packaging agreements, and annual financial reports of computer-industry corporations.
- Use of word-processing software, advanced use of database packages and spreadsheets.

EXPERIENCE:
June 1988–May 1993:

Computer and Patent Law Paralegal
Bryan, Steen & Bates, Attorneys-at-Law, Vista View, OR.

EDUCATION:
Certificate in Paralegal Studies
Specializing in Computer and Patent Law
Vista View State College, Division of Extended Studies
Vista View, OR, 1988

References on request.

Tom Lewein

79 Brook Road
Orange, CA 92000
(714) 555-1212

GOAL
A position in the insurance field as an AS/400 computer operator using personal computer support systems, using my experience in a Novell Network environment.

SOFTWARE
Lotus 1-2-3, dBase, PowerPoint, WordPerfect, Paradox, Excel, Ventura Publisher, and PageMaker.

HARDWARE
- #100M, #101EM, AS/400, VM/MVS operator.
- IBM-compatible PC, and Novell technical environment.

DOCUMENT CONTROL EXPERIENCE

October 1990–1993
LORE INSURANCE INC., Orange, CA
Computer Operator
- Operated AS/400 computers for four hours daily for three years in an insurance environment.
- Operated #100M, #101EM, VM/MVS (and IBM-compatible computers for PC support) in an insurance environment four hours daily for three years. Heavy use of Novell Network technology.
- Maintained department archives.
- Tracked and reported policy title status.
- Maintained all documentation in databases using a variety of dBase, word-processing, data entry, and spreadsheet software.
- Performed first level problem recovery/resolution for client base. Strong customer service orientation.

June 1988–May 1993
PRIME TITLE INSURANCE CO., Orange, CA
Word-Processing Specialist
- Administrative support included heavy use of WordPerfect.

EDUCATION
A.S., Records Management and Office Information Systems
Orange Community College, June 1990

References available on request.

Commander Tim Warden, U.S. Navy (Ret.)
90 Muncie Street
San Francisco, CA 91509
(415) 555-9008

OVERVIEW

Experienced computer security investigator and researcher with 30 years' military intelligence security background seeks affiliation with computer security investigation or research team of major corporation or national computer security investigation firm.

COMPETENCIES

INSTITUTIONAL
* Military police officer in the U.S. Navy.
* Naval intelligence officer, computer security services.
* Knowledge of computer security law and law enforcement.
* Experienced computer systems analyst and scientific programmer.
* Systems troubleshooting and repair technology for U.S. Navy computer systems. Top Secret security clearance.

RESEARCH
* Government computer security files.
* Systems network investigation.
* Software investigation.
* Personal interviewing.
* Telephone investigation.

SURVEILLANCE
* Military intelligence evidence gathering.
* Computer security issues evidence gathering.
* Video, network, recording, and photographic techniques.
* Documentation of research.

EXPERIENCE

June 1973– July 1993: Computer Security Analyst, U.S. Navy
May 1963–June 1973: Military Police Officer, U.S. Navy
June 1961–May 1963: Computer Security Analyst,
                    University of California, Berkeley, CA

EDUCATION

Bachelor of Science in Computer Science
University of California, Berkeley, CA, 1961

References available on request.

LOUISE DESOLA
7352 Mt. Elbrus Ridge
Brooklyn, NY 11234   (212) 555-9007

EDUCATION   Associate in Applied Science
Computer Technology and Repair
Brooklyn Community College, 1984

OVERVIEW   Nine years of experience, with increasing responsibilities, as a
computer technician, with in-depth exposure to motherboard
troubleshooting and repair of IBMs and Macs. Heavy network
experience and knowledge of Unix operating systems. Focus on
data and voice installation. Certification in PDS systems and
Fiber. Two years' PC maintenance experience in a Novell
Network environment. Seeking a position on an MIS team as a
computer repair technician.

ABILITIES

Hardware:

* Provide liaison between manufacturers and users on warranty
  services backing installations of more than $900,000 in value.
* Perform diagnostics on PCs and peripheral equipment to troubleshoot
  problems—down to the component level.
* Install/upgrade PC components such as network cards, memory
  chips, disk drives, and modems.
* Configure PC memory and network drivers.
* Coordinate cabling/wiring projects.
* Place and monitor service calls for equipment repair.
* Expedite licensing issues.
* Maintain and repair IBM and Macintosh computer systems.
* Maintain and repair Novell Network computer systems.
* Maintain and repair PDS, Fiber, and Unix operating systems.
* Configure and support systems, and inventory equipment.

Software:

* Microsoft Windows, WordPerfect, Paradox, Lotus 1-2-3,
  Quatro Pro, Lotus Freelance, and Harvard Graphics.

EMPLOYMENT

June 1985-Present: Computer Repair Technician,
MIS Analysis Systems, Inc.
New York, NY.

July 1984-June 1985:   Computer Repair Technician,
Coral Gardens Computer Store,
Coral Gardens, FL.

References on request.

Jim Patton

766 Sands Road • Biloxi, MI 22000•(814) 555-7312

OBJECTIVE
A position with a mortgage banking firm as a database manager or WAN systems manager.

SOFTWARE
dBases in Datatrieve, Fortran, Paradox, Excel, and Unix.

HARDWARE
IBM-compatible PC, Novell environment, and VAX/VMS/DCL.

DATABASE MANAGEMENT EXPERIENCE

October 1986–1993
FIRESTONE MORTGAGE BANKING, INC., Biloxi, MI
WAN Systems Manager/Database Manager
- Responsible for managing the technical databases utilizing WAN systems within the mortgage banking department of a large financial corporation.
- Retrieved databases containing technical, financial, and analytical operations, and disseminated information.
- Managed LAN databases.
- Utilized MS-DOS operating systems, multiple network technologies, and PC-based toolsets.
- Managed databases in a multiple-site PC-LAN environment.
- Managed remote access and remote LAN databases.
- Utilized various hardware platforms to retrieve and upgrade data.
- Hands-on experience in a Unix client-server environment.
- Improved productivity in a high-volume records management environment.
- Searched financial, legal, technical, and business databases. Supplied clients with packaged information.
- Utilized competitive intelligence database retrieval techniques.
- Disseminated the latest information for mortgage banking clients.

EDUCATION
Associate in Science Degrees:
1) Records Management, 1986
2) Computer Science and Information Systems, 1988
Biloxi Community College, Biloxi, MI

References available on request.

Joan Ebekson

442 Mt. Abernathy Court
Darby, PA 21123
(214) 555-9977

EDUCATION

Certificate in Data Entry Operations
Midfair Adult Continuing Education Division
Darby Community College District, 1992
(Certificate at 12,000 KPH)

Certificate in Desktop Publishing/Word Processing
Midfair Adult Continuing Education Division
Darby Community College District, 1991
(Certificate at 60 WPM)

OVERVIEW

Two years of increasingly responsible data entry experience testing at 12,000 keystrokes per hour. Mainframe computer experience. Seeking a permanent, full-time position during daytime hours as a data entry operator.

ABILITIES

Hardware:
- Operated mainframe computers.
- Entered data at tested 12,000 keystrokes per hour.
- Operated IBM-compatible PCs for data tracking.
- Operated IBMs for word processing.
- Operated ten-key adding machine.

Software:
- Managed mailing lists utilizing Microsoft Windows, WordPerfect, Paradox, Lotus 1-2-3, Quatro Pro, Lotus Freelance, PageMaker, dBase, and Ventura Publisher Software.
- Keyboarded correspondence at 60 WPM using WordPerfect.
- Expedited numeric and clerical duties using spreadsheets.
- Entered and tracked orders using dBase.

EMPLOYMENT

June 1992–Present: Data Entry Operator, Mailing List Management, Inc., Darby, PA.

May 1991–June 1992: Order Entry Clerk, Greene Software Development Co., Inc., Darby, PA.

Victoria Preston
6834 Linden Street
San Diego, CA 92115
(619) 555-1387

EDUCATION

Associate in Applied Science
Desktop Publishing/Office Information Systems
Miramar College, San Diego, CA, 1992
Certificate in Commercial Art
San Diego City College, 1991

OVERVIEW

Four years of assignments as a desktop publisher with increasing responsibilities utilizing IBM and Macintosh personal computers. Focus on electronic publishing text layout and graphics design of software manuals and training materials. Two years' experience using Imagesetter, Linotronic, and Selectset. Seeking a position as a desktop publisher designing text and graphics in the electronic publishing industry.

SOFTWARE

- Design text, graphics, slides, and multimedia presentations electronically using CorelDraw!, Ventura Publisher, Ventura AdPro, WordPerfect for DOS or Windows, PageMaker, Toolbook for Windows, PhotoShop, and WordPerfect Presentations (with bitstream fonts).
- Design multimedia presentation graphics using QuarkXPress, Adobe Illustrator, PhotoShop, and Freehand software.
- Computer tracing from original art.
- Create color separations and slides.
- Convert WordPerfect for Windows text and graphics to Ventura Publisher or Aldus PageMaker text and graphics.

HARDWARE

- IBM and compatible computers, Macintosh computers; color or B & W scanners; color, laser, or inkjet printers.
- Operate Imagesetter. Knowledge of Linotronic and Selectset.

EMPLOYMENT

June 1991–Present: Desktop Publisher, Electra Software Manual Corporation, San Diego, CA.

August 1989–June 1991:   Desktop Publisher, Courseware Textbooks, Inc., Miramar, CA.

References on request.

Kyle A. Redding

909 Butterworth Drive
El Cajon, CA 92121
(619) 555-7854

JOB OVERVIEW:
Corporate desktop video, animation, and special effects producer covering the computer industry seeks a multimedia creative position with an ad agency or video/multimedia production company utilizing computer graphics design. Six years' experience in creating special effects on Amiga computers using the Video Toaster and Genlock peripherals. Winner of 1993 Frank Award for best animation for cable TV commercials created on a personal computer. Experienced with video cameras and editing equipment.

HARDWARE:
- Amiga, IBM, Macintosh computers.
- Genlock peripherals
- Video Toaster used with Amiga for animation and special effects design.
- JVL broadcast and industrial quality video cameras.
- VHS video conversion.
- Videotape editing using a variety of equipment.

CORPORATE ANIMATION EMPLOYMENT:
1991–1993:
Desktop Video Producer, Multimedia Infomercial and Animation Production Company, Inc., El Cajon, CA.
1989–1991:
Desktop Animation Creative Director, Computer Productions (Ad Agency), El Cajon, CA.
1987–1989:
Special Effects Designer/Producer, Barstow Video Productions, Inc., New Orleans, LA.

PROFESSIONAL ASSOCIATIONS:
- Computer Graphics SIGGRAPH of ACM
- International Society of Animators

EDUCATION:
A.S., Computer Graphics Video
Grossmont College, El Cajon, CA, June 1993.

REFERENCES ON REQUEST.

Ariadne Abbot

7799 Cable Court • Los Angeles, CA 90028 • (213) 555-9734

JOB TITLE: DIGITAL TECHNOLOGIES SPECIAL EFFECTS PRODUCTION

SPECIAL EFFECTS:
- Created cutting-edge computer and video technologies to create exotic visual effects.
- Produced own multimedia entertainment and education products for a variety of electronic media.
- Translated sounds and images into computer code to alter the way films, television programs, and advertisements are produced.
- Created next-generation video games, animated films, simulator rides, and computer software programs.
- Established an in-house digital special effects company at Interactive Television Corp. in Los Angeles.
- Created mechanical and animated characters for films.
- Developed a library of digital images.
- Marketed digital effects-based characters.
- Built an interactive animation system and other creative tools that enabled movie directors to directly manipulate the actions in an animated scene, saving the company $900,000 in creative expenses during 1993.
- Expanded computing operations into special effects to build alliances between the software and entertainment companies. Interactive Television Corp. and Smorth Inc. of Hollywood.
- Located cable TV partners for a variety of firms entering the interactive TV arena.
- Developed special effects image manipulation.

EXPERIENCE:
June 1985–October 1993:

Digital Special Effects and Image Manipulation Producer, Interactive Television Corporation, Los Angeles, CA.

EDUCATION:
Master of Fine Arts, Animation and Special Effects
University of California, Los Angeles, CA, 1988
Bachelor of Science, Computer Science, Fine Arts Minor
University of California, Los Angeles, CA, 1985

References on request.

187

Thera Ellis

1756 West First St.
Rowe, IA 30206
(310) 555-0977

GOAL

Communications document production manager's position in
an engineering consulting firm.

HIGHLIGHTS OF QUALIFICATIONS

— Knowledgeable in all phases of document production.
— Experienced in managing a staff of over 20 reprographics personnel.
— Excellent word-processing, editing, and graphic design skills.
— Planned and scheduled production of proposals, reports, and studies
   in a time-sensitive, high-volume environment, using internal
   resources and outside services efficiently.
— Optimized use of hardware and software.
— Developed and maintained quality- and cost-control systems.
— Interfaced with corporate professionals at all levels in a variety of
   specialties.
— Managed cutting-edge document production technologies.
— Developed realistic budgets to control costs.

RELATED EXPERIENCE

1978–Present:
Crowe Engineering Consulting, Inc., Rowe, IA.
Fifteen years' experience, with increasing responsibilities, in document
production positions with one firm. Successfully managed document
production teams generating high-quality products under tight deadlines. Excellent communications skills.

EDUCATION AND SPECIALIZED TRAINING

Bachelor of Arts Degree,
Major in Creative Studies: English, with writing emphasis,
and graphic design/commercial art
Rowe Liberal Arts College
Rowe, IA, June 1978

References on request.

Mai Ling Chan
410 Newton Street
Washington, DC 30206
(202) 555-0977

OVERVIEW
CADD project manager and senior medical designer/draftswoman with five years' medical design and OSHPD procedure experience seeks immediate opening using knowledge of computer-aided drafting.

QUALIFICATIONS

* Knowledgeable in all phases of computer-aided drafting.
* Utilized virtual reality computer technology to draft and design 3-D medical simulations.
* Experienced in drafting building drawings, construction, drainage, street improvement, site development plans.
* Use intergraph, PC, pencil, ink, Leroy pins, and templates.
* AutoCAD software experience and graphic design skills as an AutoCAD drafter in medical and engineering model simulation for Medical Drafting Specialists, Washington, DC.
* Planned and scheduled production of blueprints, designs, and drawings in a time-sensitive, high-volume environment, using internal resources and outside services efficiently for medical, architectural, and engineering drafting projects.
* Developed and maintained quality- and cost-control systems and computed realistic budgets.
* Interfaced with corporate professionals at all levels.

RELATED EXPERIENCE
1988–Present:
Senior Medical Designer/Drafter, Medical Drafting Specialists, Inc.,
Washington, DC

Five years' experience in progressively responsible medical and engineering drafting/design projects with one firm. Successfully used AutoCAD software to draft and design high-quality blueprints and designs under tight deadline pressure. Excellent communications skills. Successfully trained staff in OSHPD procedure while working on medical drafting projects.
Naturalized U.S. citizen from Taiwan.

EDUCATION
Associate in Science Degree,
Architectural Computer-Aided Design and Drafting
Taiwan Junior College, Taiwan, 1986

REFERENCES ON REQUEST.

James B. Marstoni
918 Bard Street
Buffalo, NY 02122
(716) 555-0977

FOCUS
Systems engineering drafter specializing in production and development of instrumentation systems drawings, designs, and blueprints seeks a position as an intermediate drafter.

OVERVIEW
Five years' experience using computers to create and modify engineering drawings according to military and government standards. Experience in drafting TACTS/ACMI range instrumentation systems for an instrumentation production firm.

QUALIFICATIONS
• Knowledgeable in all phases of computer-aided drafting, including CADDS 4X and AutoCAD software. Familiar with wireframes and E/M assemblies. Strong CADKEY skills.
• Created and modified engineering drawings in compliance with IAW MIL-STDs.
• Generated and incorporated engineering change orders.
• Five years' electro/mechanical drafting experience.
• One year in AutoCAD release 10.0 and higher software.
• Knowledge of engineering terminology.
• Knowledge of government military standards (MIL-STDs), military specifications, and basic math.
• Ability to read and understand engineering drawings, sketches, schematics, blueprints.
• Skilled with scanning equipment.

RELATED EXPERIENCE

1988–Present:
Intermediate Drafter, Instrumentation Systems, Inc., Buffalo, NY.

EDUCATION
A.S., Drafting
Buffalo Community College, 1988

REFERENCES ON REQUEST.

Fasulya Zakia Hanny

171 Lyon Street
New York, NY 10122
(212) 555-0977

OVERVIEW
Consumer production fashion and textile designer/software stylist seeks a senior designer's position. Experienced in developing lines for home furnishings and gifts apparel industry. Fashion design utilizing computer software includes heavy experience designing infant to preteen clothing for child clothing manufacturer. Experienced in computer grading and production.

EXPERIENCE
Eight years' experience using computers to create and modify children's clothing and textiles. Developed 11 lines for home furnishings, six lines for gifts apparel, and 20 lines for individual infant to preteen clothing for one children's clothing manufacturer. Extensive computer experience for designing, styling, grading, and production tracking.

ABILITIES
· Knowledgeable in all phases of fashion design and styling software.
· Utilized and modified grading and production software.
· Generated and incorporated design change orders.
· Five years' experience designing and styling home furnishings and textiles.
· Three years' children's clothing design experience.
· Knowledge of garment industry terminology.
· Knowledge of grading and production standards.
· Designing patterns with software.
· Sewing samples from sketches.

RELATED EMPLOYMENT
1985–Present:
Designer/Stylist, Gregory Garment and Home Furnishing Design Industries, Inc., New York, NY.

EDUCATION
A.S., Fashion Design
Fashion Institute of Technology
New York, New York, 1985

References available upon request.

191

Jim Thompson
1900 Glendale Drive
Brooklyn, NY 11230
(718) 555-9087

OVERVIEW: Professional systems analyst in the health care industry seeks position interacting with all levels of personnel.

PROGRAMMING LANGUAGES: COBOL, ASSM.

SOFTWARE/HARDWARE SYSTEMS ANALYSIS EXPERIENCE:

• Seven years' experience in two multi-institutional health care systems consulting firms performing the following applications using superior analytical and project management skills:
  • Modified and upgraded installed systems.
  • Adhered to QA and systems management control disciplines.
  • Managed internal/external resources, work products, and project time schedules.
  • Oversaw application design, development, and maintenance in compliance with IS standards.
  • Performed application coding and system tailoring.
  • Maintained and administered databases.
  • Informed users on the status of enhancements, releases, and alternate solutions.
  • Conducted project meetings.
  • Maintained complete documentation of project materials.
  • Developed, implemented, and maintained applications.
  • Analyzed systems. Programmed computers.
  • Structured and implemented systems designs.

EMPLOYMENT:
August 1988–Present:
Information Services Systems Analyst, Berg Healthcare Services, Flushing, NY.
June 1986–August 1988:
Information Services Systems Analyst, Sands Hospital Systems, Brooklyn, NY.

EDUCATION: Master of Science
                   Computer Science and Systems Analysis
                   Brooklyn College, Brooklyn, NY, 1986

References on request.

Skye Owis
PO Box 4333   San Diego, CA 92164   (619) 555-3087

OVERVIEW: Independent interactive multimedia computer game, entertainment, instructional designer working in the following platforms: compact disc, interactive (CD-I), compact disc, read-only memory (CD-ROM), 3-Dimensional Optical Technologies (3DO), interactive broadcast television production and development, interactive feature film production, videodisc players scriptwriting and design, and writing intructional material for interactive multimedia learning as entertainment materials. Computer game designs emphasize learning values.

CREATIVE EXPERIENCE:
- Wrote documentary films for training.
- Wrote instructional plan book known as a bible for three feature films and animation.
- Wrote interactive multimedia mystery novel series.
- Designed interface and whole package with interlocking branches of several suspense novels turned into interactive multimedia computer games.
- Wrote comic books and animation series.
- Hired and trained coauthors to write scripts for computer game companies.
- Wrote character-driven stories and scripts for computer games, 3-dimensional optical technologies, and new interactive broadcast television productions
- Developed interactive designs and scripts for videodisc players using new interactive language flow charts and 3-D thinking strategies.
- Wrote and designed books and stories for CD-ROM.

EMPLOYMENT:
June 1993–Present:
> Independent Computer Game Designer/Writer,
> Three Dimensional Optical Animation and Multimedia, Inc.,
> San Diego, CA.

January 1979–June 1993:
> Cartridge computer game designer and scriptwriter,
> Learning As Entertainment Corporation,
> San Diego, CA.

EDUCATION:
> Master of Arts degree,
> English, (creative writing emphasis)
> San Diego State University
> San Diego, CA, December 1978

REFERENCES ON REQUEST.

Anne Antonis
1756 First Weston Drive
Edmonton, Alberta, Canada T6K 4C6
(403) 555-8764

OVERVIEW:
Novelist/Scriptwriter seeks staff or freelance position as a computer interactive multimedia fiction writer for a software manufacturer. Telecommuting preferred.

FICTION WRITING EXPERIENCE:

1991–Present:	*Magazine of Ancient Historical Fiction*: Author of 12 short stories on CD-ROM and CD-Interactive laser disc.
1985–1991:	Interactive computer game script, *The Adventures of Dr. Chuan*, and seven science fiction suspense novels. Thorndine & Co., Inc. Publishing, New York, NY. Each project sold over 60,000 copies annually since 1985.
1983–1985:	Two novels: *Time Traveling Buccaneers* and *Bellydancer-Nun-Psychiatrist*, Science Fiction Suspense Press, Inc. Toronto, Canada, 1983, 1984

SOFTWARE EXPERIENCE:
Wrote book on applications software uses for home-based business owners, published by Ole & Lane, NY, 1985.

Wrote video script training teachers in the operation of the Eric computer system for educational research, Edmonton Education Department, Media Center, 1976.

EDUCATION:
M.A., English (Scriptwriting Emphasis),
University of Alberta, Edmonton, December 1979

B.S., English Education
University of Alberta, Edmonton, October 1964

LIST OF ADDITIONAL PUBLISHED WORKS ATTACHED

REFERENCES ON REQUEST

Michael Enivel

33 Bright Boulevard
Far Rockaway, NY
(716) 555-7375

GOAL

Marketing communications coordinator specializing in computer presentation graphics seeks a position with a leading document imaging company.

OVERVIEW

Five years' marketing experience as a communications coordinator in a high-tech industry specializing in computer presentation graphics and document imaging. Excellent communication and organizational skills. Computer literate with IBM-PC hardware and applications software. Self-motivated. Three years' experience as a marketing proposal writer and representative for a hand-held computer products corporation. Specialized in trade show planning, sales demonstrations, and advertising.

ACHIEVEMENTS

- Coordinated collateral development and trade show participation.
- Developed corporate presentations.
- Maintained press relations.
- Disseminated all marketing communications and computer presentation graphics imaging.
- Wrote marketing proposals.
- Acted as manufacturer's representative.
- Planned trade shows and demonstrated equipment on sites.
- Supported manufacturer's representatives in VAR and OEM sales networks.

EMPLOYMENT

1988–Present: Marketing Communications Coordinator and Computer Graphics Presentations Software Publicist
Document Imaging, Inc., New York, NY.

1985–1988:   Marketing Representative and Proposal Writer
Systems Corporation, New York, NY.

EDUCATION

B.A., Communications, marketing minor,
New York University, NY, 1988

References on request.

Xandra Tyler

899 Brink Blvd. · Newport Beach · CA 90023
(714) 555-0998

OVERVIEW

Four years of experience as a computer sales and marketing manager. In-depth exposure to business and financial software. One year in customer and territory development; two years in personnel recruitment and training; and one year in office management, budgeting, and advertising. Strong sales, problem-solving, coordinating, organizing, planning, and verbal communications skills.

DIRECT SALES EXPERIENCE

* Trained sales staff in cold calling, canvassing, telemarketing, and retail sales of personal computers.
* Surpassed sales quotas in first six months of employment.
* Won four saleswoman-of-the-month awards, one for each year worked.
* Recruited, hired, and trained computer sales force.
* Designed forecasts, budgets, and expense controls.
* Wrote marketing brochures and direct marketing letters.
* Coordinated and worked end user/dealer trade shows.
* Improved customer service, tripling gross annual sales during first year of employment.

PRODUCT DEVELOPMENT

* Developed new product line, including system definition, pricing, and implementation plans.
* Budgeted vertical products within specific time frameworks.
* Organized and trained sales staff in computer sales and marketing strategies.
* Gave four national annual computer graphics presentations to executives, dealers, and sales staff, utilizing public speaking skills.
* Monitored the performance of a national sales staff through field trips throughout the United States, China, Japan, and Malaysia. Traveled 60 percent of the time.

EMPLOYMENT

June 1989–Present:
Marketing and Sales Manager, Cost Effective Computers, Inc.,
Newport Beach, CA.

EDUCATION

Bachelor of Science Degree, Marketing
California State University, Irvine, CA, 1989

References available upon request.

Robert B. Dyne
898 Warsaw St.
Goldsboro, NC 25730
(919) 555-0975

JOB OBJECTIVE

Registered medical records technician (A.R.T.) with degree and certification seeks a position as a medical records software manufacturer's representative presenting medical records software to hospitals. Willing to travel nationally.

OVERVIEW

One year of experience using medical records technology software for coding and records administration in the medical records department of a large, general hospital.

QUALIFICATIONS

Accredited Medical Records Technician (A.R.T). Knowledge of coding of diseases, retrieval, preparation for legal procedures with medical records, tumor registry, insurance coding, medical terminology, physiology and anatomy, medical records software, records management, databases, spreadsheets, statistical typing, word processing with WordPerfect, and medical transcription.

RELATED EXPERIENCE

1993–Present: Medical Records Technician, St. Michael's Hospital, Goldsboro, NC.

1980–1993: Medical Transcriptionist, St. Michael's Hospital, Goldsboro, NC.

EDUCATION AND SPECIALIZED TRAINING

Associate in Science Degree, Medical Records Technology
Goldsboro Community College, Goldsboro, NC, 1993
A.R.T. Certification, 1993

Certificate in Medical Transcription
Goldsboro Community College, Goldsboro, NC, 1980

REFERENCES ON REQUEST

Tatiana Kutkowsky
2616 Clareina Blvd. / La Jolla CA 92037 / (619) 555-1419

JOB OVERVIEW
Certified Medical Transcriptionist seeks a position with a health care systems company, medical office, or hospital using radiology medical terminology. Prefer to telecommute.

SOFTWARE
WordPerfect, Microsoft Word, dBase, Lotus 1-2-3, and medical transcription software, including medical terminology spelling and grammar checking software dictionaries on IBM-compatible PC or Macintosh computers.

MEDICAL TRANSCRIPTION EXPERIENCE
October 1988–1993
Radiologic Surgery Clinic, La Jolla, CA

RESPONSIBILITIES:
· Used medical transcription software on an IBM computer to accurately transcribe medical treatment and procedures from recordings on magnetic tape cassettes.
· Utilized practical knowledge of medical terminology, anatomy, physiology, internal organization of medical reports, medical report standards and requirements, and the medicolegal significance of medical transcripts.
· Transcribed medical histories, physicals, consultations, operative reports, discharge summaries, referral letters, and documentation in radiology subspecialties.
· Typed 90 words per minute with no errors from the spoken word using an IBM-compatible computer. (Recent certificate attached.) Excellent auditory skills.
· Proofread and edited for accuracy of medical records.
· Used a variety of equipment to transcribe in many different types of medical settings, including hospitals and offices.

EDUCATION
Certificate in Medical Transcription and Medical Office Administration (one-year program)
Mesa Community College
San Diego, CA, 1988

References on request.

Rabina Diades
9880 Serendipity Road
Seattle, WA 95023
(206) 555-0498

OVERVIEW

Four years of experience as a midi synthesizer computerized music composer, multimedia desktop publisher and video producer specializing in color separations and computer presentation graphics. Seeking a position as a multimedia designer/producer using graphics, music, video, and text.

ABILITIES

* Improved customer service, increasing gross annual sales during first year of employment by $850,000.
* Utilized DigitalMedia Studio desktop video publishing system combining hardware and software to provide 24-bit, full screen, full motion, 30-frame-per-second digital editing and production for Macintosh computers.
* Utilized desktop publishing software for color separation.
* Designed multimedia shows using midi synthesizer music, Roland synthesizers, and Amiga or IBM animation programs for technical trade show presentation graphics.
* Produced multimedia videos for electronics trade shows.
* Composed background music for courseware design in multimedia training productions for computer trade shows.
* Designed multimedia budgets, forecasts, and expense controls to meet production/promotion requirements.
* Coordinated and worked end user/dealer trade shows.

PRODUCT DEVELOPMENT

* Developed new video product line, including multimedia system definition, pricing, and implementation plans.
* Budgeted vertical products within specific time frameworks.

EMPLOYMENT
June 1989–Present:

Multimedia Producer/Designer, Multimedia Presentation Graphics, Inc., Seattle, WA.

EDUCATION

B.S., Computerized Music Composition
University of Washington, Seattle, 1993

A.S., Desktop Publishing/Desktop Video
Seattle Community College, 1989

References on request.

Kendall Kewn

996 Bedford Hwy.
Atlanta, GA 25730
(819) 555-0125

OVERVIEW

Certified Novell Network Engineer in Novell Network services seeks a position as a network systems engineer designing, implementing, installing, troubleshooting, maintaining, and modifying local area networks. Knowledge of network services.

EXPERIENCE

Two years' experience using Novell Netware 2.1x, 2.2, and 3.11, 3-Com networks, D-Link peer-to-peer networks, Artisoft LANtastic networks, TCP/IP, Unix, and Apple etal network. Support Netware Lite and LANtastic networks. LAN-to-LAN and home-to-LAN with modem systems installed and supported in a variety of locations.

QUALIFICATIONS

* Design, install, maintain, troubleshoot, and repair computer systems and peripherals.
* Supervise in the process of configuration, assembly, and testing of computer systems.
* Provide training for technicians and field service personnel.
* Assist in sales presentations.
* Evaluate new products.
* Design circuits.
* Provide customized solutions in terms of hardware and software to fit customer's requirements.
* Familiar with many bus technologies, network topologies, and protocols.
* Six years' experience maintaining telephone equipment and devices.

RELATED EMPLOYMENT

1991–Present: Network Systems Engineer
Greystone LAN Corporation, Atlanta, GA.
1985–1991:   Network Systems Engineer and Systems Analyst,
Nevada Bell Telephone Company, Reno, NV.

EDUCATION

B.S., Computer Science and Electronics
University of Georgia, Atlanta, GA, 1985

References available upon request.

Victoria Tiffany Meghan

56 First Avenue
Boise, Idaho 80776
(208) 555-1589

OVERVIEW

Neural networks and fuzzy logic heuristics specialist in biology seeks a research associate or assistant position linking computer programming skills with pharmacology, where both programming skills and biological sciences degree will be utilized.

ABILITIES
* Background in both biology and mathematics.
* Experience in and knowledge of computer programming.
* Interested in animal models to study the disposition of anticancer therapeutics.
* Experience with cell culture related to computing.
* Experience with the use of radioactive materials.
* Knowledge of neural networks applied from biological sciences to computer science and fuzzy logic.

EXPERIENCE

One year of experience as a research assistant in molecular genetics and yeast biology. Knowledge of recombinant DNA techniques, growth maintenance, DNA transfer, and identification of recombinants.
Computer programming with mathematical models using neural network and fuzzy logic principles to apply biological research. Focus on animal models and computing.

EMPLOYMENT
1992–Present:
Research Assistant, General Networks Corporation, Boise, Idaho.
1987–1992:
Computer Programmer, Genetic Engineering Corporation, Boise, Idaho.

EDUCATION
Bachelor of Science with special major in Biology and Mathematics
(minor in Computer Science)
University of Idaho, Boise, ID, 1992

References on request.

Robert Dalle

26 Reina Blvd. • El Cajon, CA 92121 • (619) 555-1889

OVERVIEW
Computer numeric control (CNC) technician in computer industrial technology seeks a position in computerized manufacturing, specializing in robotics technology.

ABILITIES
- CNC machine operator able to program computers to manufacture parts.
- Computer programmer.
- Drafter.
- Basic mathematics and physics knowledge.
- Developed computer-aided manufacturing software.
- Obtained maximum productivity from machines.

EXPERIENCE
One year of experience as a computer numeric control operator for one of the world's largest manufacturers of arc welding products and robots and a major producer of electric motors and thermal cutting equipment. Realized maximum potential of computerized equipment by training technicians in CNC operation. One year of prior experience as a computer programmer and machinist for same firm.

EMPLOYMENT
1992–Present: **CNC Operator and Robotics Technician**
Sands Electric Motor Company, El Cajon, CA.

1991–1992: **Computer Programmer and Machinist**
Sands Electric Motor Company, El Cajon, CA.

EDUCATION
Associate in Science
Computer-Aided Manufacturing Technology
Center for Applied Competitive Technologies
San Diego City College
San Diego, CA, 1991

Associate in Science
Computer Science and Information Systems
San Diego City College
San Diego, CA, 1989

References upon request.

ESTHER SANCHEZ
9998 Sweetwater Blvd.
Chicago, IL 60636
(312) 555-9575

OVERVIEW

Human resource manager seeks a personnel management position in a sophisticated, fast-paced electronic technology environment.

RELATED EXPERIENCE

Five years' experience in human resources in a high-volume manufacturing environment with two years in a supervisory position. Fluent in English and Spanish. Previous personal computer experience includes heavy spreadsheet and word-processing packages. Former trainer in industrial psychology.

RESPONSIBILITIES

Managed the human resources department, which included the following responsibilities:
— Recruitment.
— Salary and benefits administration.
— Training and development.
— Employee services.
— Recognition and safety program management.

EMPLOYMENT

1988–Present: **Personnel and Human Resources Manager**
Computercorps, Inc., Chicago, IL

1986–1988: **Bilingual (English/Spanish) Trainer in Industrial Psychology**
Computer College, San Juan, Puerto Rico

1980–1986: **Bilingual Personnel Clerk**
Personnel Department
University of Chicago Medical Center, Chicago, IL

EDUCATION

B.A., Industrial Relations Psychology/Personnel Management
University of Chicago
Chicago, IL, 1980

REFERENCES ON REQUEST

Mereet deCordoba
111 Lemon Drive
Key West, FL 30398
(305) 555-9589

OVERVIEW
Diverse programmer and hardware/software systems administrator seeks a position with a product or service-based corporation.

SOFTWARE/HARDWARE
Knowledge of PCs, Lantastic, Novell, dBaseIV+, C, EDI, DOS, and Unix. FoxPro/Windows multi-user. FoxBASE/Macintosh multiuser. SQL and Windows software.

ABILITIES
- Program.
- Manage all systems.
- Train users.
- Maintain and repair equipment.
- Write software user manuals.
- Team player.

EXPERIENCE
FoxPro Windows: Three years' experience programming FoxPro multi-user. Three years' experience programming with SQL and Windows software. Unix: Three years' experience supporting PC-based Unix with strong customer service skills. Two years' experience with FoxBASE Macintosh computer programming. Two years' experience programming with FoxBASE multi-user. Two years' experience in technical writing: software user manuals.

EMPLOYMENT
1988–Present: Computer Programmer and Systems Administrator
Control Inc., Key West, FL
1986–1988:   Computer Programmer and Technical Writer
Hawley Computers, Inc., Key West, FL

EDUCATION
Bachelor of Science Degree
Computer Science Programming
University of Miami, Miami, FL 1986
Certificate in Technical Writing, 1984

JAMES VINCENTE
890 Foxgrove Lane
Philadelphia, PA 17898
(215) 555-8764

JOB OVERVIEW:
Seeking a position as director of quality and regulatory affairs. Thirty years' experience in regulatory compliance overseeing strategic regulatory affairs quality control. Reported directly to the CEO in one of the nation's largest electronics firms.

EXPERIENCE:

1981–Present: **Director, Quality and Regulatory Affairs**
Quality and Configuration Manager: Managed Class II critical devices and supporting disposables. In-depth understanding of and experience with current GMPs, SMDA of 1990, and 510 (k) submissions, including DMR and DHR content/management. Configured software.

1975–1981: **Senior Manager in Medical Device Quality Control**
Managed complex, software-driven, electromechanical products.

1963–1975: **Quality Control Technician**
Quality inspector of hearing aids. Electronic circuit knowledge. Hands-on soldering, troubleshooting, and problem solving.

EMPLOYMENT:

1981–Present: **Director, Quality and Regulatory Affairs**
Infusion Med-Instruments, Inc., Philadelphia, PA.

1975–1981: **Senior Manager, Medical Device Quality Control**
Star Medical Instruments, Inc., Philadelphia, PA.

1963–1975: **Quality Control Technician**
Serendipity Hearing Aids, Inc., Philadelphia, PA.

EDUCATION:
Associate in Sciences Degree, Quality Control and Assurance
Philadelphia Technical College, Philadelphia, PA, 1963

References available upon request.

MARTIN MOSS
23 Bloomfield Street
Dearborn, MI 48128
(313) 555-3899

OVERVIEW

Robotics technician position wanted installing, troubleshooting, and repairing robots. Specialist in robot applications and maintenance.

EMPLOYMENT
1984–1993
EXPERIENCE

AUTOMATED COMPUTERS, INC., Dearborn, Michigan
Robot Repair Technician
Installed, diagnosed, maintained, and repaired robots and robotic systems in factories where robots lift heavy loads.
• Interfaced with welding engineers and industrial designers to troubleshoot and solve problems.
• Utilized robotics software systems to operate, control, and repair robots.
• Diagnosed computer problems for builders and users of robots.
• Trained electricians and mechanics to repair robots on-site in factories.
• Repaired robot-related automated factory equipment and computers used to control robots.
• Repaired defense robots used by the military.

1980–1984

U.S. NAVY   Stationed at Long Beach, CA
Underwater Robotics Technician
• Maintained, diagnosed, and repaired underwater robots while serving in the Navy. Trained in the Navy's extensive underwater robotics programs.

EDUCATION

Bachelor of Science Degree
Robotics and Manufacturing Technology
Northrup University
Los Angeles, CA 1984

Associate in Sciences Degree
Industrial Technology
Henry Ford Community College
Dearborn, MI 1980

MEMBERSHIP

Robotics International of the Society of Manufacturing Engineers, Dearborn, MI.

The Robotics Institute, Pittsburgh, PA.

REFERENCES ON REQUEST.

JEANNE D'ARCY
561 Orange Avenue
Nashville, TN 45138
(615) 555-9589

CAREER GOAL
Field sales representative seeks an assigned territory selling hardware and software multimedia products for the personal computer.

ACHIEVEMENTS
- Marketed professional development seminars to dealers that resulted in a 50 percent increase in sales.
- Designed new market penetration and sales to computer manufacturing industry, thereby securing an agreement for the largest dollar volume contract in present company's history.
- 250 percent of sales quota 1985
- 175 percent of sales quota in 1984
- 188 percent of sales quota in 1983
- Established tenth company office, expanding business beyond tenth year projections by 260 percent.
- Obtained the first marketing program with Fortune 500 companies, generating a 75 percent increase in new revenue base.
- Created and implemented multimedia market by establishing relationships with major chain reseller stores.
- Provided information interface between company and customers.
- Attended user group meetings and industry events.
- Directed sales of personal computers and peripheral products.

EMPLOYMENT

1980–Present: Field Sales Representative
Multimedia Marketing, Inc.
Nashville, TN

1978–1980:   Sales Manager
Computer Events, Inc.
Nashville, TN.

1964–1978:   Field Sales Representative,
Marketshare Corp.,
Baton Rouge, LA.

EDUCATION
Bachelor of Business Administration Degree
Marketing Management
University of Tennessee
Nashville, TN, June 1964

REFERENCES ON REQUEST

June Langst

60 Elmwood Place
Rockville, MD 20854
(301) 555-8960

JOB OBJECTIVE:
To find a challenging scientific programming position that utilizes my master's degree in mathematics.

EXPERIENCE:
Computer security analyst with 31 years' experience in computer research toward developing better security systems. Expertise in scientific computer programming and mathematical analysis. Specialist in designing mathematical models for security problem interpretation and solution. Knowledge of operations research and development.

SOFTWARE:
FORTRAN, PL/1, C, C++, Assembly, Pascal.
Lisp, DEC. Neural Networks, Fuzzy Logic, Artificial Intelligence applications software, heuristics.

HARDWARE:
Cray Supercomputers and IBM PCs.
VAX-11/750 and above, PDP, DGM600, CDC, MODCOMP.

ACCOMPLISHMENTS:
* Created a study resulting in higher assurance of computer security.
* Designed a relational database to analyze classified military security computer operating system requirements using operations research statistical techniques.
* Developed mathematical models specializing in research development.
* Presented statistical breakdowns for survey questionnaire.

EMPLOYMENT:
1962–Present: Security Analyst Programmer,
                     Data Security Dynamics, Inc.,
                     Rockville, MD

EDUCATION:
Master of Science Degree in Mathematics
Johns Hopkins University, Baltimore, MD, 1962

Bachelor of Science Degree in Mathematics
Johns Hopkins University, Baltimore, MD, 1960

References available upon request.

BARRY MINTON
8990 Santa Cruz Blvd.
Santa Cruz, CA 95143
(408) 555-9889

OVERVIEW: Software engineer experienced in system definition seeks a challenging opportunity to utilize applications development, data communications, graphics, relational databases, and systems engineering in project management.

ACHIEVEMENTS:
* Prepared detailed technical documentation.
* Made oral presentations to customers and company management.
* Developed software within DOD and commercial environments.
* Designed software.
* Implemented, tested, documented, and integrated COTS/GOTS.

SOFTWARE: Unix, C language, Unix workstations, Program Design Language (PDL), GUI. Macintosh software: Think c, MPW, MacApp., and Tool Box.

HARDWARE: IBM and Macintosh computers.

ANALYSIS AND DESIGN:
Structured analysis and design utilizing RDBMS (e.g., Sybase), CASE tools, and DOD-Std-2167A.

SECURITY CLEARANCE:
Top Secret. Eligible for access to classified information.

EXPERIENCE: Eight years' experience in a commercial environment. Experience in all areas of development (functional specifications, design, program specifications, programming, and testing).

EMPLOYMENT: 1985–Present: Software Engineer,
Government Software Engineering, Inc., Cambria, CA.

EDUCATION: Bachelor of Science Degree
Computer Science
University of California, Santa Cruz, CA, 1985

REFERENCES: On request

Marcia Destinee Whisper
1744 Bright Blvd., Eugene, OR 98254
(503) 555-9432

CAREER GOAL   SOFTWARE TALENT AGENT STAFF POSITION

SOFTWARE EXPERIENCE

- **Wrote book on software talent agenting** for public relations agency owners, published by West & West, Marketing Promotions Press, London, England, 1988.
- **Weekly national newspaper columnist** for *The Talent Agent's News* (for owners of software talent agencies).

SOFTWARE AGENTING EXPERIENCE

- 1980–Present: Account Executive, Dynamic Software Talent Agency Inc., Eugene, OR.

Ten years' experience operating a software talent agency for absentee owner with over 150 clients. Specialist in marketing and promoting patented and copyrighted software for independent software designers, manufacturers, and consultants.

ABILITIES

- Find software designers for leading manufacturers.
- Package software created by independent contractors.
- Recruit software talent for software firms.
- Copyright and patent software for designers.
- Refer software designers and engineers to jobs.
- Consult and counsel software talent seeking markets.
- Create promotions, publicity, ad campaigns, marketing programs, and press kits for software designers, writers, artists, or manufacturers.
- Train software designers in packaging, distributing, marketing, and selling their software.
- Track software audiences for market research.
- Research software markets and create mailing lists.
- Locate publishers and producers for software writers, multimedia or video artists, and software designers.

EDUCATION

Master of Arts in English (Writing emphasis)
University of Oregon, Eugene, OR, December 1980

REFERENCES UPON REQUEST

ROBERT A. SHELDON
876 Rayna Lane
Chicago, IL 60603

(303) 555-1999

OVERVIEW
Software test manager seeks an innovative intrapreneurial environment in which to develop products, create market acceptance, provide hands-on leadership, and to develop software test methods from the ground up.

RESPONSIBILITIES
- Selected and implemented test methods.
- Determined and controlled test environments.
- Wrote software test suites.
- Documented test results.
- Managed the testing of new products.
- Implemented systems around a client/server model on a PC under Windows and OS/2.
- Verified designs of complex software products.
- Developed software test plans.
- Prepared test procedures.
- Documented test results.

EXPERIENCE
Two years' software engineering development experience managing the following software testing procedures:

- Tested voice annotation software and toolkits that connect data and phone networks to provide multimedia services (voice and data) to the desktop personal computer.
- Connected local area networks (LAN) to wide area networks (WAN).
- Implemented systems using client/server models on customized VME-based servers operating under VxWorks and UNIX.
- Tested tools and methods using knowledge of automated regression.

RELATED EMPLOYMENT
June 1991–Present
Software Test Manager
Innovative Software Corporation, Chicago, IL.

EDUCATION
Bachelor of Science degree,
Computer Science and Information Systems
University of Chicago, Chicago IL, 1991

REFERENCES AVAILABLE UPON REQUEST.

SALLY TUCKER
971 Sunshine Lane
Chicago, IL 60603
(303) 555-1589

CAREER GOAL
Software user manual writer seeks a creatively technical environment in which to develop, write, and edit software user manuals from the ground up.

RESPONSIBILITIES
* Planned software user manuals to meet the needs of users.
* Organized and transcribed interview notes from programmers and software designers.
* Increased the number of potential software customers by making complex steps easier to understand.
* Documented use of manuals by novice users.
* Designed software user manuals.
* Wrote user manuals to make the software stand out from the crowd.
* Reduced the amount of after-sale support required by dealers by making the manuals easy to use.
* Tracked sales increase in manuals from dealers.
* Reduced the number of technical support personnel publishers had to hire, and saved the company $50,000 through improved manuals.

EXPERIENCE
Two years' software user manual writing/editing experience managing the following procedures:
* Planned the revision of COBOL and other software manuals.
* Determined audience and training requirements.
* Organized and outlined manuals by researching operation of the programs.
Progressively detailed each draft of manuals.
* Coordinated programmers with other writers and illustrators to plan the software design and the manual together.

RELATED EMPLOYMENT
June 1991–Present: Software User Manual Writer
                      Kyleberg and Stetson Computer Training Corporation
                      Chicago, IL.

EDUCATION
Bachelor of Science Degree
English Education
New York University, NY, 1991

REFERENCES ON REQUEST.

MARINA SABRET

2432 Elysian Glen
Palo Alto, CA 94587
(415) 555-1875

OVERVIEW: Systems analyst will provide sales and technical support for your on-line report viewing software.

EXPERIENCE: Ten years' experience in training system administrators and end users at customer sites in the operation of MVS/CICS-based application.
IBM mainframe systems analyst and programmer with knowledge of JCL. Traveled throughout the United States.

DUTIES: Performed analysis, evaluation, architecture definition, trade-off studies, customer presentation and interface, proposal preparation and generation.

HARDWARE: Imagery Intelligence Processing Systems. Open systems POSIX compliant client server architecture. Two-bit workstations.

SOFTWARE: Unix/C software and communications protocols.
GUI, relational DBMS (Sybase); CASE Tools, DOD-Std-2167A.

EMPLOYMENT:

1988–Present:	Systems Analyst and Trainer, Info-Development, Palo Alto, CA.
1986–1988:	Programmer and Systems Analyst, Training Systems, Inc., San Francisco, CA.
1983–1986:	Systems Analyst/Systems Engineer, Image Systems, Berkeley, CA.

EDUCATION: Bachelor of Science Degree
Computer Science
California State University,
San Francisco, CA, 1983

REFERENCES ON REQUEST

Louise Mendoza
1995 Ward Ave./Austin, TX 78754
(512) 555-5921

OVERVIEW:
Systems engineer experienced in weather systems analysis and design seeks a challenging opportunity to perform system requirements in hardware and software integration.

ACHIEVEMENTS:
- Performed functional decomposition.
- Made/bought analyses.
- Performed COTS component trade-off studies and selections.
- Designed and executed time and sizing studies.
- Conducted reliability, availability, and maintainability analyses.
- Integrated software and hardware.
- Provided vendor/subcontractor coordination.
- Prepared technical proposals.
- Made oral presentations to customers and company management.
- Presented oral and written design reviews.

SOFTWARE/HARDWARE:
C computer language, UNIX and MS-DOS. IBM computers and LAN/WAN technologies.

SYSTEMS ENGINEERING:
Systems engineering requirements analysis. Integration and testing of distributed workstation-based systems. Knowledge of automated weather systems. Familiar with military standards, DOD engineering drawings and lists. Experience with communications protocols, (X.25/ADCCP).

EXPERIENCE:
Four years' experience in a commercial environment. Experience in all areas of development (functional specifications, design, program specifications, programming, and testing).

EMPLOYMENT:
1989–Present: **Systems Engineer,** Great Weather Systems Engineering Inc., Austin, TX, 1989

EDUCATION:
Bachelor of Science Degree
Electrical Engineering and Computer Science
University of Texas, Austin, TX, 1989

REFERENCES:
Upon Request.

ZACHARY WESTLAND
895 Plains Ave.
St. Louis, MO 63100
(314) 555-3971

JOB OVERVIEW: Tape librarian experienced in legal and news source
                       on-line services and database retrieval/searching, seeks
                       position with timeshare data transmission firm.

EXPERIENCE:
1981–Present: Reference and Source Tape Librarian

- Serviced database companies by providing them with a way to transmit their data.
- Created abstracts of articles, placing them on-line within timesharing computer
  services to be accessed by computer users.
- Transmitted data by modem and fax as well as by tape, audio, and video-conferencing.
- Stored reports and records, and maintained archives and database tapes/disks.
- Maintained on-line services offering database producers a network to reach users.
- Compiled and wrote a directory of on-line databases.
- Organized and maintained tapes of legal abstracts, contest and sweepstakes entries,
  academic research article abstracts, electronic news sheets, and dissertation abstracts.
- Managed numerical and textual reference databases and referred users to primary
  sources.
- Transmitted both reference and source data. Created channels for transmission.
- Managed reference and source databases.

EMPLOYMENT:
1986–Present: Tape Librarian
                       Computer Bank Tape Library
                       St. Louis, MO.
1981–1986:   Tape Librarian
                       Cranshaw Legal Library
                       St. Louis, MO.

EDUCATION:

                       B.A., Public History
                       University of Kansas, Kansas City, MO, 1981

REFERENCES ON REQUEST

TILLIE FOSTER
(614) 555-1453

7780 Pine Road
Columbus, OH 43231

OVERVIEW
Technical illustrator seeks permanent position in the computer industry. Excellent training in technical illustration, drafting, engineering graphics, architectural illustration, computer-aided drafting and design, industrial design, and presentation graphics. Expertise in computer applications of technical illustration on Cadds 4X, Macintosh, IBM, and Amiga computers.

COMPETENCIES
- Advanced technical illustration methods.
- Architectural drafting and advanced design.
- Assembly drawing.
- Airbrush.
- Basic blueprint reading.
- Computer-aided design and computer applications in drafting and technical illustration (advanced).
- Dimensioning and tolerancing.
- Electronic design and illustration.
- Engineering graphics.
- Engineering design.
- Industrial design. Developed complex concepts in graphic arts.
- PCB (circuit board) design (advanced).
- Presentation graphics.

SOFTWARE/HARDWARE
Presentation graphics on Macintosh computers using Adobe Illustrator, Freehand, and Quark software. AutoCAD and CorelDraw! software on the IBM. Technical illustration on Cadds 4X computers.

EMPLOYMENT
June 1993–Present: Technical Illustration Intern, Site Engineering, Inc., Columbus, OH.

EDUCATION
Associate in Arts Degree
Technical Illustration
Columbus Community College, Columbus, OH, 1993

REFERENCES ON REQUEST

JOAN BEDFORD
377 Park Place
Raleigh, NC 27699
(919) 555-9326

TECHNICAL WRITER

EXPERIENCE

1983–1993: <u>Wrote two books per year on applications software uses</u> for home-based business owners, totaling 20 books published by Simon & Schuster, Arco, VGM, and numerous other major career book publishers.
<u>Independent Computer Career Book Writing</u>: Author of numerous published books on computer graphic design and technical writing careers for major NY career book publishers.
<u>Word Processing and Desktop Publishing</u>: Owner of a private word processing, desktop publishing, and technical writing home-based business specializing in computer career information using WordPerfect, CorelDraw!, Ventura AdPro, and Ventura Publisher software on an IBM.

1973–1983: <u>Reporter</u> and weekly national newspaper columnist for *The Small Business Entrepreneur's News*. Wrote business strategies advice columns and software reviews.

1963–1973: <u>Wrote three video scripts per year</u> to train teachers in the operation of the Eric computer system for educational research, and numerous other computer database systems for the Raleigh Education Department, Media Center, as an independent contractor.

EDUCATION

Master of Arts Degree in English
New York University, New York, NY
June 1963.

LIST OF PUBLISHED WORKS ATTACHED
REFERENCES ON REQUEST

Leslie Stephens

78 Green Street
Boston, MA 02114
(617) 555-8317

OVERVIEW:
Technical trainer seeks a staff position as a software applications instructor.

EXPERIENCE:
Developed, designed, and presented on-site and in-house training courses for diverse corporate clients in group and tutorial settings and for community college business and computer students.

SOFTWARE:
Word Processing software training:
WordPerfect, Microsoft Word (IBM or Macintosh computers).
Windows or DOS.
Printer techniques for word processing.
Use of scanners in word processing.
Advanced word-processing methods.

Desktop Publishing software training:
Ventura Publisher
Aldus PageMaker
First Publisher
WordPerfect Presentations (presentation graphics software)
Ventura Publisher AdPro
Color separation techniques in desktop publishing.
Printer techniques for desktop publishing.
Scanners in desktop publishing.

EMPLOYMENT:
1981–Present:
Software Applications Instructor, Department of Office Education
Boston Community College, Boston, MA.

EDUCATION:
M.A., Business Education
University of Massachusetts, Boston, MA, 1981

References available on request.

Jason Jared

1137 Meridian Street • Denver, CO 80275 • (303) 555-1914

GOAL: Computer video games designer specializing in virtual reality simulations seeks staff position with educational, entertainment, or computer games software manufacturer.

EXPERIENCE: Ten years' experience designing computer cartridge video games as a video games artist for entertainment and educational software manufacturers. One year of experience in virtual reality games design.

ACHIEVEMENTS:

- Produced digital multimedia games in simulated virtual reality.
- Created Amiga-based special effects advanced digital multimedia software.
- Converted comic strip characters into 3-D computer games.
- Designed background and character movements.
- Illustrated games software.

HARDWARE: IBM, Amiga, Video Toaster, Virtual Reality Simulation peripherals, and Macintosh.

SOFTWARE: CorelDraw!, Freehand, Quark, PhotoShop, Virtual Reality Simulations, Adobe Illustrator, Tool Box. Advanced animation software for Amiga computers and Video Toaster peripherals. Deluxe Paint software for the Amiga computer. Harvard Graphics software. Multimedia software.

EMPLOYMENT:

1988–Present: **Computer Video Games Designer,** Virtual Reality Games Software, Denver, CO.

1986–1988: **Video Games Artist,** Multimedia Systems, Inc., Denver, CO.

1983–1986: **Special Effects Artist,** Image Magic Digital Multimedia, Boulder, CO.

EDUCATION: Bachelor of Science Degree
Special Major in Computer Graphics
University of Southern Colorado, Pueblo, CO, 1983

REFERENCES UPON REQUEST.

Kevin Zimms

1784 Queens Highway
Prairie Village, KS 66200

(913) 555-1114

OVERVIEW: Teleconferencing executive seeks a position utilizing multimedia teleconferencing equipment to motivate, inspire, persuade, and influence the growth of international firms.

EXPERIENCE: Three years' experience selling and marketing electronic satellite network communications services and videoconferencing equipment.

RESPONSIBILITIES:

- Produced video conferences for executives in worldwide corporations utilizing electronic satellite communications to transmit data.
- Planned and created computer conferences, telephone confer-ences, and video conferences between Pacific Rim nations and the United States.
- Designed video conferences to link colleges with home-based students in 24 states.
- Sold video-conferencing equipment to Fortune 500 corporations, saving the companies a total of $50,000 annually in travel expenses.
- Linked corporations worldwide by telephone, computer, and video cameras via satellite communications.
- Edited all videotape for conferences.

HARDWARE: Knowledge of industrial and broadcast-quality video cameras, Genlock equipment, IBM and Macintosh computers, modems, scanners, fax, and electronic satellite communications.

SOFTWARE: WordPerfect, PageMaker, Ventura Publisher, dBase IV, and Lotus 1-2-3 spreadsheet software.

EMPLOYMENT:

1993–Present: Video conference equipment rental and sales manager, Teleconference Computer Corporation, Prairie Village, KS.
1990–1993: Video conference coordinator, Lawrence Communications, Lawrence, KS.

EDUCATION: Bachelor of Arts Degree, Telecommunications and Film, University of Kansas, Lawrence, KS, June 1990

REFERENCES AVAILABLE ON REQUEST

Karen Leeds

560 Medallion Highway
Gainesville, FL 32600
(904) 555-5310

OVERVIEW:
Virtual reality interactive, computer-generated, three-dimensional graphics simulation production position wanted by recent college graduate interested in producing 3-dimensional models for architects, court medical presentations, animation, education, health care training, and entertainment.

EXPERIENCE:
* Created interactive, computer-generated 3-D graphics simulations on military jet fighter pilot training computer games.
* Designed games for active participants in computer-generated world in real time with 360 degrees of action.
* Operated virtual reality equipment, such as Virtuality 1000CS machine, made by Horizons Entertainment in Missouri.
* Operated virtual reality games at demonstrations and trade shows instructing players how to project 3-D images onto a liquid crystal screen using a head visette.
* Adjusted system images and sounds in response to player's movement.
* Designed computer video games.
* Acted as recruiter for an electronic university, training sales managers in virtual reality demonstration and machine monitoring.

HARDWARE:
Virtuality 1000CS machine operation.

EMPLOYMENT:
1993–Present:
Virtual Reality Design Intern, High Tech Simulations, Simulations Inc., Gainesville, FL.

INTERNSHIP:
Completed one-year internship in virtual reality production, design, and sales departments for a high-tech virtual reality training and entertainment corporation.

EDUCATION:
Bachelor of Arts Degree
Special Major in Medical Illustration and Computer Science
University of Florida
Gainesville, FL, June 1993

REFERENCES ON REQUEST

James Keystone
1170 Mt. Everest Place
Barrington, IL 60012
(708) 555-9635

OVERVIEW: Corporate telecommunications management position wanted. Wireless transmission executive seeks position building, designing, promoting, or selling global cellular systems.

EXPERIENCE: Two years' experience marketing cellular networks in the United States and overseas to open global links. One year of experience designing, maintaining, and repairing foreign cellular networks.

DUTIES:
- Installed, maintained, and repaired cellular networks and systems for electronic publishing companies in the United States and abroad.
- Marketed distance teaching cellular systems to rural public schools in the United States.
- Sold international wireless telecommunications equipment for multimedia, linking over 50 nations in 1992.
- Retained customers and alleviated customer dissatisfaction in a high-call work environment.
- Worked closely with customer service personnel, financial services, and dealer care departments. Trained staff in customer service skills.

EMPLOYMENT:

1991–Present: Marketing Manager,
International Wireless Communications, Inc.,
Barrington, IL.

1990–1991: Wireless transmission technician,
Global Hotlinks, Inc.,
Barrington, IL.

EDUCATION: Associate in Sciences Degree
Computer Science and Electronics
Chicago Community Technical College
Chicago, IL, 1990

REFERENCES AVAILABLE UPON REQUEST

IRENE HART

1245 Village Street
San Diego, CA 92106
(619) 555-8166

OVERVIEW

Word-processing specialist, supervisor, and staff trainer experienced in high-tech document production seeks high-growth corporate environment. Five years' experience in the word-processing department of a computer manufacturer, with increasing responsibilities.

COMPETENCIES

- Advanced level word processing with WordPerfect software on the IBM and compatible computers.
- Mail merging, sorting, labeling, custom mailing, and text editing of direct mail marketing material.
- Electronic publishing and data transmission utilizing word-processing and desktop publishing software, including: Ventura Publisher for Windows and PageMaker on the IBM and compatible computers.
- Statistical keyboarding and integration of tabular material and graphics into word-processing documents and desktop publishing software, including spreadsheets and dBase programs.
- Use of software spelling checkers, dictionaries, grammar-checking software, and editing software.
- Record keeping utilizing dBase IV and Lotus 1-2-3 spreadsheet software.
- Integration of spreadsheets and database programs into word-processing text and/or graphics.
- Experience with laser printers, label printers, fax machines, scanners, modems, and electronic transmission networks.
- Text entry keyboarding speed of 80 words per minute (certificate holder) using WordPerfect software.
- Editing and proofreading of all documents.
- Staff training and supervisory ability.

EMPLOYMENT

1988–Present: Word-Processing Specialist
Lennody Computers, Inc., San Diego, CA.

EDUCATION

Certificate in Word Processing and Desktop Publishing
San Diego City College
San Diego, CA, 1988

REFERENCES ON REQUEST

11

STEERING STRATEGIES

To what companies will you send your résumé? You can find a listing of all the software and hardware companies in the United States or Canada in your public library. Look in the industrial directories under computer hardware, software, or on-line companies. For a quick listing, you can find excellent databases of U.S. software, hardware, and on-line companies on Parson's Technology software, "Address Book for Windows." You could then compile your list using that software.

Address Book for Windows is an expandable database for storing names, addresses, and phone numbers of organizations or individuals and includes the capability to dial the phone numbers automatically. It also contains databases of airlines, motels, and other names, addresses, and phone numbers you'll need for travel or job relocation. You can write for further information to: Parson's Technology, One Parson's Drive, P.O. Box 100, Hiawatha, Iowa, 52233-0100.

Think Small

Are you willing to try new search techniques to interest an employer? Then target smaller companies. As the larger corporations downsize to cut costs, smaller businesses are less likely to lay off as frequently, according to a recent poll taken by the American Management Association (New York).

By the year 2000, Virginia employment trends and labor forecaster, Marvin Cetron, optimistically predicted that the services industry will employ 88 percent of the American workforce. Cetron stated to Perri Capell, associate editor of the *Wall Street Journal's Managing Your Career* (a college edition of the *National Business Employment Weekly*) in the spring 1993 article, "Hiring Demand Shows Signs of Life," that "We'll have a completely different economy, where computerization and literacy will be absolutely essential."

The computerized world economy now focuses on the growth of export trade businesses. Your résumé will have a better chance if sent to divisions of companies that show growth.

Therefore, seek out small to mid-size firms that are growing fast. A good indicator of a healthy company is export volume. For example, SunMicrosystems Inc. of Mountain View, CA, showed a 44 percent growth in exports during 1992.

Check a company's growth rates before mailing your résumé by looking at *Hoover's Handbook of American Business* (Reference Press Inc.).

The handbook charts ten-year sales and earnings growth and total debt ratio for more than 500 major employers, according to Capell's article.

Another reference book you should look through before sending out your résumé is the *Bond Guide* (Standard & Poor's). You can find these reference publications in any major public or college library. The monthly *Bond Guide* is a booklet that rates thousands of corporate bonds based on whether a company can pay principal and interest by the due date. If you see a corporation rated less than BB, think carefully before you send it your résumé.

Professional employment researchers, career consultants, trend forecasters, college counselors, and résumé specialists look at investment analysts' current reports to research financially sound firms. Investigative reporters covering employment trends read computer industry trade journals to get the most timely information for similar research.

Try "Investext." It's a computerized anthology, a CD-ROM database of professional analysts' reports. It's available from Information Access Company, 362 Lakeside Drive, Foster City, CA 94404, 1(800)227-8431.

Investext is available on-line through many computerized news services, or you can find it on CD-ROM in several major libraries. Information Access Company also offers "The General Business File." This database contains full-text articles taken out of trade magazines as well as full-text stock analysts' reports.

Use trade journals to network with others in your field. Most major public and college libraries maintain a current collection of trade journals listing companies and names of key personnel in management. Read the trade journals' help wanted advertisements. Many trade magazines also run a category for job seekers called positions wanted.

An index of trade journals and industry-oriented magazines, including those for the computer industry, is listed in *Gale's Directory of Publications*. Computer industry professional and business associations are included with other types of associations in *The Encyclopedia of Associations*.

If you are looking for a job in the computer mail order business there are library reference books that list the small to medium-sized high growth companies such as Dell Computer Corporation, a pioneer in the computer mail-order business.

Sometimes, when you can't find such information in your public or college library, you can ask university placement directors for it (a small fee may be charged if you're not a student). Many offer such information sources and databanks to the public as well as to their students.

If you want to obtain the names, addresses, and phone numbers of top executives in major corporations so you can direct your résumé to a particular person in your field, your library may contain *The Greenwich Register* (Hunt-Scanlon Publishing Company).

By checking these reference books or databases, you can send your résumé to the company most likely to be hiring in your niche.

As has been emphasized throughout this book, the best way to put your résumé in the right hands is to network. Build a team of business contacts by joining industry groups in your specialization. Track the trends.

EPILOGUE

This update presents a cross-section of tips, thoughts, and ideas that reflect some of the latest thinking about job seeking within the computer industry and related electronic enterprises.

According to career consultant Connie Baher, U.S. Business Communications of San Diego, an excellent strategy for job seekers in a tight market is to "adopt" your favorite company. Learn all you can about the firm by asking for information instead of asking for a job.

Baher suggests asking for perspective on a company. For example, introduce yourself to a company by stating, "I'm not looking for a job. I'd like to know more about your organization."

Baher emphasizes that the hidden job market includes tips you get from your lawyer, doctor, accountant, tax preparer, or business associates who have a variety of clients who may have additional referrals or know of jobs soon to open in their clients' workplaces.

Uncover the hidden job market by networking with your peers who attend these business mixers, socials, conferences, and seminars sponsored by your local chamber of commerce or by professional associations, trade shows, and trade journal publishers and advertisers in your field of interest.

Branch out in the methods you use to find job leads from business contacts and close friends. Employers like to hire from within the company in order to give employees the feeling that they're working towards goals and advancement. However, if you are coming from outside the company you adopt or walk in off the street, you may be hired if there's no one inside the company who is qualified for that job.

Age Discrimination

Because of age discrimination against emerging mature writers and artists, such creative people may feel shut out of fields like Hollywood scriptwriting or animation. Discrimination by Hollywood-type agents and producers is especially directed against older scriptwriters, novelists, or artists who didn't break in or move to Hollywood when they were young.

A good resource to cope with this issue is the International Documentary Association's 18-minute video, "The Hollywood Grey List," on age discrimination against Hollywood scriptwriters. The video is available for rental from the organization.

"Elderheroes" can appear as superheroes in instructional design of software that challenges the imagination in users of all ages. If you are over 50 years old and your career is centered on creative expression, consider jobs in imaginative or educational software for home computers and for instruction as entertainment.

To counteract age discrimination against persons in the arts, the computer industry now offers a future in multimedia, particularly interactive multimedia, to writers and artists who can work with computers and video instead of only videotape or film. In interactive multimedia, we are all one. There is neither old nor young designer or marketer. Only the freshest, most profitable ideas are acquired through hands-on training, skill, and innovative thinking.

New Opportunities

Sometimes the emerging technology is so new that no one has much experience in it, and the doors are wide open to the inexperienced. Emerging digital technologies offer many branches of entry to the older worker with fresh ideas in creative, expressive, or software design jobs. Some of the creative jobs include writing hyperfiction for interactive multimedia, CD-ROM, computer games, or desktop video training and education scriptwriting.

The computer industry's interactive multimedia emphasis combines telephone lines, personal computers, fax machines, modems, local and wide area networks with home VCRs or videocameras, cable, satellites, electronic music, animation, scriptwriting, adventure stories, and games. Instructional courseware design combines software with video-conferencing equipment and brings distance teaching into homes or links schools around the globe. Job opportunities are being created for people in all stages of personal growth, from teenagers to the elderly.

Interactive multimedia is so new that there are not yet stereotypes, myths, or prejudices against the older creative writer, software designer, or animation artist as there are in the Hollywood scriptwriting arena.

Risk and Problem Solving

Today, it is common to see frequent employee turnover. Temporary or contingency work is growing rapidly. The average worker now goes through eight or more jobs in a lifetime, often wondering, "Why was I hired or not hired?"

According to Connie Baher, you are usually hired for one of two main reasons:

     1. to be the solution to an employer's problem or
     2. you present the lowest possible risk of all applicants.

Those who are hired pose the least risk and solve the most problems.

You are hired for the company's reasons, not yours. However, it helps if you persist in showing your enthusiasm and imply, "I'm so eager to work for this company that I made it my business to learn all about your firm and the benefits and advantages of your products."

Making yourself the lowest possible risk may mean working in temporary jobs for the company, serving an internship, applying as a freelancer, independent contractor, intrapreneur, or volunteer, or offering to help the company in new and creative ways.

Also, the lowest possible risk has done similar work before. It's a lower risk to hire someone with a high school education who has done accounts payable clerking than it is to take on an unemployed M.A.-level English teacher, and wonder whether that person will make mistakes and demonstrate a lack of enthusiasm about the job duties.

It's hard to pass over the unemployed professional with only slight or new knowledge of computer skills but who desperately needs the job, is a single parent, is facing covert age discrimination from other employers, or is in a financial crisis. In the end, however, the person who does get hired is the one who poses the lowest risk to the employer's investment in the applicant's salary.

If you are hired at $30,000 annually, for example as a technical writer of user manuals for desktop publishing software, the employer may risk an investment approaching $100,000 in salary and benefits until you have proved your worth. That's why the person presenting the lowest possible risk to the employer is hired.

Final Points to Ponder

1. *Look for opportunities in emerging technologies* that few people have experience with, and thus where competition isn't so great. Seek out new start-up businesses. Adopt them when they're about to join in partnerships with larger computer firms to develop new interactive software and hardware, or new applications, such as home entertainment that plays compact discs on TV and stereo.

2. *Look at companies that develop products for home entertainment* combined with learning that allow students to complete home work assignments, watch movies, listen to music, look at electronic photo albums, and play video games all on the same machine that uses compact discs for educational software

3. *The living room is a learning center.* The workplace is a training center. Learning has become entertainment. The joy of play leads to technical or human relations job skills. Training leads to production. These are the goals of interactive multimedia in the computer industry.

4. Systems analysts who rise to the top of their niches are more like *autonomous consultants.* Their purpose is to troubleshoot and redesign, always hungering for change and breaking away from routine.

5. During this decade, *computer personnel will see the health-care field growing* and seeking more résumés from trainers and equipment designers. Technology has reached a critical point where simulation may be played as reality because of vast leaps in the quality and quantity of data transmittal through fiber optics. This is the first generation of a new technology known as interactive multimedia in the computer industry. Coss-training will increase. Promotion of reentry programs will tap into previously untouched sources of future employees. Networking will increase the flow of résumés.

As you finish this book, remember one thought above all: The computer industry runs on the competitive edge, but it emerges on the cooperative curve.

APPENDIX A

RÉSUMÉ TRACKING FOLLOW-UP WORKSHEETS

(For mass mailings, use or copy this form for your files.)

Date _____

Company _____

Name _____

Address _____

_____

_____

_____

Phone _____

Interview _____

Interview Comments: _____

_____

_____

Follow-up Letters _____

_____

Job Offer _____

Referrals _____

Related Information _____

_____

_____

Quarterly Follow-Up _____

_____

Results_____

_____

RESUME TRACKING FOLLOW-UP WORKSHEET

(For smaller mailings, use or copy this form for your files.)

Resume Tracking   Interview or Follow-Up History

Name_____   Date_____

_____

Title_____

_____   Organization_____

  _____   _____

_____   _____

Address_____

_____   _____

_____   _____

Phone_____

_____

Date Mailed _____

_____

COMMENTS

Follow-Up Letter Mailed	Reject Job	Accept Job
Date _____	_____	_____
Name _____	_____	_____
Title _____	_____	_____
Organization _____	_____	_____
Address _____	_____	_____
_____	_____	_____
_____	_____	_____
_____	_____	_____
Phone _____	_____	_____

APPENDIX B

COMPUTER INDUSTRY ASSOCIATIONS

Advertising/Multimedia

Association of Independent Commercial Producers
Kaufman Astoria Studios
34-12 36th St.
Astoria, NY 11106
(718) 392-2427

International Chain of Industrial and Technical Advertising
Agencies
C/O Poppe Tyson
201 Littleton Rd.
Morris Plains, NJ 07950
(201) 539-0300

Young Professionals Division
C/O Lintas: New York
1 Dag Hammarskjold Plaza
New York, NY 10017
(212) 459-5690
(Jr. professionals in advertising, marketing, and public relations under age 30 or with less than two years' professional experience. Affiliated with Advertising Club of NY.)

Artificial Intelligence

American Association for Artificial Intelligence
445 Burgess Dr.
Menlo Park, CA 94025
(415) 328-3123

Banking
American Bankers Association
1120 Connecticut Ave. NW
Washington, DC 20036
(202) 663-5000

Electronic Banking Economics Society
1317 Third Ave.
New York, NY 10021
(203) 295-9788

Electronic Funds Transfer Association
950 Herndon Pkwy., Ste. 390
Herndon, VA 22073
(703) 435-9800

Bar Coding

Automatic Identification Manufacturers
634 Alpha Dr.
Pittsburgh, PA 15238-8753
(412) 963-8588

Uniform Code Council
8163 Old Yankee, Ste. J
Dayton, OH 45458
(513) 435-3870

CD-ROM, CD-Interactive, and Multimedia

Association for the Advancement of Computing in Education
(Publisher of *Ed-Tech Review*)
P.O. Box 2966
Charlottesville, VA 22902
(804) 973-3987

Electronic Artists Group
P.O. Box 580783
Memphis, MN 55458
(612) 331-4289

Interactive Multimedia Association (IMA)
3 Church Circle, Ste. 800
Annapolis, MD 20401
(410) 626-1380

International Interactive Communications Society (IICS)
P.O. Box 1862
Lake Oswego, OR 97035
(503) 649-2065

Multimedia Publishers Group
Advanced Strategies
60 Cutter Mill Rd., Ste. 502
Great Neck, NY 11021
(516) 482-0088

San Francisco-Multimedia Development Group
2601 Mariposa Street
San Francisco, CA 94110
(415) 553-2300
Fax (415) 553-2403

CD-Interactive Publishing

Optical Publishing Association
P.O. Box 21268
Columbus, OH 43221
(614) 793-9660

Optical Publishing Association
7001 Discovery Blvd. #205
Dublin, OH 43017

Phillips Consumer Electronics Co.
1 Phillips Drive
Knoxville, TN 37914
800-223-7772 (CD-I consumer information)
(Not an organization, but a prime manufacturer of CD-I software and machines.)

Software Publishers Association
1703 M St. NW, Ste. 700
Washington, DC 20036
(202) 452-1600

Communications

Computer and Communications Industry Association
666 11th St. NW, Ste. 600
Washington, DC 20001
(202) 783-0070

Council of Communications Management
Oak West Office Plaza
17W703 E. Butterfield Rd.
Oakbrook Terrace, IL 60181
(708) 268-0707

International Communications Association
12750 Merit Dr., Ste. 710-LB-89
Dallas, TX 75251
(214) 233-3889

International Interactive Communications Society (IICS)
P.O. Box 1862
Lake Oswego, OR 97035
(503) 649-2065

Networking Institute
505 Waltham St.
West Newton, MA 02165
(617) 965-3340

Society for Technical Communication
901 N. Stuart St., Ste. 304
Arlington, VA 22203
(703) 522-4114

Computational Linguistics

Association for Computational Linguistics
445 South St.
Morristown, NJ 07960
(201) 829-4312

Computer Consulting
Independent Computer Consultants Association
933 Gardenview Office Pkwy.
St. Louis, MO 63141
(314) 997-4633

Computer Graphics and Animation

National Computer Graphics Association
2722 Merrilee Dr., Ste. 200
Fairfax, VA 22031
(703) 698-9600 or (800) 225-6242

Special Interest Group on Computer Graphics
C/O Lois A. Blankstein
Association for Computing Machinery
1515 Broadway
New York, NY 10036
(212) 869-7440

World Computer Graphics Association
2033 M St. NW, Ste. 399
Washington, DC 20036
(202) 775-9556

Computer Press/Journalism

American Business Press
675 Third Ave., Ste. 400
New York, NY 10017
(212) 661-6360

American Medical Writers Association
9650 Rockville Pike
Bethesda, MD 20814
(301) 493-0003

American Society of Business Press Editors
4445 Cilmer Lane
Cleveland, OH 44143
(216) 531-8306

Associated Business Writers of America
1450 S. Havana, Ste. 620
Aurora, CO 80012
(303) 751-7844

Association of Editorial Businesses
116 4th St. SE
Washington, DC 20003
(202) 543-1800

Association of Professional Writing Consultants
3924 S. Troost
Tulsa, OK 74105
(918) 743-4793

Aviation/Space Writers Association
17 High St., Ste. 1200
Columbus, OH 43215
(614) 221-1900

Computer Press Association
1260 25th Ave.
San Francisco, CA 94122
(415) 681-5364

Council of Biology Editors
Illinois Center, #200
111 E. Wacker Dr.
Chicago, IL 60601-4298
(312) 616-0800

Disabled Journalists of America
484 Hammond Dr.
Griffin, GA 30223
(404) 228-6491

Editorial Freelancers Association
P.O. Box 2050
Madison Sq. Station
New York, NY 10159
(212) 677-3357

Freelance Editorial Association
P.O. Box 835
Cambridge, MA 02238
(Includes desktop publishers.)

Multimedia Publishers Group
Advanced Strategies
60 Cutter Mill Rd., Ste. 502
Great Neck, NY 11021
(516) 482-0088

National Association of Science Writers
P.O. Box 294
Greenlawn, NY 11740
(516) 757-5664

Society for Technical Communication
901 N. Stuart St., Ste. 304
Arlington, VA 22203
(703) 522-4114

Society of American Business Editors and Writers
P.O. Box 838
University of Missouri
Columbus, MO 65205
(314) 882-7862

Software Publishers Association
1703 M St. NW, Ste. 700
Washington, DC 20036
(202) 452-1600

Women In Scholarly Publishing
C/O Marilyn Campbell
Rutgers University Press
107 Church St.
New Brunswick, NJ 08901-1242
(908) 932-7396

Computer Security

International Association for Computer Systems Security
6 Swarthmore Lane
Dix Hills, NY 11746
(516) 499-1616

Computer Service and Repair
National Computer Service Network
3524 Telfair Way NE
Atlanta, GA 30319-1974

North American Computer Service Association
100 Silver Beach, #918
Daytona Beach, FL 32118
(904) 255-4040

Computer Users (General Interest)

PC-Special Interest Group
1030 E. Duane Ave., Ste. D
Sunnyvale, CA 94086
(408) 730-9291
(IBM-compatible computer users.)

Data Communications

Electronic Mail Association
1555 Wilson Blvd., Ste. 300
Arlington, VA 22209
(703) 875-8620

Independent Data Communications
Manufacturers Association
1201 Pennsylvania Ave. NW
Washington, DC 20004
(202) 626-6600

International Facsimile Association
4023 Lakeview Dr.
Lake Havasu City, AZ 86403
(602) 453-3850

Data Entry

Data Entry Management Association
101 Merritt 7, 5th Fl.
Norwalk, CT 06851
(203) 846-3777

EDP Auditors Association
455 E. Kehoe Bvd., #106
P.O. Box 88180
Carol Stream, IL 60188
(708) 682-1200

Database Management

International Data Base Management Association
10675 Treena St., Ste. 103
San Diego, CA 92131
(619) 578-3152 or 1(800)767-SHOW
(Promotes the database management industry. Conducts hands-on computer workshops and seminars.)

National Center for Automated Information Retrieval
165 E. 72nd St., Ste. 1B
New York, NY 10021
(212) 249-0760

Data Processing

Black Data Processing Associates
P.O. Box 7466
Philadelphia, PA 19101
(215) 843-9120

Newspaper Systems Group
C/O Clark Lambert
The Kansas City Star
1729 Grand Ave.
Kansas City, MO 64108
(816) 234-4273
(Newspaper data processing executives.)

Special Interest Group for Business
Data Processing and Management
C/O Association for Computing Machinery
11 West 42nd St.
New York, NY 10036
(212) 869-7440

Digital Photography

American Society of Media Photographers
419 Park Ave. South
New York, NY 10016
(212) 889-9144
(Electronic imaging and digital technology.)

Entrepreneurship

Young Entrepreneurs Organization
1010 N. Glebe Rd., Ste. 600
Arlington, VA 22201
(703) 527-4500
(Entrepreneurs under age 40 who have either founded or own a firm with annual gross revenues exceeding $1 million.)

VFEA International Trade Association (Computers)
10229 N. Scottsdale Rd., Ste. B
Scottsdale, AZ 85253
(602) 951-8866

Fashion Design with Software

Costume Designers Guild
13949 Ventura Blvd., Ste. 309
Sherman Oaks, CA 91423
(818) 905-1557

Council of Fashion Designers Of America
1412 Broadway, Ste. 1401
New York, NY 10018
(212) 302-1821

Games and Simulation (Computer)

International Simulation and Gaming Association
C/O Steven E. Underwood
University of Michigan
4110 E.E.C.S. Bldg.
Ann Arbor, MI 48109
(313) 764-4333

North American Simulation and Games Association
C/O John delRegato
Pentathlon Institute
P.O. Box 20590
Indianapolis, IN 46220
(317) 782-1553

Hardware

ABCD: The Microcomputer Industry Association
1515 E. Woodfield Rd., Ste. 860
Schaumburg, IL 60173-5437
(708) 240-1818

AM/FM International (Computers)
14456 E. Evans Ave.
Aurora, CO 80014
(303) 337-0513

American Society of Computer Dealers
1255 23rd St. NW
Washington, DC 20037
(202) 785-4990

Associated Minicomputer Dealers of America
3101 N. Central Ave., Ste. 560
Phoenix, AZ 85012
(602) 265-1699

Center for Office Technology
1800 N. Kent St., Ste. 1160
Roslyn, VA 22209
(703) 276-1174

Computer and Business Equipment
Manufacturers Association
311 1st St. NW, Ste. 500

Washington, DC 20001
(202) 737-8888

Computer Dealers and Lessors Association
1212 Potomac St. NW
Washington, DC 20007
(202) 333-0102

Digital Dealers Association
107 1/2 S. Main St., Ste. 202
Chelsea, MI 48118
(313) 475-8333

National Computer Dealer Forum
C/O National Office Products Association
301 N. Fairfax St.
Alexandria, VA 22314
(703) 549-9040

Human Resource Management

Association of Human Resource System Professionals
P.O. Box 801646
Dallas, TX 75380-1646
(214) 661-3727
(Includes automated human resource systems, data processing professionals, and payroll/data processing personnel.)

Institute for International Human Resources
606 N. Washington St.
Alexandria, VA 22314
(703) 548-3440

Society for Human Resource Management (SHRM)
606 N. Washington St.
Alexandria, VA 22314
(703) 548-3440

Information Technology

Information Industry Liaison Committee
5430 Grosvenor Lane, Ste. 200
Bethesda, MD 20814
(301) 564-4505

Information Technology Association of America
1616 N. Fort Meyer Dr., Ste. 1300
Arlington, VA 22209
(703) 522-5055

Management/Technology

Association of University Technology Managers
71 East Ave., Ste. S
Norwalk, CT 06851
(203) 852-7168

Marketing Research

American Telemarketing Association
5000 Van Nuys Blvd., #300
Sherman Oaks, CA 91403
(818) 995-7338, 1(800)441-3335

Biomedical Marketing Association
310 N. Alabama Ave., Ste. A100
Indianapolis, IN 46204
(317) 237-9100

Marketing Research Association
2189 Silas Deane Hwy., Ste. 5
Rocky Hill, CT 06067
(203) 257-4008

Technical Marketing Society of America
4383 Via Majorca
Cypress, CA 90680
(714) 821-8672

Marketing Communications

CIMA Marketing Communications Council
111 E. Wisconsin Ave., Ste. 940
Milwaukee, WI 53202
(414) 272-0943

Color Marketing Group
4001 N. 9 St., Ste. 102
Arlington, VA 22203
(703) 528-7666
(Marketing, researching, and communicating about how color trends influence business.)

Medical Transcription
American Association for Medical Transcription
P.O. Box 576187
Modesto, CA 95357-6187
(800) 982-2182

Music (Computerized)

Computer Musician Coalition
1024 W. Wilcox Ave.
Peoria, IL 61604
(309) 685-4843

International MIDI Association
5316 W. 57th St.
Los Angeles, CA 90056
(213) 649-6434

Networking

International Association of Telecomputer Networks
660 E. Hwy. 434, Ste. A
Winter Springs, FL 32708
(407) 327-7777

Networking Institute
505 Waltham St.
West Newton, MA 02165
(617) 965-3340

Office Information Systems

Office Automation Society International
6348 Munhall Ct.
P.O. Box 374
McLean, VA 22101
(703) 821-6650

Society for Information Management
401 N. Michigan Ave.
Chicago, IL 60611-4267
(312) 644-6610

Special Interest Group on Office Information Systems
C/O Prof. Carson Woo
University of British Columbia
Faculty of Commerce
2053 Main Mall
Vancouver, BC, Canada V6T 1Z2

Robotics

American Defense Preparedness Association
2101 Wilson Blvd., Ste. 400
Arlington, VA 22201-3061
(703) 522-1820
(Military artificial intelligence/robotics.)

Robotics Industries Association
P.O. Box 3724
900 Victors Way
Ann Arbor, MI 48106
(313) 994-6088

Robotics International
of the Society of Manufacturing Engineers
P.O. Box 930
Dearborn, MI 48128
(313) 271-1500

Secretarial

American Society of Corporate Secretaries
1270 Ave. of the Americas
New York, NY 10020
(212) 765-2620

Software

Business Software Alliance
1201 Pennsylvania Ave. NW, Ste. 250
Washington, DC 20004
(202) 737-7060

Software Maintenance Association
P.O. Box 12004, #297
Vallejo, CA 94590
(707) 643-4423

Software Publishing

Software Publishers Association
1703 M St. NW, Ste. 700
Washington, DC 20036
(202) 452-1600

Software Talent Agenting

Association of Talent Agents
9255 Sunset Blvd.
Los Angeles, CA 90069
(213) 274-0628

National Conference of Personal Managers
210 E. 51st St.
New York, NY 10022
(212) 421-2670

Society of Photographers and Artists
Representatives (Agents)
1123 Broadway, # 914
New York, NY 10010
(212) 924-6023

Technical Illustration

National Computer Graphics Association
2722 Merrilee Dr., Ste. 200
Fairfax, VA 22031
(703) 698-9600

Society for Technical Communication
901 N. Stuart St., Ste. 304
Arlington, VA 22203
(703) 522-4114

Telecommunications

North American Telecommunicators Association
2000 M St. NW, Ste. 550
Washington, DC 20036
(202) 296-9800

Satellite Broadcasting and Communications Association
C/O Charles C. Hewitt
225 Reinekers Lane, Ste. 600
Alexandria, VA 22314
(703) 549-6990

Society of Satellite Professionals International
2700 Prosperity Ave.
Fairfax, VA 22031
(703) 204-4537

Society of Telecommunications Consultants
P.O. Box 810776
Boca Raton, FL 33481-0776
(407) 852-7071

Telecommunications Association
858 S. Oak Park Rd., Ste. 102
Covina, CA 91724-3625
(818) 967-9411

Telecommunications Industry Association
2001 Pennsylvania Ave. NW, Ste. 800
Washington, DC 20006-1813
(202) 457-4912

Telecommunications Industry Forum
C/O Exchange Carriers Standards Association
5430 Grosvenor Lane, Ste. 200
Bethesda, MD 20814
(301) 564-4505

Teleconferencing

International Teleconferencing Association
1150 Connecticut Ave. NW, Ste. 1050
Washington, DC 20036
(202) 833-2549

Training

American Society for Training and Development
P.O. Box 1443
1640 King St.
Alexandria, VA 22313
(703) 683-8100

Association for the Advancement of Computing in Education
(Publisher of *Ed-Tech Review*)
P.O. Box 2966
Charlottesville, VA 22902
(804) 973-3987

Center for Computer-Assisted Legal Instruction
229 19th Ave. S
Minneapolis, MN 55455
(612) 373-5352

Commission on Instructional Technology
C/O Superintendent of Documents
U.S. Government Printing Office
Washington, DC 20402
(202) 275-2051

Educating Computing Council (ICIA)
3150 Spring St.
Fairfax, VA 22031
(703) 273-7200

National Association of Industrial
and Technical Teacher Educators
Dept. of Practical Arts and Vocational Education
University of Missouri
Columbia, MO 65211
(314) 882-3082

Society for Applied Learning Technology
50 Culpepper St.
Warrenton, VA 22186
(703) 347-0055

Training Media Association
198 Thomas Johnson Dr.
Folk, MD 21702
(301) 662-4268

Video

International Television Association (ITVA)
6311 North O'Connor Rd. DB51
Irving, TX 75039
(214) 869-1112

National Cable TV Association
1724 Massachusetts Ave. NW
Washington, DC 20036
(202) 755-3550

Society of Motion Picture and Television Engineers (SMPTE)
595 West Hartsdale Ave.
White Plains, NY 10607
(914) 761-1100

Video Software Dealers Association
303 Harper Dr.
Morristown, NJ 08057-3229
(609) 231-7800

Vidion/International Association of Video
1440 N St. NW, Ste. 601
Washington, DC 20005
(202) 328-9346

Videotex

Videotex Industry Association
8403 Colesville Rd., Ste. 865
Silver Spring, MD 20910-3366
(301) 495-4955

Virtual Reality

Cyber Society
C/O Greg Klein
2016 Main St., Ste. 1207
Houston, TX 77002-8843
(713) 752-0761
(Clearinghouse for virtual reality products and technology.)

Wireless Communications

National Association of Cellular Agents
1716 Woodhead St.
Houston, TX 77019
(713) 522-0528

National Communications Association
7 Park Ave., Ste. 14-3
New York, NY 10016
(212) 725-0248

Telocator, The Personal Communications Industry Association
1019 19th St. NW, Ste. 1100
Washington, DC 20036
(202) 467-4770
(Cellular phone companies.)

Wireless Cable Association
2000 L St. NW, Ste. 702
Washington, DC 20036
(202) 452-7823

Women's Associations

Association for Women in Computing
41 Sutter St., Ste. 1006
San Francisco, CA 94104

Executive Women International
Spring Run Executive Plaza
965 E. 4800 South, Ste. 1
Salt Lake City, UT 84117
(801) 263-3296

Women in Scholarly Publishing
C/O Marilyn Campbell
Rutgers University Press
107 Church St.
New Brunswick, NJ 08901-1242
(908) 932-7396

Word Processing

National Association of Professional
Word Processing Technicians
110 West Byberry Rd., Ste. E2
Philadelphia, PA 19116
(215) 698-8525
(Word processors and computer operators.)

APPENDIX C

COMPUTER INDUSTRY TRADE PERIODICALS
(Software, Technical & Trade Systems)

ACM Transactions on Computer Systems
ACM Transactions on Database Systems
ACM Transactions on Programming Languages and Systems
Association for Computing Machinery
11 W. 42nd St., 3rd Fl.
New York, NY 10036
(212) 869-7440

ADAPSO
The Computer Software and Services Industry Association
1300 N. 17th St., Ste. 300
Arlington, VA 22209-3899
(703) 522-5055

AEC News Report
Association of Electronic Cottagers (AEC)
P.O. Box 1738
Davis, CA 95617-1738
(916) 756-6430

Canadian Datasystems
Maclean Hunter Ltd.
777 Bay St.
Toronto, ON, Canada M5W 1A7
(416) 596-5906

Computer Consultant
Schueler Communications, Inc.
208 N. Townsend St.
Syracuse, NY 13203
(315) 472-1008

Computer Daily
Computer Age
EDP News Services, Inc.
7043 Wimsatt Rd.
Springfield, VA 22151-4080
(703) 354-9400

Computer Industry Report
International Data Corporation
5 Speen St.
Framingham, MA 01701
(617) 872-8200

Computer Industry Update
IMR, Inc.
P.O. Box 681
Los Altos, CA 94022
(415) 941-6679

Computer Language
Miller Freeman Publications
500 Howard St.
San Francisco, CA 94105
(415) 397-1881

Computer Service and Repair
California Service Dealer
C/O Harry Midkiff
P.O. Box 202
Hawthorne, CA 90250
(213) 679-9186

Computerworld
CW Publishing, Inc.
375 Cochituate Rd.
P.O. Box 9171
Framingham, MA 01701-9171
(617) 879-0700

Computing Reviews
Computing Surveys
Association for Computing Machinery
11 W. 42nd St., 3rd Fl.
New York, NY 10036
(212) 869-7440

Datamation
Cahners Publishing Company
275 Washington St.
Newton, MA 02158-1630
(617) 964-3030

Datapro Applications Software Solutions
Datapro Research Corporation
1805 Underwood Blvd
Delran, NJ 08075
(609) 764-0100

Dataworld
Faulkner Technical Reports
6560 N. Park Dr.
Pennsauken, NJ 08109-4374
(609) 662-2070

Dr. Dobb's Journal
M & T Publishing, Inc.
501 Galveston Dr.
Redwood City, CA 94063
(415) 366-3600

EDP Weekly
Computer Age
EDP News Services, Inc.
7043 Wimsatt Rd.
Springfield, VA 22151-4080
(703) 354-9400

High Technology Careers
4701 Patrick Henry Drive, Suite 101
Santa Clara, CA 95054
(408) 492-0777

The Independent
Independent Computer Consultants Association
P.O. Box 27412
St. Louis, MO 63141
(314) 997-4633

InfoWorld
1060 Marsh Rd., Ste. C-200
Menlo Park, CA 94025
(415) 328-4602

The Inputer
Capstone Publishing, Inc.
2368 Fairlane Dr., Bldg. E., Ste. 37
Montgomery, AL 36116
(205) 277-7266

Micro Moonlighter
4121 Buckthorn Ct.
Lewisville, TX 75028
(214) 539-1115

Micro Software Marketing
P.O. Box 380
Congers, NY 10920

MIS Quarterly
University of Minnesota
Carlson Schoool of Management
MIS Research Center
271 19th Ave. S
Minneapolis, MN 55455
(612) 624-2029

Software Maintenance News
Software Maintenance Association
56 Bay St., Ste. 400
Staten Island, NY 10301
(718) 816-5522

Software Protection
Law & Technology Press
1112 Ocean Dr., Ste. 103
Manhattan Beach, CA 90266
(213) 372-1678

Worksteader News
2396 Coolidge Way
Rancho Cordova, CA 95670
(916) 635-8764

Computer/Electronic Service News

CESN Publications
P.O. Box 428
Peterborough, NH 03458
(603) 924-9457

Electronic Products
645 Stewart Ave.
Garden City, NY 11530
(516) 227-1300

Electronics Today International
300 Don Mills Rd.
Toronto, ON, Canada M3B 3M8
(416) 445-5600

The Illinois Word
Electronic Service Dealers Association of Illinois
4621 N. Kedzie Ave.
Chicago, IL 60625
(312) 463-2499

Intertec
Intertec Publishing Corporation
P.O. Box 12901
Overland Park, KS 66212
(913) 888-4664

ISCET Update
International Society of Certified Electronics Technicians
2708 W. Berry, Ste. 8
Fort Worth, TX 76109
(817) 921-9101

Micro Marketworld
174 Concord St., Ste. 21
Peterborough, NH 03458
(603) 924-9471

Modern Electronics
76 N. Broadway
Hicksville, NY 11801
(516) 681-2922

NASD News
National Association of Service Dealers
C/O National Association of Retail Dealers of America
10 E. 22 St.
Lombard, IL 60148
(312) 953-8950

NCSN Network News
National Computer Service Network (NCSN)
90 Crossways Park West
Woodbury, NY 11797
(516) 682-5300

NESDA Member Memo and *NESDA Update*
Professional Electronics
National Electronic Sales and Service Dealers Association
(NESDA)
2708 W. Berry St.
Fort Worth, TX 76109
(817) 921-9061

Readout
North American Computer Service Association
506 Georgetown Dr.
Casselberry, FL 32707
(305) 331-0181

Technical Notebook (Quarterly)
International Society of Certified Electronics Technicians
2708 W. Berry, Ste. 8
Fort Worth, TX 76109
(817) 921-9101

Technician Association News
Electronics Technicians Association, International (ETA)
604 N. Jackson
Greencastle, IN 46135
(317) 653-3849

Computer Magazines (General, Mass-Market, Computer-User)

AMIGA WORLD
TechMedia Publishing Inc.
80 Elm Street
Peterborough, NH 03458
(603) 924-0100

Byte
McGraw-Hill
1 Phoenix Mill Lane
Peterborough, NH 03458
(603) 924-9281

MacUser
Ziff-Davis Publishing Company
P.O. Box 56986
Boulder, CO 80322-6986
(800) 627-2247

MacWEEK
Coastal Associates Publishing
P.O. Box 1766
Riverton, NJ 08077-7366
(609) 461-2100

MACWORLD
Macworld Communications, Inc.
501 Second Street, 5th Floor
San Francisco, CA 94107
(415) 243-0505

PC Magazine
Ziff-Davis Publishing Company
P.O. Box 54093
Boulder, CO 80322-4093
(800) 289-0429

PC WORLD
PC World Communications, Inc.
501 Second Street, #600
San Francisco, CA 94107
(415) 243-0500

COMPUTER GRAPHICS

Computer Artist
PennWell Publishing Company
Subscription Services
P.O. Box 3188
Tulsa, OK 74101
(918) 831-9423

Computer Graphics World
PennWell Publishing Company
One Technology Park Drive
Westford, MA 01886
(508) 692-0700

Computer Pictures
Montage Publishing Inc.
701 Westchester Ave
White Plains, NY 10604
(914) 328-9157

MacArtist
MacArtist, Inc.
901 E. Santa Ana Blvd., Ste. 103
Santa Ana, CA 92701
(714) 973-1529

Step-By-Step Design
Step-By-Step Publishing
6000 North Forst Park Drive
Peoria, IL 61614
(309) 688-2300

Verbum
The Gosney Company, Inc.
670 Seventh Ave., 2nd Fl.
San Diego, CA 92101
(619) 233-9977

DESKTOP PUBLISHING/DESKTOP VIDEO

Desktop Communications
International Desktop Communications Ltd.
P.O. Box 941745
Atlanta, GA 30341
(404) 493-4786

Publish
Integrated Media, Inc.
P.O. Box 55400
Boulder, CO 80322
(800) 274-5116

MULTIMEDIA, CD-INTERACTIVE, AND CD-ROM

CD-ROM Professional
Pemberton Press, Inc.
462 Danbury Road
Wilton, CT 06897
(800) 248-8466

Ed-Tech Review
P.O. Box 2966
Charlottesville, VA 22902
(804) 973-3987

New Media
Hypermedia Communications Inc.
901 Mariner's Island Blvd., Ste. 365
San Mateo, CA 94404
(415) 573-5170

QuickTime Forum
Multi-Facet Communications
110 West Iowa Ave.
Sunnyvale, CA 94086
(408) 749-0549

MULTIMEDIA ELECTRONIC MUSIC AND AUDIO

Electronic Musician
Act III
P.O. Box 41094
Nashville, TN 37204
(800) 888-5139

Keyboard
Miller Freeman, Inc.
Box 58528
Boulder, CO 80322-8528
(800) 289-9919

Mix
Act III
P.O. Box 41094
Nashville, TN 37204
(800) 888-5139

Recording Engineer/Producer
Intertec Publishing Corp.
9221 Quivira Road, P.O. Box 12901
Overland Park, KS 66212
(913) 541-6628

VIRTUAL REALITY

PCVR
1706 Sherman Hill Rd.
Unit A
Laramie, WY 82070
(307) 742-7675

APPENDIX D

SOFTWARE DIRECTORIES

The Computer World Buyers Guide
Computerworld Communications, Inc.
375 Cochituate Rd.
Box 880
Framingham, MA 01701

Data Sources
P.O. Box 5845
Cherry Hill, NJ 08034

The Datapro Directory of Microcomputer Software
1805 Underwood Blvd.
Delran, NJ 08075

Datapro Directory of Software
1805 Underwood Blvd.
Delran, NJ 08075

ICP Software Directory
International Computer Programming
9000 Keystone Crossing
P.O. Box 40946
Indianapolis, IN 46240

International Software Directory of Mini Computers
Imprint Software
1520 S. College Ave.
Fort Collin, CO 80524

PC Clearing House Software Directory
PC Clearing House, Inc.
11781 Lee Jackson Hwy.
Fairfax, VA 22033

APPENDIX E

RECOMMENDED SOFTWARE

Calera WordScan Plus
475 Potrero Ave.
Sunnyvale, CA 94086
(408) 720-0999
OCR products that work with leading desktop scanners and fax cards.
Microsoft Windows compatible.

IdeaFisher
IdeaFisher Systems, Inc.
2222 Martin St., Suite 110
Irvine, CA 92715
(714) 474-8111
Helps find and brainstorm ideas.

MarketPlace
Three University Office Park
Waltham, MA 02154
(617) 894-4100
Database of nearly 8 million names and addresses of businesses to help
find potential employers or clients and help perform market analysis on
CD-ROM, where you may subscribe to updates. Creates lists by type of
business, geography, number of employees, annual sales, year started,
new/update status, etc.

Working Together Side-By-Side
Institute for Management Development, Inc.
1330 Orange Ave.
Coronado, CA
(619) 435-1331

ZyImage
ZyLab, 100 Lexington Drive
Buffalo Grove, IL 60089
(708) 459-8000
Complete document imaging and text retrieval software.

ZyIndex for Windows
ZyLab, 100 Lexington Drive
Buffalo Grove, IL 60089
(708) 459-8000
Highly recommended for résumé and cover letter retrieval. It's the fastest,
most powerful document retrieval system for personal computers (IBM
compatible with Windows). Ideally suited for frequently changing text or
for networks. Documents retrieved based on their content rather than on
name or location. Powerful search options widen or narrow
requests.Compares personality types, management, and learning styles.

INDEX

ABOUT THE AUTHOR

Anne Cardoza is president and founder of Personality Assessment Features, an instructional design, career development, and psychological type consulting and research firm specializing in writing computer industry career books and books on career and personal development. She frequently writes about creative expression jobs in the computer industry and is recognized as a national expert in CD-I multimedia and instructional design. Cardoza also researches computer graphics, reviews software, and writes newspaper and magazine columns about computer industry issues and trends.

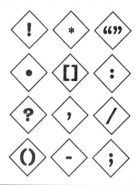

BARRON'S POCKET GUIDES—

The handy, quick-reference tools that you can count on—no matter where you are!

ISBN: 4843-1
$6.95 Canada $8.50

ISBN: 4285-9
$5.95 Canada $7.95

ISBN: 4381-2
$5.95 Canada $7.95

ISBN: 4404-5
$5.95 Canada $7.95

ISBN: 4845-8
$6.95 Canada $8.95

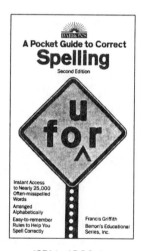

ISBN: 4380-4
$6.95 Canada $8.95

ISBN: 4382-0
$6.95 Canada $8.95

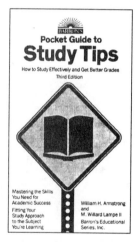

ISBN: 4488-6
$6.95 Canada $8.95

 EDUCATIONAL SERIES, INC.
250 Wireless Boulevard
Hauppauge, New York 11788
In Canada: Georgetown Book Warehouse
34 Armstrong Avenue
Georgetown, Ont. L7G 4R9

ISBN PREFIX : 0-8120

Prices subject to change without notice. Books may be purchased at your bookstore, or by mail from Barron's. Enclose check or money order for total amount plus 10% for postage and handling (minimum charge $1.75, Can. $2.00). N.Y. residents add sales tax. All books are paperback editions.